TREEHOUSES

KNACK

TREEHOUSES

A Step-by-Step Guide to Designing & Building

a Safe & Sound Structure

Text and Principal Photography by Lon Levin

Treehouse construction and technical review by Dan Wright

Guilford, Connecticut
An imprint of Globe Pequot Press

Copyright © 2010 by Morris Book Publishing, LLC

ALL RIGHTS RESERVED. No part of this book may be reproduced or transmitted in any form by any means, electronic or mechanical, including photocopying and recording, or by any information storage and retrieval system, except as may be expressly permitted in writing from the publisher. Requests for permission should be addressed to Globe Pequot Press, Attn: Rights and Permissions Department, P.O. Box 480, Guilford, CT 06437.

Knack is a registered trademark of Morris Book Publishing, LLC, and is used with express permission.

Editor in Chief: Maureen Graney
Editor: Katie Benoit
Project Editor: Tracee Williams
Cover Design: Paul Beatrice, Bret Kerr
Interior Design: Paul Beatrice
Layout: Nancy Freeborn
Cover Photos: Lon Levin and courtesy of Barbara Butler Artist-Builder Inc., Alsadair Jardine As, and Tree Top Builders, Inc.
Interior Photos: Lon Levin with exception of those listed on pages 238 and 239
Illustrations and diagrams by Lon Levin

Library of Congress Cataloging-in-Publication Data
Levin, Lon.
  Knack treehouses : a step-by-step guide to designing & building a safe & sound structure / text and principal photography by Lon Levin.
     p. cm.
  Includes index.
  ISBN 978-1-59921-783-3
  1. Tree houses. I. Title. II. Title: Treehouses.
  TH4885.L475 2010
  690'.89—dc22
                              2009043608

The following manufacturers/names appearing in *Knack Treehouses* are trademarks: ACR® (Anti-Camout Ribs), baumraum®, Deck Mate®, Dremel®, Eco-Safe®, Evercoat®, Kynar®, Lexan™, Ondura®, Plexiglas®, SawStop®, Teflon®, Tree-Grip™

Printed in China

10 9 8 7 6 5 4 3 2 1

The information in this book is true and complete to the best of our knowledge. All recommendations are made without guarantee on the part of the author or Globe Pequot Press. The author, builders, and Globe Pequot Press disclaim any liability in connection with the use of this information.

TreeHouse Workshop, Inc. does not support all of the building practices shown in this book.

For my wife and best friend Joanne; this book would never have gotten off the ground without her love, loyalty, and support.

Acknowledgments

No project like this one is the effort of one person; it took countless people some of whom I don't even know to make this book a reality. I thank all those people and their efforts for making this project come to life. Specifically, I want to recognize Brooks Sumberg for his friendship and support, Alan Jones for his brilliance and talent, Maureen Graney, Katie Benoit, Tracee Williams, and the Globe Pequot Press team for all their help and last but not least thanks to my children Alexx, Asher, and Josh for inspiring me to do great things.

CONTENTS

Introduction..viii

Chapter 1: Treehouse Dreams
Treehouse Possibilities............................... xii
Treehouse Dream Designs............................ 2
Treehouse Design Statements 4
Treehouse Art & Study Centers...................... 6
Treehouse Industry 8
Treehouse Resorts 10

Chapter 2: Treehouse Styles
Single-Trunk Treehouse...............................12
Two-Tree Treehouse 14
Three-Tree Treehouse 16
Four-Tree Treehouse 18
Trees & Posts...20
Unique Treehouse Supports 22

Chapter 3: Rustic Treehouses
Basic Treehouses.......................................24
Treetop Playhouses....................................26
Treetop Forts & Outposts 28
Specialty Treehouses..................................30
Found Object Treehouses.............................32
Stunning Treehouses 34

Chapter 4: Tree Selection
Best Varieties 36
Vertical Trees 38
Branching Trees..40
Using Multiple Trees 42
Tree Health 44
Tree Diseases 46

Chapter 5: Planning
The Plan...48
Codes & Regulations..................................50
Working the Plan 52
Respect the Tree 54
Building Supplies & Timber 56
Supports 58

Chapter 6: Platforms & Supports
Radiating Spokes 60
Flexible Brackets.......................................62
Suspension Systems 64
Support System Innovations.........................66
One of a Kind...68
Post Supports 70

Chapter 7: Treehouse Access
Tree Steps 72
Tree Stairs 74
Rope Ladders...76
Tree Handles 78
Adventurous Accesses................................80
Unique Accesses 82

Chapter 8: Windows & Doors
Doors 84
Different Doors 86
Windows 88
More Windows 90
Custom Windows.......................................92
Custom Doors & Openings 94

Chapter 9: Treehouse Roofs
Wood Roofing...96
Alternate Roofing Types 98
Metal Roofing 100
Recycled Roofing......................................102
Unique Roofing..104
The Future..106

Chapter 10: Fun Features
The Fort 108
Bridges & Walkways..................................110
Pulleys, Beds, Hammocks 112
Fun Accessories.......................................114
More Fun Accessories.................................116
More about Fun 118

Chapter 11: Tools
Hand Tools 120
More Hand Tools 122
Power Tools. 124
More Power Tools. 126
Specialty Tools. 128
More Specialty Tools 130

Chapter 12: Hardware
Bolts. 132
Screws 134
Nails. 136
Braces & Brackets 138
Adhesives & Glues 140
Special Fasteners 142

Chapter 13: Materials
Lumber. 144
Posts 146
Roofing. 148
Decking 150
Siding 152
Railings. 154

Chapter 14: Support Construction
Prep the Site. 156
Bolt Support System. 158
Setting the Beams 160
Attaching Joists. 162
Blocking. 164
Cleanup 166

Chapter 15: Platform Building
Decking Materials 168
Set Decking in Place 170
Decking around the Tree. 172
Trimming the Deck Edges 174
Cleanup 176
Double-Check Everything 178

Chapter 16: Framing & Walls
Organizing the Lumber 180
Base Plates & Framing. 182
Erecting the First Wall. 184
Raising the Walls. 186
Siding 188
Stain & Finish 190

Chapter 17: Roofing
Roofing Types 192
Framing the Rafters. 194
Attaching the Roofing 196
Trim the Roof 198
Attaching the Rubber Gasket 200
Troubleshoot the Roof 202

Chapter 18: Access
Stair Support 204
Framing the Platform 206
Stringers. 208
Stringers & Treads. 210
Railing. 212
Extras. 214

Chapter 19: Additional Options
Doors 216
Windows 218
Electricity. 220
Furniture 222
Lighthearted Fun 224
Accessories. 226

Chapter 20: Resources
Resources 228

Photo credits 238
Index. 240

INTRODUCTION

In most people the word treehouse conjures up a feeling that takes them right back to their childhoods. Whether you actually had a treehouse or not, you know that feeling. It's the same feeling you got when Johnny the ice cream man showed up at the playground or your Little League team won a championship. You're transported back to a time when all of one's imaginary worlds were real, and when all it took to become a pirate, cowboy, or wizard was a good friend to play along.

My first treehouse was actually a clubhouse my younger sister and I built in the rafters of our garage. I can't remember how we actually built it, but I do remember that I always felt a great pride of ownership every time I ventured up there. Dirty, dusty, and hot, it was nevertheless ours.

These days things have changed. Owning a treehouse is as often a status symbol as it is a child's retreat. Celebrities like Julianne Moore, Val Kilmer, Donna Karan, and Sting all own highly designed treehouses that are literally works of art. Designers, architects, and treehouse builders all over the world have challenged themselves to keep building bigger, better, and more ingenious treetop structures. You have only to spend some time at the Canopy Cathedral in Pennsylvania or the $7 million treehouse restaurant at Alnwick Gardens in England to see how magnificent treehouses can be. There are countless examples of builders working with nature, building treehouses to help us all understand the world in which we live.

Perhaps Whitman said it best: "After you have exhausted what there is in business, politics, conviviality . . . what remains? Nature remains." And that may be the ultimate draw to the world of treehouses: freedom from the constraints of everyday life. I jumped at the opportunity to put this book together, in part because I saw it as a chance to both revisit my childhood dreams and to clarify my personal relationship to nature.

Constructing a book while deconstructing preconceptions

Little did I know that the challenging experience of writing about treehouses would forever change my life and the way I view the world. Like most people who will read this book, I thought treehouses are for kids. How wrong I was. Some of the most sophisticated, futuristic, and eco-friendly buildings in the world are being placed in trees, appealing to adults every bit as much as children. Whether perched in a poplar, elm, or pine, whether built from natural wood,

wood composites, or metal, the houses themselves take on all shapes, sizes, and colors. And the builders are world-class designers, architects, and carpenters, men and women whom its been a privilege to interview and get to know.

When I first met with builders Dan Wright and Gary Koontz at our treehouse site in Pennsylvania, I knew my preconceptions were going to be challenged. Here were these two guys who were faced with building an amazing treehouse in an impossibly short length of time, and they looked, well, they looked like your everyday carpenters. It was cold and crisp, and the sun was poking through a patch of poplar trees. We were all wearing jackets and gloves. As we stared out at the Delaware River, I realized how lucky I was to be working on such a project. I found Dan to be a thoughtful man and dedicated to his work. Gary was already working, setting up his tools and making the area usable. I already sensed that he was the "Energizer Bunny," always moving, never standing around and waiting for something to do. In fact, following him around on behalf of the book was tricky, in part because he'd finish things before I could take pictures or ask questions. I had to slow him up sometimes. It wasn't until I sat down to write a few weeks later that I realized how much I had learned from Gary.

It took us five days to complete the project chronicled in this book. As the treehouse took shape in front of my eyes, I thought about the children who would one day be using this masterpiece on the river, scooting up and down the stairs, swinging from the platform, zipping in and out of the trees scattered around the property. It made me smile. In this age of iPods, iPhones, and video games, how nice it was to think that some children were going to get a chance to experience the world as it should be, outdoors in the sunlight, playing from dawn until dusk in a treehouse by the Delaware River.

The nuts and bolts

Somewhere around day three, George showed up on the job. An ex-military man, he was going to be the nuts-and-bolts guy, helping Gary and Dan by cutting studs, measuring trim, and doing everything else they needed done. George was a bit easier to follow because he was more methodical and deliberate in his building process. He and I had many discussions that had little to do with treehouses and more to do with life and politics. But he was invaluable in helping me understand the building process and the importance of each step. He was the perfect complement to Dan and Gary. Together, the three of them couldn't have made my job more enjoyable. It was an important lesson to learn, that the work should be shared with someone. The joy of putting together a treehouse is enhanced by sharing it with a good buddy, a son, a daughter, or a dad. It creates a lasting bond that may last well beyond the life of the treehouse.

The gifts of nature married with innovation

The trees are there, just as they always have been, waiting for us to come to them. The islanders of New Guinea built in the trees thousands of years ago, seeking shelter from floods and wild animals. The Romans arranged platforms in the trees to monitor activity along their borders. The English nobility built treehouses to entertain their guests. And now we, too, can raise our own structures into the limbs and leaves.

Given the innovations that have proliferated over the last decade, treehouse building has come of age. You no longer have to harm a tree to build in it. Structural engineers like Charlie Greenwood, innovators like Michael Garnier and S. Peter Lewis, and designers like Simon Torquil, Simon Mitchell, Tom Chudleigh, Dustin Feider, Barbara Butler, and Pete Nelson have all taken treehouse building to an entirely new level. People like us, the backyard builders, are the beneficiaries.

The road map to our dreams

What you have in your hands now is a road map more than an architectural plan. It represents the cumulative knowledge of hundreds of people who have dedicated themselves in one way or another to treehouse construction. I am the lucky conduit who had the opportunity to take the journey. Standing on the shoulders of these treehouse giants, I've come to feel a little closer to the Earth. When I look at a tree today, I see more than a simple plant, more than an arrangement of roots and limbs. I see a living creature giving us gifts, protecting us from the elements, providing shade, and producing the air we breathe. Thanks to this book I've come to appreciate trees in a way I hadn't before. To build a treehouse in this self-contained world without harming it is to both pay tribute to the world and to participate in it. The trees are waiting for us with open arms, welcoming our aspirations and dreams.

This volume contains as much written information as could be packed into the format, but the photographs tell the real story. Every person I approached to be part of this book willingly donated his or her work to make this effort a success. From little Katie Ellis in Maryland to Andreas Wenning, master architect in Germany, each one of them was anxious to introduce me to their world, to let me wander around in the delights of treehouse building. And now it's your turn. I hope you enjoy.

TREEHOUSE POSSIBILITIES

A treehouse can be a playhouse, a relaxing getaway, or a commitment to green living

Whether you're eight or eighty, pounding your first nail into a board or finishing a degree in engineering, there's something alluring about treehouses. Something that appeals to the child in all of us. Maybe it's that basic urge to climb high and look down, to rule the backyard from a crow's nest in the leaves, or maybe it's more an instinct toward retreat and

camouflage, an urge to hide briefly from a parent or boss or even a ringing phone. No matter. Treehouses speak to that basic part of us that fantasizes about going out on a limb, about simultaneously taking risks and hiding away. They're the stuff dreams are made of.

The most basic treehouses, the ones you had when you

Storybook Treehouse

- This treehouse was inspired by the Hugh Comstock "Hansel House." It was built for a family with three children.

- The access to the treehouse is via a ladder that leads to the platform.

- The interior of the treehouse is approximately 160 square feet and it features a small sleeping loft.

- It was built with 90 percent reclaimed materials, including refurbished windows and salvaged cedar siding, by TreeHouse Workshop, Inc. of Seattle, WA.

A Relaxing Getaway

- The treehouse is perched between two trees using a combination of fixed, knee brace, and cable supports.

- Textured plywood was used for siding along with corrugated roofing and pressure-treated lumber. The materials for this style of treehouse can be found anywhere.

- The flap-style awning windows are a nostalgic touch. Plywood may not last long so opt for cedar boards.

- The sunburst pattern in the railing is attractive but has spaces greater than 4 inches near the top, which may not meet local codes.

were a kid, can be thrown up by a dad who is handy with a handsaw and hammer. But most of the treehouses that adults are drawn to require real expertise to build. Rather than starting with just a few boards between limbs, these are structures that might spread across multiple branches, hang from the tree, or even be built right into the body of the tree itself.

What draws people to live in a tree? Maybe they want to help save the environment by sitting in a protest hut in a tree. Or try to recapture a lost childhood. Regardless of the motivation, and whether the treehouse is functional or whimsical, affordable or extravagantly expensive, there is no end to the magical variety of forms a treehouse can take.

Combining architecture and landscaping, imaginative builders create treehouses that mix into their surroundings and preserve the health of the trees that support them. Some treehouses blend a classic look with contemporary angles, clean lines, and modern design elements. These tree-top dwellings mix with their natural settings and are often customized to client specifications.

The Eco-friendly Treehouse

- German landscape architect Rudolf Doernach developed treehouse-building techniques that he broadly called "biotecture" or "agritecture."

- These methods are set up to be largely self-sustaining.

- Eco-friendly treehouses use minimal external energy while providing maximum agricultural yield.

- With proper knowledge, the architect believes, you can grow your own house. These are the ultimate in low-cost, low-maintenance, zero-energy homes.

San Diego Treehouse

- Just as a gazebo or pool house can provide extra space for entertaining and relaxing, a treehouse can have a practical as well as a whimsical function.

- Built in a live oak grove, this 1,000-square-foot tree-house features a full bath, kitchen, running water, fireplace, and a washer and dryer.

- The railings and siding were all milled on site from felled, standing dead oak.

- Everything was built on site by TreeHouse Workshop, Inc. of Seattle, WA.

TREEHOUSE DREAM DESIGNS

An imaginative treehouse design can be not only functional but also innovative

For an artistic soul, there is nothing more satisfying than seeing your creative urges realized in a physical construction. Treehouses can provide one of the most satisfying outlets for the desire to express yourself.

The movable and sturdy Free Spirit Spheres, designed and manufactured by Tom Chudleigh of British Columbia, can be hung from almost anything, including trees, buildings, and rock walls. A unique system of webbing and ropes anchors the spheres to their locations. Each sphere or pod is waterproofed and built to be impact-resistant. The surface is composed of an internal laminated wood frame and clear fiberglass exterior.

Free Spirit Spheres

- The spheres are designed to fit harmoniously into a forest setting without altering it.

- Inside the sphere, walls and ceiling become one in a single continuous shell.

- A web of rope connects the sphere to the trees, reflecting a connectedness to the ecosystem.

- Suspended spheres reduce the human footprint. The sphere's web attaches at multiple points, and its stretchiness enables sphere and trees to move freely, producing a feeling of floating while in the sphere.

The 4Treehouse

- The design lets the existing trees set the parameters of the project. The treehouse was constructed around the bases of four existing trees.

- The intent of the project was to minimize the impact on the trees and the site.

- A swing was suspended from above, forming the structural foundation.

- The tall, tubelike structure allows visitors to ascend up an interior staircase beside the tree. Three platform levels vary in transparency, allowing for various levels of illumination.

The 4Treehouse is situated to accommodate four existing trees on the site. This project successfully works around the existing natural site conditions.

The O2 Sustainability Treehouse design turns the conventional treehouse on its ear. The archetypical square wooden structure is replaced with an eco-friendly geodesic dome.

The Terreform FabTreehabitat is a dwelling composed of 100 percent living nutrients. The idea is to grow homes from native trees, allowing them to interact with native ecosystems

The O2 Treehouse

The Terreform FabTreehabitat

- The most intriguing aspect of the O2 Treehouse is its ability to adapt to large-scale designs and a wide variety of sites.

- With the integration of graywater systems and solar and wind energy systems, the O2 Treehouse becomes an economical alternative to summer camps, traditional travel destinations, and ecoresorts.

- Only local materials were used in construction.

- Treehouses can be used to observe nature, hold meetings, and conduct team-building exercises.

- Looking to the future, the next stage in treehouse evolution is a living treehouse.

- The design utilizes "pleaching," a gardening technique in which tree branches are woven together to form living archways.

- Trees such as elm, live oak, and dogwood bear the heavier loads, while vines, branches, and plants form a lattice for the walls and roof of the house.

- The interior structure is made of cob (clay and straw).

TREEHOUSE DESIGN STATEMENTS

An imaginative, artistic design can complement the surroundings rather than distract from them

Some of the most talented designers in architecture have turned to treehouses as a fresh palette on which to indulge their creative instincts. From prefabricated designs to sweeping, interpretive creations, there is no end to the inventiveness of these treetop Michelangelos.

Andrew Maynard designs prefab treehouses that are passionately inventive. He is a model for any aspiring designer. Maynard created his Global Rescue Station to fasten semipermanently to the body of three trees. The design shelters and protects environmental protesters during their demonstrations. If a logger dares to cut down its supports, the structure will potentially harm anything beneath or around it.

The Global Rescue Station

- A pristine wilderness in southwestern Tasmania, the Styx Valley Forest is home to the tallest hardwoods in the world.

- Many of the trees are over four hundred years old. Less than 13 percent of the original forest remains.

- A large area of Tasmania's wilderness is protected. Unfortunately the Styx Valley falls just outside of this protected area.

- Much of the wood that is logged is reduced to wood chips that are exported to Japan.

Tentvillage—Revisited

- Dutch artist Dré Wapenaar created a "Tentvillage" that, when clustered together, look like a colony of wild mushrooms.

- Canvas tents were arranged on multilevel platforms. They formed both an autonomous sculpture and a functioning campsite.

- Initially sold to four campgrounds in the Netherlands, one cluster of the tent village was repurchased and refurbished by the artist.

- The refurbished tents were used as a hangout and chill site during the city of Nantes's famous biennial.

The Sybarite Treehouse project designed by Torquil McIntosh and Simon Mitchell conforms to the landscape. The foundation and supports are designed to reduce impact on root systems. Rainwater collection, solar panels, and a wind energy system are also integrated, for energy independence.

Finca Bellavista is a treehouse community in the Southern Zone of Costa Rica, created to maintain ecological balance within the rain forest. Each structure in the community must utilize a rainwater catch system, hydroelectric power system, and treat waste with biodigestors.

ZOOM

The Sybarite Treehouse project has caught on with at least one buyer in England's West Country. From above, it pokes through a thick covering of trees like a structure from a science fiction movie or an alien spaceship that has landed in the trees. The house is a flexible modular system designed to be elevated just above the natural treeline.

The Sybarite Treehouse

- The flexible floor plans encourage an organic approach to country living. The treehouse capitalizes on the beauty of its setting while minimizing its impact.

- The layout, along with panoramic windows, maximizes the benefits of the sun's path. The kitchen enjoys morning light, whereas the living and bedroom spaces have the pleasure of sunset.

- The prefabricated sections allow for various configurations.

- The treehouse is designed to be 70 percent energy self-sufficient.

El Castillo Mastate

- This octagonal dwelling located in Finca Bellavista is a sight to behold. The master bedroom is situated 90 feet off the forest floor in a giant Mastate tree.

- An 80-foot-long suspension bridge connects the treehouse to a raised knoll on the forest floor.

- A stilt-built casita houses a full kitchen and bath as well as a dining area.

- Special features include hardwood bamboo floors, custom tile finishes, and bright skylights.

TREEHOUSE ART & STUDY CENTERS

A treehouse can provide an atmosphere that makes learning and art appreciation fun

A well-designed treehouse can be more than a child's playhouse or a place where Dad goes to read a good book. It can host a children's environmental school or be an art studio where classes can be taught in the inspirational setting of a forest. At the end of the day, there are almost as many uses for treehouses as there are for traditional structures. New York's

Madison Square Garden, for instance, took on a Swiss Family Robinson feel in 2009 when an art exhibition called "Madison Square Tree Huts" was installed. The collection consisted of a series of small wooden structures, an arrangement of treetop art meant to shake up our preconceived notions of public space and how it interacts with urban life.

Morocco Treehouse

- Roderick Romero built this project in collaboration with TreeHouse Workshop, Inc. and the 212 Society, a nonprofit school that trains Moroccan orphans in carpentry and metalwork.

- A documentary, entitled the *Tangier Treehouse*, chronicles their efforts.

- The unique platform was built in a huge black fig tree over two hundred years old. Lebanese cedar from Tangier was used for beams.

- The bolts, brackets, and hardware were paid for by donations from Sting, Russell Simmons, and Donna Karan.

The Yellow Treehouse Restaurant

- Pacific Environments Architects wanted its treehouse to be one we all dreamed of as children but see realized only as adults.

- The eighteen-seat café is 30 feet wide and 36 feet high, with kitchen and lavatories on the ground.

- G-beams are a great choice for green building with less waste and a smaller carbon footprint than standard materials.

- The project is located on a rise near the edge of a wood overlooking a stream.

The Yellow Treehouse Restaurant by New Zealand–based Pacific Environments Architects Ltd. (PEL) is a stunning architectural feat perched high above a redwood forest. Appearing for all the world like an enormous chrysalis grafted onto a 120-foot redwood tree, the project is constructed of plantation poplar slats and redwood railing milled at the site. It makes extensive use of natural lighting throughout. Taking a cue from its surroundings, it was inspired by many forms found in nature, including a cocoon, an onion or garlic clove, a lantern, and a sea shell with the open ends spiraling to the center.

Samantha Sherwood, a third-year architectural student from Oxford Brookes University, was the winner of a competition to design an arboreal concept for the New Forest Treehouse Study Center at Beaulieu, Hampshire. One of the key aims of the center is to provide a stimulating environment in which children from inner-city areas can get close to nature and experience the range of activities that the Countryside Education Trust (CET) offers. The center opened in 2008.

Samantha's Treehouse School

- The design features a biomass boiler, solar panels, rainwater collection, and a glass roof.

- Given that the size of the structure's carbon footprint was a concern, construction materials were acquired locally wherever possible.

- A walkway suspended 16 feet from the ground enables students to move readily from one classroom to the other, increasing the enjoyment of their studies.

- Only the bathrooms and the facility's office are located on the ground.

CET's Forest Learning Center

- The new learning center replaced two dilapidated classrooms that the center had acquired second-hand.

- The Countryside Education Trust (CET) in England commissioned two classrooms-on-supports, giving ten thousand children a year the opportunity to experience rural life.

- With an eco-minded design, the treehouse project is a catalyst for environmental awareness.

- Twenty-two-year-old Samantha Sherwood worked closely with professionals to develop her plans.

TREEHOUSE INDUSTRY
Builders are increasingly attracted to treehouses, making for a burgeoning, eco-friendly business

For those inclined to forgo a nine-to-five work week and start up their own business (perhaps indulging their childhood dreams while they're at it), few things can be as satisfying as forming a treehouse-building company, creating a treehouse bed and breakfast, or even establishing a treetop theme park. There are many talented individuals to look to for inspiration.

Armed with superior woodworking skills and an MBA, Dan Wright has created over one hundred treehouses of all types. He makes a good living from his constructions, but the real payoff is seeing the children of a client climb up the ladder for the first time to enjoy their treetop fort.

In addition to his internationally famous Out 'n' About

Tree Top Builders, Inc.

- Trained as a carpenter, Dan Wright made the decision to professionally build treehouses in 1999.

- Wright has built treehouses from California to Texas to Maine.

- Dan and his partner typically support treehouses with knee braces, fixed and floating, or custom designed cable support systems.

Michael Garnier's Out 'n' About

- Garnier's Treehouse Institute offers comprehensive instruction in engineering, design, and construction methods for treehouses.

- Out 'n' About's theme-based treehouses include the Swiss Family Complex, the Cavaltree, and the Cabintree.

- Michael fought an eight-year zoning battle with county officials in Oregon. He sold one-of-a-kind "treeshirts" to raise money for his defense.

- An innovative engineer, Garnier has developed many custom construction elements.

Treesort (a licensed bed and breakfast), Michael Garnier has also created the Treehouse Institute of Arts and Culture in Takilma, Oregon. But he's most famous for the "Garnier Limb," an eponymous device that is used around the world as a main support in treehouse building.

Longwood Gardens near Kennet Square, Pennsylvania, a beautiful park once owned by Pierre DuPont and the DuPont family, features three custom treehouses by TreeHouse Workshop, Inc. and Forever Young that provide hours of fun and enjoyment for the whole family. The outdoor gardens and conservatory are open at 9 a.m. and 10 a.m., respectively, every day of the year, and close at 6 p.m. from April through October and 5 p.m. from November through March. Admission price is $8 to $15 for adults, $6 for youths ages sixteen to twenty, $2 for youths ages six to fifteen, and free for children under age six.

Although Longwood is a huge facility, it can serve as an inspiration for those looking to incorporate treehouses into their business lives. Every backyard enthusiast might one day start his or her own eco-friendly business in the treetops.

Longwood Gardens

- Open to the public, the treehouses on display in these historical gardens are an inspiring tribute to what can be accomplished by a builder.

- The salvaged wood, scalloped trim, doweled fasteners, and shellac finishes can be used by any builder.

- Set picturesquely around the gardens are the Lookout Loft by Forever Young, and the Canopy Cathedral and the Birdhouse by TreeHouse Workshop, Inc. of Seattle, WA.

- The gardens have their roots in the DuPont family fortune.

Alnwick Gardens

- The treehouse in Alnwick Gardens is the world's largest all-wood treehouse at 6,000 square feet. It's composed of walkways, cottages, shops, a restaurant, and play areas.

- More than thirty lime trees support the structure.

- The main building sits on a platform of yellow balau hardwood decking.

- When the structure was designed, freeform sketches were used rather than CAD architectural renderings.

TREEHOUSE RESORTS

In your search for innovative treehouse ideas, a treetop-themed vacation can show you the world

Building a living area in the trees is an idea that has arisen in any number of cultures. Before constructing your own treehouse, and if you're feeling self-indulgent, a treehouse-themed vacation can provide just the inspiration you need. From Fiji to New Zealand to the forests of Oregon, different regions offer their own unique approach to treetop building.

Most of the differences in the treehouse construction are based on available materials, climate, and the expertise of the local builders. If you are looking to build something unique to your region, take care to use materials that will weather well in your area

At Matangi Private Island Resort, three split-level treehouses

Matangi Resort Treehouses

- A privately owned 240-acre horseshoe-shaped island serves as the setting for a trio of unique thatch-roofed treehouses.

- Exotic hardwoods such as giant bamboo provide a durable alternative to most domestically available materials.

- Treehouses have been part of the Fijian culture for thousands of years but have been modified here to accommodate tourism.

- The first treetop dwellers sought refuge in trees from harmful animals and potential flooding.

Out 'n' About Treehouses

- Out 'n' About sees itself as a summer camp for the family.

- The resort staff teaches a ropes course, horseback riding, and rafting.

- Craft courses are taught on site by local artists and

include classes on everything from tie-dye to tile-making.

- A library houses a number of books about treehouses, from instructional how-tos to the history of the specific treehouses on the premises.

hold their own in the midst of volcanic rock formations and a tropical jungle. The treehouses are built with native evergreen trees and covered in thatch. They have easy access and are set high enough above the ground to provide stunning views. Featured on a Travel Channel segment entitled, *Tremendous Tree Houses,* these treehouses would have to be called "world famous."

For a resort in the woods, Michael Garnier's Out 'n' About Treesort features eighteen thematically unique treehouses. Platforms, seven swinging bridges, zip lines, and a swimming pool complete the experience.

The fifteen villas in Daintree Raintree Resort in Queensland, Australia, are sequestered amid one of the world's oldest rain forests. Each treehouse retreat features carved cedar furniture, luxury double showers, kitchen facilities, stained glass windows, sunken double spas, and private balconies with barbecues. Daintree is home to the spiritual ancestors of the Kuku Yalanji tribe, and the resort strives to harness that spiritual energy by creating a unique healing environment.

Daintree Treehouse Resort

- The resort features an art gallery called "Julaymba," displaying authentic aboriginal and nonindigenous art.

- Visitors can learn the traditional stories and customs of the Kuku Yalanji people by taking Bimalbu Arts and Crafts.

- Artists can create their own aboriginal-inspired masterpieces using earthy colors from a nearby waterfall.

- Bird watchers who visit Daintree Valley will see species like the great billed heron, black bittern, little tern, and beach stone curlew, among others.

Treehouse Resorts

- When you're looking to go on a treehouse resort vacation, first choose the area of the world you'd like to visit.

- Most resorts offer outdoor activities as well as relaxing spas and meditation services. Price amenity services to avoid sticker shock after arrival.

- It's always a good idea to talk to people who have been to the resort. Don't be afraid to ask the management for referrals.

- Most treehouse resorts have Web sites that are very detailed. Some even offer videos that you can view online.

SINGLE-TRUNK TREEHOUSE
Building in a single tree is the simplest and easiest way to begin construction

For the beginner or casual builder, it's usually best to start your treehouse experience with construction in a single tree. There are various single-tree styles, from the elementary to the quite sophisticated, but the more you know about the variations, the easier it will be for you to decide what type of treetop getaway you should construct.

The most obvious style of house design surrounds the tree's trunk. The tree should be a durable, live tree with thick branches and, preferably, the makings of a platform within a safe distance of the ground. You can get a great feeling of treetop adventure even when you are only a few feet high. The trunk should be at least 1 foot in diameter at the base.

Illinois Treehouse

- The entrance deck is in the front area. The structure occupies 90 square feet in the back, all of which is built around the tree.

- Prehung windows and screens allow for ventilation, essential to a treehouse built where the summers can be hot and humid.

- A simple wooden ladder leads to the deck, providing for a great view of the backyard and neighborhood forest.

- The platform system is knee braced to the tree trunk with a bolt-and-bracket system.

Havertown Treehouse

- Despite utilizing only a single trunk, the treehouse is large enough to accommodate a few children and adults for a sleepover.

- The structure is firmly seated with steel cables attached to lag bolts, eyebolts, turnbuckles, and knee braces.

- A simple ladder takes you directly to the deck and the treehouse's Dutch door.

- The interior has a loft bed and several prehung windows that are designed to allow for lots of light.

After choosing a tree, the most essential step is to create a strong, level platform for your treehouse. The most common system for a safe platform support is "spokes" that radiate outward from the trunk. The spokes themselves can be supported either with knee braces underneath or from cables or braces above. Tension braces work in a similar manner to upside-down knee braces with the treehouse suspended underneath.

Although there are disadvantages to building around a single trunk, there are still enormous possibilities.

Treehouse Chronicles

- A hexagonal steel collar, a set of suspension cables, and wooden trusses combine to provide exceptional stability.

- The two hundred-year-old white pine divides into two trunks 37 feet above the ground.

- The collar-cable-truss (CCT) system provides great strength and stability and was utilized to avoid drilling holes in the tree.

- The system was developed by S. Peter Lewis specifically for this project, given that the structure weighed over three tons.

Tips for Tree Prep

- While laying out the platform, bumps in the limbs can be flattened with a saw.

- Cut off bumps or branch stumps only if they are dead.

- The most important step in building in one tree is to erect a strong, stable platform.

- Using a standard bubble level, all structural beams should be leveled several times.

TWO-TREE TREEHOUSE

Using two trees allows for a builder to choose between a wider variety of floor plans

Common sense says that if one tree is good, two must be better. And indeed, the creative possibilities multiply with the addition of another trunk. It's possible, for instance, to build the main treehouse in one tree and a deck in the other. To connect them, consider a rope bridge or a stairway. If the two trees grow close enough together, a treehouse can be built between them, thus eliminating a trunk running through the middle of your structure. The extra room provided by the absent trunk can allow for new ways to access the treehouse, be it a rope ladder, escape hatch staircase, rock wall climbs, or a wooden ladder.

The trees you select should be strong, healthy trees at least

Playahead Treehouses

- Playahead is a family-run business established over ten years ago. Its main focus is safe, outdoor playhouses for children.

- Their two-tree treehouses feature verandas, raised walkways, and secret platforms that provide access farther up into the trees.

- They use softwood logs that give the decor a rustic feel, while the rounded corners and edges ensure there are no gaps to trap small fingers.

- Doors, window shutters, and a lined roof weatherproof the interior.

Glenmoore Treehouse

- The treehouse and its lookout platform utilize two trees by spanning a bridge from one structure to the other.

- When building separate structures, a rope net bridge can be a fun, relatively inexpensive way to connect them.

- The zip line from lookout deck to a separate tree 75 feet away can hold an adult of over two hundred pounds.

- An escape hatch ladder accesses the main treehouse, making for an efficient use of floor space.

10 inches in diameter. Unless you're connecting them to a bridge, they should be at least 6 to 8 feet apart.

The first step in building in your two trees is to lay down the support beams. Depending on the final size of the structure, 2-by-6 or 4-by-8 beams are usually adequate. When in doubt, err on the side of caution and choose the larger beams. Or better yet, consult a professional builder. The beams should straddle the two trees and be attached with lag bolts or lag screws. It's always best to use a fastener that will handle more than your intended load.

Once you've erected the beams, you can start building the support platform with 2-by-6 joists. It's often most efficient to build the platform on the ground and then hoist it onto the support beams. With the platform in place, the next decision is to choose between knee braces or a suspension system. After all of this is behind you, you're ready to build your treehouse.

The Canopy Cathedral at Longwood Gardens

- Inspired by a Norwegian church, custom-made posts and railings provide an opportunity for one-of-a-kind hand carvings.

- There are many creative exit and entrance points.

- A clear lacquer finish water-proofs the wood, while fasteners tie rafters and trim together. The center rafters are scalloped, giving the interior a storybook look.

- To preserve the trees, a Diamond Pier pin foundation system was used, technically making the Canopy Cathedral a no-tree treehouse.

More about Longwood Gardens

- Longwood Gardens has two other treehouses called the Birdhouse and the Lookout Loft.

- The Lookout Loft features rounded logs fitted together with notches and wood fastenings. It's a combination of modern design and rusticity.

- The Birdhouse is a three-story treehouse fashioned out of recycled timber. The top deck offers terrific views.

- The property features one of the largest conservatories of plant life in the world.

THREE-TREE TREEHOUSE

Although an architectural challenge, building between three trees can offer many aesthetic rewards

If two trees are better than one, are three better than two? The addition of an element certainly offers a greater variety of potential floor plans as well as further latitude in choosing amenities, including decks and bridges. You can use all three trees to form a triangular platform, you can use one tree for a lookout deck, or you can build any platform shape you like as long as your supports can handle the weight. You can also build between three branches of the same tree, using the same support system you would have used on separate trees. The branches need to be at least 6 to 8 inches in diameter and strong enough to support the weight.

The first step in building a triangular platform is to cut the

The Lookout Loft at Longwood Gardens

- A metal post system supports the three-tree wood pavilion, providing extra support.

- The log posts and railings were notched and fitted together with hidden wood and bolt fasteners.

- Because the gardens receive hundreds of thousands of visitors per year, safety is of paramount importance. The Lookout Loft is lined with solid, round-post railings.

- A walkway leads to the second pavilion, a modern-looking, shake-covered structure built around a single tulip tree.

Joanne and Harry Neely Treehouse

- An archetypical triangular platform has been bolted and bracketed to each tree at the angled ends of the boards.

- A rectangular platform sits on top of the triangular support and is bolted to the trees behind. Floor joists provide additional support and stability.

- A ladder to the deck provides simple access.

- Windows around the entire structure provide for fantastic views, while a smaller decorative hexagonal window is inset into the facing of the roofline.

beams to fit the three sides. Each end should be cut at an angle to fit into the neighboring beams. Once the beams are cut, drill holes in the trees where each bolt will fasten. Make sure the beams are level and leave enough board jutting beyond the tree to fit with the boards that will complete the triangle. Use screws to fasten the ends of the beams together. Check your level and then attach the joists. As soon as the platform is finished, you are ready to build your main structure on top of it.

To build a rectangular platform on three trees or tree branches, the best method is to affix 2-by-4 triangular braces to each tree or branch with lag bolts. The sharpest angle of the triangle should be facing downward, leaving enough board area to support your platform's joists. The platform can usually be built on the ground and then hoisted onto the support system. Fasten the platform to the supports using appropriate fasteners and begin building your treehouse.

Mis Ojos Miran la Catarata

- Supported by a trio of trees, this model treehome in the Finca Bellavista community has two separate, free-floating levels.

- The downstairs has a full kitchen and lounge area while the upstairs has a bedroom and full bath. Special features include a retractable staircase and terrestrial dining gazebo.

- The ground level is perched 60 feet off the ground.

- Both levels have balconies with sensational views of a 40-foot waterfall and the zipline canopy travel system.

A Dan Wright–built Three-tree Treehouse

- One of these three trees has two large branches, making for a rectangular platform support. Two large beams bolted to the tree provide support.

- The platform is supported by a cable system from above, leaving the bottom of the platform free for a wraparound staircase.

- The main beams are supported by large treehouse fasteners, and the long cantilever in the front is supported by overhead cables.

17

FOUR-TREE TREEHOUSE

Using four trees for a foundation is unusual but can have beautiful results

Finding four trees arranged in such a way as to form a suitable treehouse foundation is a tough prospect. In the rare instance that four similar-size trees grow in proximity, however—neither too close nor too far apart, forming a rectangular shape—then it's possible to build a stunning and stable treehouse with plenty of interior space, unimpeded by trunks poking through the structure. Typically, however, a four-tree construction requires the handiwork of an expert builder, if only to find ways to accommodate the movements of four trees.

Brackets provide the stability, while cables are good for awkward, swaying conditions.

A Dan Wright–built Four-tree Treehouse

- Platform beams bolted with a bracket assembly to each of the four trees create a secure foundation.

- Three of the walls of the main structure were built flush to the support beams, while the fourth wall, containing the entry, was set back to accommodate the deck and railing.

- A wooden bridge stretches from the main structure to a platform, providing access to the ground.

- The cable system splits the load between the upper and lower parts of the trees.

Four-tree Sky Room, Cheshire, England

- Special flexible joints were used to allow each of the four trees to move independently.

- Rounded log joists were built into the platform to give it extra stability. The deck was then fastened onto the platform.

- A flexible wood tread-and-rope ladder provides access. The ladder was constructed with braided white rope threaded through the treads.

- An open structure without formal windows allows for 360-degree views.

In the likely case of four trees not arranged in a rectangular pattern, the best scenario might be to construct the treehouse between two or three of the trees and use a bridge to incorporate the remaining trunk or trunks. A single-trunk treehouse connected to a lookout platform or crow's nest via a bridge or zip line is also a possibility. Keep things simple if possible to avoid having to deal with the difficult maintenance that four trees can cause in the future.

Four trees allow for an infinite variety of treatments, limited only by your imagination.

YELLOW LIGHT

Use caution when building in different tree species. Different species grow at different rates, both vertically and horizontally. A good rule of thumb is to keep conifers and deciduous trees separated in the building process, unless they support separate structures. Consult an arborist about the specifics of your trees if you have questions.

Eric Akers's Treehouse

- Six 4-by-4 posts and two 4-by-4 beams created a structure strong enough to support four stories of treehouse.

- The trees were not large enough to use as supports, so the structure was built freestanding, but with trees weaving through its boards.

- The treehouse was built by Eric and his father but inspired by artist Lebbeus Woods.

- Sited in Florida, the platform was built to provide plenty of room for the trees to sway, allowing for potential hurricane weather.

Eric Akers

- This treehouse is more than just a treehouse; it represents a memory for Eric.

- He and his father built the treehouse together, learning a little about treehouses and a lot about their relationship.

- The end result was a monument to their persistence and love for each other.

- Lebbeus Woods's artwork plays with the idea of construction and deconstruction.

TREES & POSTS

When a site doesn't allow for building between trees, posts are an acceptable substitute

Is a treehouse really a treehouse if it uses posts to help support the structure? What about building a structure without using tree support at all? Integrating trees into a structure set above the ground, for all intents and purposes, provides the same atmosphere and experience of an actual treehouse (minus the swaying, of course).

The use of posts can allow for a very inventive approach, unconstrained by the limitations of the trees themselves. Generally, 4-by-4 posts are used for most small to mid-size treehouses. Round poles at least 5 inches in diameter are also good, particularly when young children might be bumping against sharp edges.

Ellis Treehouse

- A rectangular platform is fastened by lag bolts to four 4-by-4 posts.

- Because the treehouse was built on a hill, the posts were shorter in the back, making it very important to make sure the platform was level once it was set on top of the posts.

- To give the playhouse a treetop feel, one small tree was integrated into the front deck and railings. The branches poke through the structure itself.

- Clear plastic, corrugated polycarbonate roofing provides ambient lighting.

Papua Green House

- Located in the rain forests of Papua, New Guinea, the builders—the Korowai and Kombai tribes—were discovered by the outside world just thirty years ago.

- Set between 36 and 150 feet off the ground, the structures are high enough to catch the breeze, providing relief from the stifling tropical heat.

- The vista allows the inhabitants a terrific vantage point.

- One of the most common trees in New Guinea is the Indian devil tree. It's often used in treetop construction.

When using a combination of trees and posts, it's usually preferable to have the trees in the back of the treehouse where they can be integrated into the structure, leaving the front access point clean and easy to use. Treated posts should be used, preferably set into concrete. The holes should be at least 36 inches deep. When setting the posts, level them first, brace them, then pour the concrete into the holes. Even a slight tilt on the posts can cause headaches down the road. At least twenty-four hours should be allowed for the concrete to cure before any structures are fastened to the posts.

The Birdhouse

- A creative fusion of materials, the supporting posts are steel set in concrete, while the staircase and framing are recycled warehouse lumber.

- This magnificent structure, located at Longwood Gardens in Pennsylvania, has hundreds of visitors a day.

- The refinished warehouse door is from Alaska. The gate and railings are made of natural tree branches. The bench is a finished cross section of a tree trunk.

- This treehouse was designed and built by TreeHouse Workshop, Inc. of Seattle, WA.

More on Posts

- In regions where the ground freezes, "heaving," or soil expansion caused by freezing, can cause instability.

- To avoid heaving, the posts should be set below the frost line.

- Treated wood posts have to meet industry specifications for retention and chemical penetration relating to decay, fungi, and insects.

- Any type of wood can be treated at various wood-preserving companies.

UNIQUE TREEHOUSE SUPPORTS

Every one-of-a-kind treehouse needs its own uniquely designed system of support

Even more than typical ground structures, treehouses inspire innovation in the builders. From parade floats to pirate ships, each new design requires a new approach to the engineering problems that arise.

Some of the world's most forward-thinking builders and architects are exploring the possibilities of treetop homes.

In England, a company called Sybarite is developing eco-friendly, self-sustaining treetop modular structures that are built on steel stilts.

In central California, Daniels Wood Land specializes in designing, fabricating, and installing interactive-themed environments for family entertainment centers, theme parks, and

KNACK TREEHOUSES

The Pirate Treehouse

- Built by Peacemaker Treehouses, Captain Jack's Flying Pirate Ship sails 10 feet off the ground.

- The triangular platform was built above two low branches on the south side of the main trunk and anchored at the front of the ship by 4-by-4 posts.

- Diagonal braces provide additional support.

- The ship comes complete with cabin, masts, rigging, and gun ports.

- Company founder John Carberry studied architecture and then turned to building treehouses.

Found Object Treehouse

- Utilizing scavenged wood, owner and builder Horace Burgess built this ten-story treehouse for less than $12,000.

- Started in 1993, it's still a work in progress, utilizing donated or discarded wood.

- All the scavenged or donated wood is sorted through to make sure it's not warped, full of nails, or cracked.

- The square footage is estimated to be between 8,000 and 10,000 square feet. The construction has incorporated 258,000 nails, give or take a few hundred.

other commercial outlets. Its treehouses utilize artificial trees, animated characters, shooting galleries, and more. In addition, it employs expert craftsmen who carve statues of bears, pirates, and cowboys as part of the themed treehouses. Daniels Wood Land also creates and manufactures faux trees sculpted of steel and reinforced foam. They are customized to fit the client's existing space and look as good as the real thing.

Still other builders opt for using found and salvaged materials. Their tree dwellings are meant to integrate so fully with the environment that they seem to disappear from view.

Echoing the eco-movement, artist Tadashi Kawamata's tree huts were erected in New York's Madison Square Park in 2008. They were a statement about insertion of private objects into public spaces as a method of renegotiating the meaning of both. Using treehouses evoked a childlike fascination, bringing the viewers closer to nature, if only for a moment.

Grizzly Adams Treehouse

- This whimsical design, sided with real home logs, was based on a variation of the contractor's standard treehouse.

- When builders create for children, treehouses can be playful without seeming inappropriate. The crooked shingles and rustic materi- als are adorned by a faux set of antlers.

- A carving of a cartoon bear holds up his end of the swing set.

- The construction of this child's dream house was finished with a twisty slide and tire swing.

Rose Parade Treehouse

- Two large redwood logs provide the support for this winner of the 2003 Rose Parade's Grand Marshal Trophy for most creative concept and design.

- The treehouse is made of wood and has stairs that lead up to a deck. The railing sports a rope netting.

- The float was financed by a box store and built to show how imaginative you can be using materials from the store.

- The two treehouses were connected via an elevated bridge, sitting atop two large redwood logs.

BASIC TREEHOUSES
A treehouse can make you feel like you're in the countryside or a wild jungle

A sense of style is all important when it comes to treehouse construction. A design can both reflect the builder's personality and create a certain desired mood. A rustic treehouse, one made without excessive refinements and with natural wood materials, communicates both a love for the environment and a sense of pragmatism in the builder.

Treehouses with c apboard walls and wood shake rooftops say that the builder has a real feel for the land, as do treehouses made from indigenous woods, perhaps even with thatched or hand-shingled roofs.

From Marc's Treehouse Lodge in the African bushveld, visitors can hear the gurgling of the Klaserie River, whoops of hyenas,

Marc's Treehouse Lodge

- Visitors to South Africa expect a certain level of rusticity as well as safety. Set above the banks of the Klaserie River, overlooking a bush filled with Cape buffalo, zebra, and giraffe, the lodge satisfies both requirements.

- The interiors are well

appointed with electricity, fans, and mosquito nets.

- Buffalo, zebra, and giraffe wander around the grounds.

- Sited above a lighted waterhole, the treehouse has unparalleled game-viewing possibilities.

Potomac Treehouse

- A pentagonal platform and knee braces provide exceptional support of a kind that any treehouse bu lder can imitate.

- Five beams were spoked out from the tree trunk and fastened with a large bolt-and-bracket assembly.

- Board-and-batten walls and an eco-friendly recycled roofing material allow the structure to fit easily into its surroundings.

- From the deck (railed in cedar), visitors are provided with a great view of the woods surrounding the main house.

and the soft cry of bushbabies. The native cedar and the viney fig trees create a rich green canopy over the property.

Given its tree branch railings, clapboard walls, and rough-cut beams, the Owl's Nest in the Adirondacks has a true woodsy feel. You know you're roughing it when the smell of pine trees is in the air.

The Treehouses of Hana on the Hawaiian island of Maui exude a delightful sense of tropical magic. The rich flora are integrated into the treehouses themselves with cut-branch railings and handles. You truly feel the island spirit in the treetops of Hawaii.

The Hana Treehouse

- The main room in the House of the August Moon in Maui is 13 feet by 18 feet and sits 10 feet above ground.

- A queen-size bed, a sleeping platform, and a balcony with a view of the ocean all sit perched on African tulip trees. Diagonal braces help support the platform.

- Treetops Treehouse is a deluxe unit that spreads out over 1,000 square feet on three levels.

- A small Hawaiian structure on the top deck provides shade.

Owl's Nest Adirondacks Treehouse

- Kim VanEvera ran her business, Back to Basics Lodging, until her untimely death in 2006. The rustic Owl's Nest Treehouse is an admirable part of her legacy.

- Appealing to a sense of southern Adirondacks rusticity, the structure was built between an oak tree, a cherry tree, and two ash trees.

- A cherry tree runs through the main structure and up through the roof.

- Most of the work was done with a chain saw and hand tools; the stairway was constructed from all handmade materials.

TREETOP PLAYHOUSES

Nothing appeals to a child's sense of adventure like a hideaway in the trees

For most kids, a treetop playhouse is the ultimate dream. Be it a wooden castle or a pirate's crow's nest, these treehouse creations are almost as much fun for the parents to build as for the children to play in. Given the recent revolution in treetop design and mechanics, almost any vision for a structure can now become a reality.

Daniels Wood Land, one of the top playhouse builders in the world, makes everything from wacky cabins to prince and princess castles. The company recently bought a treasure trove of giant sequoia stumps, remnants of trees that were cut down over fifty years ago. The company is now using these beautiful pieces of American history as foundations.

Malibu Treehouse

- Redwood, the main building wood, provides a nice contrast against the light wood bark of a eucalyptus tree.

- The rectangular main platform uses triangular braces on posts set in concrete.

- The deck and platform were constructed with no less than 6 inches of room between the tree and the boards, allowing for future tree growth.

- The interior of the clubhouse features custom accessories, including a fold-down desk—just the relaxing environment a child needs to do homework.

Glenmoore Treehouse

- With a focus on creating a play area, the three structures spread across two trees, incorporating both a bridge and a slide.

- The main house has a bunk bed loft and a built-in heater, making sleepovers comfortable even in winter.

- Wooden ladders access both platforms, but a fun tube rope ladder leads to the crow's nest.

- A long zip line stretches from the smaller platform to another tree 100 feet way. Young adventurers can fly across the backyard.

Barbara Butler has a company in San Francisco that builds all sorts of colorful play forts and treehouses. She's even developed a line of custom-colored wood stains for the public to use. Since 1999, Barbara's company has made donations to schools and charitable organizations around the world.

Peter Kirsch–Korff specializes in designing and building custom and high-end wood treehouses, playhouses, and forts. One of his goals is not only to provide a safe play place for children but also to plan his creations so they can easily transition into adult retreats as the children mature.

Kitty Kat Treehouse

- Wild color combinations and terrific details create a lively atmosphere for this themed play area.

- A carved image of the family cat lies just underneath and to the back of the curved-top window, adding a personal touch.

- A wide loft inside, accessed by a rung ladder, creates a warm and cozy nook.

- The front deck boasts 3-foot-high railings. The curved-top front Dutch door has a sliding peephole so the young treehouse owner can decide who can come in.

Monstro Treehouse

- Straight out of Dr. Seuss or J. R. R. Tolkien, the skewed windows, crooked roofline, and wave-patterned siding create a wonderful sense of whimsy and humor.

- An enormous (or "Monstro") 10-foot sequoia log supports the 64-square-foot clubhouse.

- A pair of tire swings allows playmates to swing side by side.

- The deck supports feature carvings of adorable bears, while the tree stumps are hollowed out to allow for a ladder access inside.

TREETOP FORTS & OUTPOSTS

Building a treehouse along a theme can allow for creative and often unexpected embellishments

Creating a treehouse along a "fort" theme appeals to the basic impulse behind treehouse construction. Using the architectural vocabulary of military outposts, the treehouse becomes both a place where a child can be in charge and a retreat where he or she can withstand assault from imaginary enemies down below. The adults who design these structures are allowed to revisit, if only for a little while, the sensibilities of their childhoods.

Using the idea of a fort as a starting point, treehouse accessories can include turrets, carved cowboys and Indians, rope ladders, swinging rope bridges, and even old movie or theatrical props. For a more colorful approach, Barbara Butler

Fort Fiesta

- Combining the idea of a tree fort with a playground, the lively color palette communicates a sense of playful, childhood fun.

- Architect Barbara Butler and her team used a color map to bring the structure to life before the building process began.

- A catwalk weaves through three trees. The idea was to make the walkway look as if it were suspended in the air.

- The King Fort is the anchor point for the structure, providing strength for the connecting bridges.

Tree Fort

- A simple design, when combined with a bridge walkway and creative use of playground materials, creates an elaborate but very functional treehouse.

- Built between multiple trees using lag bolts and brackets attached to the surrounding trunks, this construction is strong enough to last through several generations.

- The natural wood finish and brown Ondura roof blend nicely into the woods.

- The swings can be used after a peace treaty has been signed.

has created theme-based palettes and treehouses with signature names like "the Emerald Fortress," "the Tuxedo Castle," and "Casa de Arbol."

An outpost retreat where you can relax, read a good book, or finally work on that dream craft project could fulfill those dreams of a getaway without leaving your home. The best treetop builders and architects are constantly pushing the limits of their designs to combine the childhood fantasy of living in trees with an adult desire for comfort and beautiful surroundings.

For four years, designer and builder S. Peter Lewis has pursued his dreams of treetop construction. As he describes it, this is "what happens when big people decide to be kids again, and they have tools and lumber." One of the results of his passion is a two-story treehouse with all the amenities you'd want in any home and none of the typical distractions. Extras include a natural-branch chess table with chessmen made of twigs and branches. With tree branches woven through all available interior spots, the final result is truly a thing of beauty.

Treehouse Chronicles

- Before construction began, owner and builder S. Peter Lewis oversaw elaborate architectural drawings.

- One of Lewis's first priorities was to avoid drilling holes in the trees. He devised a metal collar supported by cables, suspending the structure's platform.

- An elaborate rigging system was used to bring the building materials safely and efficiently up into the tree.

- The suspension system hangs from the tree. Wooden wedges fix the distance between the trunk and the truss.

Treehouse Chronicles

- S. Peter Lewis's father built him his first treehouse over thirty years ago.

- The white pine that supports Lewis's treehouse is over 100 feet tall.

- The treehouse is 21 feet above the ground.

- White pines can live to be over four hundred years old.

- An old white pine grows less than 1/8 inch in diameter a year.

SPECIALTY TREEHOUSES

Treehouses can perform a number of specific functions tailored to an owner's needs

A meditation hut, an artist's retreat, or a meeting lounge, treehouses can be utilitarian as well as self-indulgent.

Dan Wright's Make-a-Wish treehouse was specifically requested by a young girl who wanted a Victorian treehouse with a white fence.

Treehouses can also fit the bill for a company retreat. A playful, low-key venue creates an atmosphere where groups can work on team-building and brainstorm for new ideas. TreeHouse Workshop built an amazing treehouse for the IslandWood Environmental Learning Center. It was built in collaboration with Dale West and Mithun Architects.

Some of the world's most innovative treehouse designs

IslandWood, a School in the Woods

- IslandWood is an Environmental Learning Center (ELC) that fosters innovative learning in its occupants.

- Expertly crafted, the TreeHouse Workshop, Inc. design incorporates a single Douglas fir, salvaged wood, metal railings, and superior custom woodwork.

- The ELC is covered with a scalloped, wood-shingled roof, shingled exterior skirt, and salvaged windows. A staircase leads to the reclaimed wood door.

- Situated over a bog, it functions as a classroom where children study wetland life.

Artist's Retreat

- An art installment perched in a tree, at night this Hellbron, Germany, construction lights up like a lantern.

- A staircase leads up into the structure via forks in the branches.

- The treehouse's pear tree cannot bear the complete

- weight of the treehouse, so a part of the construction was propped up by two slanting supports.

- A varnish glazing was applied to all sides. A large dormer window and sunscreens for the south-facing side complete the construction.

are being done by Andreas Wenning, principal designer of Baumraum in Germany. The company combines the creative and constructive expertise of an architect with the expert experience of a landscape architect, an arborologist, and a master craftsman. In the hands of a talented builder, a treehouse designed as an artist's retreat becomes something beyond a mere structure. It's a place that fosters creativity and inspiration.

ZOOM

Aside from writing three books about treehouses, Peter Nelson has as his most recent undertakings the Northwest Treehouse School (which instructs new treetop builders on treehouse design and construction); Treehouse Point, an environmental treehouse retreat center; and the Tree for All Foundation, a nonprofit corporation that brings disabled people into nature and treehouses. He is truly a jack-of-all-trades.

Make-a-Wish Treehouse

- This dollhouse in the woods was built for an eight-year-old girl who requested a Queen Anne Victorian look. The roof is asphalt shingle. A ladder inside leads to a loft.

- Part of the platform rests on a beam bolted to an American beech tree.

- An eyebolt-and-turnbuckle cable system gives the house a light, airy feeling.

- The little girl moved in even before the structure was finished, neatly arranging her belongings (including a beanbag chair given to her by the foundation).

Treehouse History

- The Roman Emperor Caligula often hosted banquets in a lavish treehouse.

- Small treehouses were popular throughout medieval England and remained in high demand until the late 1700s.

- Members of Florence's Medici family vied with each other to create the most magnificent marble treehouse.

- In Tudor England, Queen Elizabeth I dined in a treehouse resting in a massive linden tree.

FOUND OBJECT TREEHOUSES

Assembling a treehouse from incidental artifacts is cost-effective and reflects a builder's personality

Building a treehouse from found materials—hunting for boards, sanding and cleaning them, deciding how to incorporate them—reflects a personal, emotional investment ultimately unavailable in other methods of construction.

For kids, building a treehouse from found materials adds a dimension of joy to the construction. In the summer of 2000,

teenagers Nick McGlynn and his pal Zac started with scavenged wood and a vision, even going so far as to design their own support system. Their treehouse still stands today.

Almost two decades ago in Tennessee, local minister Horace Burgess received "a mission from God." He had a vision of an enormous treehouse, complete with almost every imaginable

Found Object Treehouses

- A found object is also called an "objet trouvé."

- Ancient islanders of Indonesia built treetop dwellings using downed timber, bamboo, and tree stumps.

- For the last twenty years, Sam Edwards has been building a found object treehouse in a 60-foot-high oak in Calhoun, Georgia.

- His treehouse has three levels and eleven rooms.

Tennessee Found Object Treehouse

- Some eighteen years ago, Horace Burgess received "a mission from God": a vision of an enormous treehouse church with almost every imaginable detail included.

- Burgess scavenged wood to create an eight-level structure enveloping the remains of an old white oak.

- Construction was begun in 1993, but it is still a work in progress.

- Burgess estimates the construction to be 8,000 to 10,000 square feet. He's used approximately 258,000 nails.

detail. The vision led to an ongoing labor of love and devotion. His hand-built cathedral now stands almost 100 feet tall.

A treehouse display in New York City was the ultimate expression of found object construction. Pieces of cast-off plywood, 2-by-4 lumber, and odd pieces of timber were haphazardly thrown together and screwed into position to create several simple hut-style treehouses perched in the trees of Madison Square Park. It served as a reminder of one's childhood fantasies as you passed through the bustling city.

ZOOM

Found objects make interesting materials to use in treehouse construction. Sam Edwards used part of a boat for a guest bedroom and a small submarine for a bathroom. More conventionally, he used pine flooring from a former slave cabin, corrugated iron from an old barn, and salvaged windows from a train depot.

McGlynn Found Object Treehouse

- Teenager Nick McGlynn spent the summer months with his friend Zac, creating a treehouse from materials they found

- The lower level is made from small saplings bound together with rope. Plywood sheets create a sturdy base level.

- The second level incorporates an ingenious system that allows the trees to move in the wind without tearing the support beams apart.

- A groove was routed in the beams, allowing for give on either side of the nails.

Incorporating Found Objects

- While building a treehouse with found objects, interesting items can be found at salvage yards, swap meets, and even yard sales.

- Use new supporting bolts, cables, brackets, and fasteners to assemble your creation.

- Carefully inspect all found objects for wood rot and general soundness.

- If possible, learn the story behind the objects you acquire.

STUNNING TREEHOUSES

An attractive treehouse is hard to achieve but is worth every effort

What is an attractive treehouse? Beauty is in the eye of the beholder, but whether you're considering a rustic, round log–style hut or a modular treetop dwelling, there are some commonalities. Expert craftsmanship, innovation, and attention to detail all play their part, especially in the three treehouses shown below, which are designed and built by TreeHouse Workshop, Inc. of Seattle, WA.

At Longwood Gardens in Pennsylvania, the builders have achieved a synthesis of beauty and practicality with three spectacular treehouses called, respectively, the Birdhouse and the Canopy Cathedral built by TreeHouse Workshop, Inc., and the Lookout Loft which was built by Forever Young.

The Ramona Treehouse in San Diego County was a fully functional home. The metal struts that co-supported the structure accepted vertical and lateral stress loads, allowing for a certain amount of "wiggle room" when the trees moved.

The Canopy Cathedral

- One of the finest classic treehouses ever built, this ornate, two-story structure was inspired by a Norwegian church.

- The interior sports Old World–style woodworking, multicolored woods, doweled fasteners, and scalloped beams.

- The staircase inside and out allows visitors easy access to all parts of the house. The centerpiece of the structure is a beautiful stained glass window.

- A wooden dragon on the lower stairs greets you when you enter. See photo on page 214.

The Ramona Treehouse

- The 1,000-square-foot treehouse was built between seven oak trees and used a combination of steel struts and trees for support.

- Full of creature comforts, the structure sat on eight acres of land in Ramona, California.

- A fully functional interior fireplace also served as a pizza oven, creating an outdoor picnic area under the house.

- Wildfires in 2007 burned down the treehouse and all the trees. Nothing remains now except the stone fireplace.

Underneath the platform, a fully outfitted eating area was created. This changed the dynamics of the groundwater availability under the treehouse, affecting, in turn, the tree growth. Provisions were taken to counteract the effect.

The Western Virginia treehouse built by TreeHouse Workshop, Inc. is an enchanting getaway for adults. In this age of quick and shoddy workmanship, their structure was pieced together with slow care and exquisite attention to detail. Truly it is a work of beauty.

Western Virginia Treehouse

- This two-story luxury treehouse was built around a single oak tree.

- The first floor features a full kitchen and sitting room complete with a gas fireplace. The second floor has a cozy bedroom and a full bathroom including a slate tiled shower.

- Natural Cedar pickets were salvaged in Washington State and the Western red cedar siding is from Alaska.

- This treehouse was designed by Pete Nelson and built by Bubba Smith and TreeHouse Workshop carpenters.

If your structure is overly large, make sure you understand how the platform is going to cover the ground and affect moisture patterns. The supply of rainwater becomes almost nonexistent for the tree supporting the structure, which can cause health problems. Strategically placed rain gutters can help mitigate this problem, directing rainwater to the tree.

TreeHouse Workshop

- In 1997, Jake Jacob and Peter Nelson formed Treehouse Workshop, Inc. in Seattle, Washington.

- Their company is dedicated to creating unique treehouses all across the country.

- The company is constantly searching for new and creative ways to build.

- Intended to be a retreat for the Boy Scouts of America, Treehouse Camp, which was donated by a philanthropist, was built by TreeHouse Workshop.

RUSTIC TREEHOUSES

BEST VARIETIES
A wide selection of tree species makes great homes for treehouses

The most important element of a treehouse is the tree itself. In order for a treetop dream to last, a builder should consider the tree's health and its capacity for future growth. Before the first board is cut to fit, a consultation should be scheduled with a certified professional arborist (not your gardener or the local tree removal guy). A good arborist can usually be found by looking in the Yellow Pages or by referencing www.isa-arbor.com. An arborist can age and type the potential tree, recommend how large a treehouse structure it can support, and predict its prospects for the future.

Certain types of trees are better suited than others for treehouses. The first decision to make is choosing between deciduous and evergreen. Deciduous trees, of course, lose their foliage, whereas evergreens keep it year-round. Most

Elm Trees

- Among the oldest tree types on Earth, elms originated in what is now central Asia.

- The most common North American species is the American elm, distinguished by its rapid growth, its adaptability to a broad range of climates and soils, and its strong wood.

- Elm wood is valued for its interlocking grain. It's also resistant to decay.

- Dutch elm disease, caused by a fungus, devastated elms throughout Europe and North America in the second half of the twentieth century.

Poplar Trees

- Although a good tree to build in, poplars are noted for their weak wood and possible limb fall.

- *Populus* species include poplar, aspen, and cottonwood. They can grow to between 45 and 150 feet tall.

- The bark of young trees is smooth. Depending on the species, older trees can either retain their smooth bark or become progressively rough and fissured.

- Poplars can be attacked by borers, bark beetles, stem cankers, fungal leaf spots, and vascular disease.

builders would probably prefer deciduous so that they can easily see if a branch is living or dead. However, particularly if viewshed is a concern, choosing a deciduous tree means limiting the construction period to certain times of the year—something to consider if the work is being done on a set schedule or in northern latitudes.

Building on a single tree, the most important factor is the diameter of the tree. Ten to 12 inches should be the minimum. A mature tree with large, well-established limbs to provide a cradle for the floor system is preferable. Larger, lower branches are best suited for safe construction. Building too high in the tree is probably not a good idea because limbs tend to get weaker the higher up you go, and tree movement in the wind is greater. When using multiple trees for the structure, it's wisest to choose trees that are all about the same size.

Sycamore Trees

- The American sycamore can reach up to 130 feet high. It's a great tree for treehouses.

- Sycamores are easily recognized by their spotty, shedding bark. The bark flakes off in irregular masses, leaving the surface mottled.

- The sycamore tree is often divided near the ground into several secondary trunks. The trunks of large trees are often hollow.

- Sycamores can endure a city environment. They grow rapidly and can serve as a shade tree.

Beech Trees

- This massive tree can eventually reach a height of 120 feet. The tree is naturally low-branched, which makes it ideal for treehouses.

- As the tree ages, the bark looks not unlike elephant skin. The wood is almost white and very resistant to decay.

- Beech grows slowly and does not require much pruning.

- Usually disease is not a serious problem. Several fungi cause leaf spots but are generally not serious enough to warrant chemical control.

VERTICAL TREES

Trees with a vertical limb configuration can be used for almost any kind of treehouse

What exactly are vertical trees? As opposed to branching trees, vertical trees don't have branches that spread the tree out in a conspicuously horizontal way. They make treehouse building, especially one-trunk treehouses, a little less complicated. In the case of multiple vertical-tree supports, the trunks serve as natural posts that stand at something very close to 90-degree angles.

Pine and sequoia are examples of vertical trees. Pines are among the most commercially important of all tree species, valued for their timber and wood pulp. Coast redwood, the common name for sequoia, is one of the most valuable timber species in California, prized for its beauty, light weight, and

Pine Trees

- Pine trees are found all over the world but are mostly native to the Northern Hemisphere.

- Very hearty trees, pines make great homes for treehouses.

- Evergreen and resinous, pines can grow to over 200 feet tall, with the majority of species reaching between 45 and 125 feet tall.

- Pines are long-lived, with the oldest species (bristlecone pine) living more than four thousand years. This makes them, generally, a good, hearty tree to build in.

Eucalyptus Trees

- Eucalyptus oil is highly flammable. Trees have been known to explode during forest fires. If a treehouse is being constructed in an area that has dense timber or a history of forest fires, the flammability should be a concern.

- Due to their resilience and fast growth, eucalyptus are often used to provide windbreaks and to resist erosion.

- The oil can be used for cleaning and functions as a natural insecticide.

- Of concern for treehouse builders, most eucalyptus are not tolerant of frost.

resistance to decay. Its lack of resin makes it resistant to fire.

Eucalyptus is another highly valued vertical tree. Native to Australia, it has more than seven hundred species, a few of which can be seen in a number of countries. The Australian mountain ash, a type of eucalyptus, is one of the tallest trees in the world and the largest of all flowering plants. Only the sequoia is taller.

Another common vertical tree is the Douglas fir. These are medium-size to very large evergreen trees, ranging from 60 to 300 feet high. They are part of the conifer family. Although the total number of species is relatively small, conifers are of immense ecological importance, being the dominant tree species over huge areas of the Northern Hemisphere. They are also of immense economic value, primarily for timber and paper production.

Another vertical tree species, spruce, ranges in size from 60 to over 300 feet tall. Spruce wood, often called "whitewood," is used for many purposes, ranging from general construction work to highly specialized uses in the building of musical instruments.

Douglas Fir Trees

- A strong tree, fir is ideal for larger treehouses.

- It is unique among all soft-wood species in that it can be used before it has fully seasoned. Many builders prefer to cut, nail, and fasten Douglas fir in a "green" or unseasoned condition, allowing it to air-dry during construction.

- The trees are subject to injury from high winds.

- They are susceptible to a number of problems, including cankers, leaf and twig blight, cottony aphids, bark beetle, and scale insects.

Spruce Trees

- The spruce is the tallest of European trees. Its straight, tapering stem and sweeping branches give it a conical outline.

- Spruces are popular ornamental trees, which are admired for their symmetrical look. For the same reason, some species are used as Christmas trees.

- The species has only moderate tolerance to flooding and drought. It grows 1 to 2 feet a year.

- The wood of the spruce is generally white, more elastic, less resinous, and light.

BRANCHING TREES
Multiple branches can provide for a wide range of treehouse variations

A mature branching tree, with its graceful, arching, vase-like form, can be beautiful to look at, reminding us of those long, hot summer days resting under a thick canopy of green leaves. But the bucolic atmosphere comes at a price because the confusion of branches can be problematic for a tree-house builder.

The typical branching tree has a trunk that splits into major branches a few feet off the ground. Unlike with a tree with a straight, simple trunk, the treehouse builder must take into consideration several branches at once. Whether you build in a sturdy cradle of limbs or with a dangerous, unequal distribution of weight, the site must be chosen carefully.

Tulip Trees

- Sturdy in structure, the tulip tree's main trunk can be as much as 20 to 30 feet in circumference with the lower branches being easily accessed.

- North American tulip wood is fine-grained and stable and commonly used for cabinets and furniture.

- Moist, well-drained soils and full sun to light shade are ideal environments for this tree. It prefers a slightly acidic soil but is quite adaptable.

- The Birdhouse in Longwood Gardens is built between huge tulip trees, each of which is over 150 years old.

Maple Trees

- Hearty and fast growing, maples are planted as ornamentals by homeowners, businesses, and many municipalities.

- There are 125 species of maple, 13 that are native to North America. The black, red, and sugar maples are the main species tapped for sap content.

- Many maples have bright autumn foliage, which makes for great leaf-watching traditions around the world.

- Maple wood carries sound waves well and is used in musical instruments.

Native to North America, the tulip tree is sometimes called the "tulip poplar" or "yellow poplar," although it's unrelated to the genus *populus*. These trees are easily recognized by their general shape, with the higher branches sweeping together in one direction. Trees from 150 to 165 feet in height are common.

A deciduous species, maple trees grow from 30 to 145 feet in height. These are especially popular trees for house construction because they are fast growing and extremely cold resistant.

Oak trees are broad-leaved and long-lived, growing up to 150 feet tall. With a famously strong wood, these trees can support even the largest of treehouses.

A branching tree par excellence, the banyan can spread out over two-thirds of an acre. Older banyan trees are characterized by their aerial prop roots, which grow into thick, woody trunks. With age, these roots can become indistinguishable from the main trunk. With so many irregular branches, it makes for a unique tree to build in because supports need to be fabricated between them.

Oak Trees

- Unusual strength and hardness with branches that are easy to access make oak a great choice for treehouse builders.

- Sudden oak death is a regional water mold that can kill oaks within just a few weeks.

- Oak wilt is also a lethal disease of some oaks, particularly the red oaks. Other dangers include wood-boring beetles as well as root rot in older trees.

- The oak is the national tree of England, France, Germany, Lithuania, Poland, and the United States.

Banyan Trees

- The banyan is actually a parasitic fig that starts its life as an epiphyte, or "air plant."

- Seeds germinate in the cracks of a host tree, giving banyan the nickname "strangler fig."

- Older banyan trees have aerial prop roots that grow into thick, woody trunks, indistinguishable from the main trunk. They can make interesting homes for treehouses.

- They extend their roots from the host branches to the ground, giving the tree the appearance of being supported by pillars.

USING MULTIPLE TREES

Let the tree types and configurations dictate the shape of the treehouse

A healthy tree has a way of silently dictating what sort of structure it will support. A builder should be very conscious of what type of trees will be serving as a foundation and their particular characteristics. As always, a professional arborist should be consulted to learn the condition of the trees. Are they all around the same age? Are they all healthy? Are they all the same type of trees, and will they grow at the same rate?

Once the decision to build has been made, the carpenter should do extensive footwork. Draw the treehouse as you imagine it will look, paying particular attention to how it will fit into the unique configuration of branches. What will the view be from the height that's been decided upon? Grab a

Conifer Trees

- Conifers, or evergreens, are vertical and do not have lower branches.

- The branches keep their foliage throughout the year. For a builder anticipating a potential view, the guesswork is eliminated.

- Building around multiple

evergreens can be more predictable than building around trees that have branches with multidirectional growth.

- Needle blight is a concern with conifers. Infected needles often have brown spots and fall from the tree.

Poison Oak Is Not a Tree

- In shrub form, poison oak can be as tall as a small vine maple. As a vine, it can grow over 150 feet high and may not have lower stems or leaves.

- Poison oak grows throughout the Pacific Northwest. Few other vines with smooth bark grow on

Pacific northwestern trees.

- The oily residue causes an allergic reaction in roughly 90 percent of humans.

- The best method of removal is to sever the vines at the base of its host tree.

ladder and climb into the tree to take a look. Do your homework and make sure the view and the orientation of the treehouse are what you want. It will be time well spent.

Having decided on the trees and a design, consult arborists to determine the impact your treehouse will have on the trees and the surrounding area. Will it affect soil compaction? The roots? The flow of nutrients to the trees? These are critical things to know to preserve the health of the trees and the longevity of your treehouse.

Deciduous Trees

- Deciduous trees display a wide array of colorful leaves before they shed their leaves in autumn. They are collectively known as "hardwoods."

- The tallest deciduous tree is the sugar maple, which can grow over 100 feet high.

- Because they are very "branchy," building in deciduous trees is easier when the trees are bare.

- Building in multiple deciduous trees can inspire building structures and platforms that are tied together with bridges, walkways, and rope climbs.

Watch Out for Poison Ivy

- Poison ivy can appear as ground cover, a shrub, or as a vine growing up a tree.

- Poison ivy grows throughout eastern North America.

- Before building in a tree with poison ivy, the vines should be ripped from the trunk to a height of 10 feet or more above the platform.

- Treatment of poison ivy consists of cleansing exposed areas with rubbing alcohol, washing the exposed areas with water (no soap), then taking a warm shower using soap.

TREE SELECTION

TREE HEALTH

Always take precautions to preserve the tree's health and the treehouse's longevity

The health of the potential treehouse's tree should be of first concern to a builder. After consulting a professional arborist and getting the go-ahead to build, a conscientious treehouse owner must continue to be aware of the tree's health, checking it periodically according to a set of certain criteria. The U.S. Forest Service recommends that each treehouse owner start a permanent inspection sheet for each tree. There are five categories to note when starting a list: leaves and buds, leaf size, twig growth, trunk deformity, and crown dieback. After establishing a baseline, continue to take note of certain "canary in the coal mine" issues. An unseasonal yellowing of leaves, for instance, could mean problems. The leaf size and

KNACK TREEHOUSES

Tree Cross Section

- A tree cross section expands the knowledge of trees and how they function.

- Xylem is the plant substance that creates wood. Its basic function is to transport water.

- The most recent annular rings of a tree are called "sapwood." The cambium layer is the growth area, whereas heartwood surrounds the core of the trunk. The pith is the central part of the trunk.

- The cambium, or outer layer, is the only layer that actually grows.

Cutting Branches

- Before destroying tree parts to make room for a treehouse, the overall health of the tree should be the first consideration. A builder should never irreparably harm a tree.

- Prior to trimming, ensure that all persons, structures, and personal property are well away from the area where debris might fall.

- Remove smaller branches first. It's safer to remove the larger limbs piece by piece.

- As a limb is trimmed down toward the stub, make sure the bark is not stripped off the tree.

shape should be recorded so any changes over time can be noted. Small leaves and abnormally shaped leaves are an indication that something might be wrong. A reduction in the extension of shoots (growth of new branches) should also be noted and is a reliable clue that the tree's health has changed for the worse. Deformed growth, mushrooms, and conks on the trunk should also be noted and dealt with immediately. A dying of the canopy or of individual limbs should be recorded, and action should be taken with appropriate treatment.

Tree Injuries

- Once a tree injury is identified, it is important to act fast to correct the problem. Injuries that expose wood or kill the bark can provide an opportunity for disease to enter the tree.

- To treat a wound, cut away the damaged bark into an elongated ellipse, which

helps to promote callous growth.

- Smooth the surface of exposed wood. Disinfect the wound and leave it open for quick healing.

- The best time to treat wounds is in the winter or late autumn.

Insect activity is another situation to monitor. If you see spotted, deformed, discolored, or dead leaves or twigs, they should be noted and watched closely. If you're not sure how to handle any type of infestation, consult a professional to deal with the problem immediately.

It's easy to think that trees are indestructible, but in fact they can be very vulnerable to a host of ailments. The key to a long-lived treehouse is the tree it calls home. So be vigilant.

Tree Terms

- "Alternate leaves" are staggered across from each other on the twig.

- A "blade" is the flat part of a leaf.

- A "bract" is a modified leaf that bears a flower. "Broadleaf" is a tree with leaves that are flat and thin.

- An "invasive" is a nonnative plant known to reproduce rapidly.

- Banyan, poison ivy, and poison oak are all invasives.

TREE DISEASES
Watch out for signs that your tree has been infected, then act quickly

Trees are living organisms, and their health is dependent on a number of factors. Even the largest trees can be destroyed by a microorganism if the infestation is left unchecked and untreated. In that sense, trees are much like humans.

As an extreme example of the devastation caused by tree ailments, a blight affecting the American chestnut decimated an entire species. At one time, it is estimated, one in every four Appalachian hardwoods was an American chestnut. Shedding tasty nuts and providing a wood resistant to rot, American chestnuts were an essential part of the ecology and culture. But because of a blight accidentally introduced to North America in the first years of the twentieth century, by 1940,

Detecting Disease

- Tree diseases are caused by pathogens such as bacteria, worms, fungi, and viruses. Disease prevention hinges on early diagnosis so the tree can be treated or destroyed.

- Visual signs and symptoms can give insight into which pathogen may have infected the tree.

- Effective diagnosis helps to determine an effective course of treatment.

- Once a course of action has been determined, it is important to monitor the progress of treatment so the tree can remain healthy, strong, and a sturdy home for your treehouse.

Chestnut Blight

- Chestnut blight fungus first appeared in 1904. Within forty years the American chestnut population was devastated—today only a few clusters of mature trees remain in California and the Pacific Northwest.

- Surviving chestnut trees are being bred for resistance

- to the blight, notably by the American Chestnut Foundation.

- The foundation aims to reintroduce a blight-resistant American chestnut.

- The fungus attacks the bark of the chestnut tree.

mature American chestnut trees were virtually nonexistent.

Dutch elm disease—identified by Dutch scientists in 1917—spread quickly through Europe, wiping out many of the continent's elms. In the 1930s, the disease spread to North America on wooden crates made with infected wood. A second introduction of the disease in North America occurred in 1945, destroying over half the remaining elm trees in eastern Canada and the United States.

Both chestnut blight and Dutch elm disease have been studied in the hope of finding a cure and preventing future contagions. Unfortunately, new and virulent diseases are developing all the time. Sudden oak death, initially attacking only tanoak in California, has been found on a widening list of trees. Even the stately redwood may be vulnerable. But more troubling than that is the possibility that the disease will make its way out of California and infect the forests of the interior United States. Scientists are working around the clock to find out where the disease got started, precisely how it spreads, and how to eradicate it.

Dutch Elm Disease

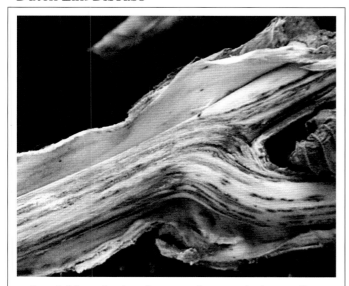

- Graceful, long-lived, and tolerant of compacted soils and air pollution, elms unfortunately can be infected with Dutch elm disease (DED).

- DED occurs when a fungus infects the water-conducting system of the tree, clogging vascular tissue.

- Because elm is so well suited to urban environments, it continues to be a valued component of the urban forest.

- DED is managed by interrupting the disease cycle early, either by sanitizing the tree or spraying insecticide.

Tree Callous

- A healthy tree will naturally recover from most minor damage, sealing off wounds through "compartmentalization."

- New bark, or callous tissues, forms around fresh wounds.

- The tree's age, species, extent of damage, and weather conditions all determine if the tree can successfully protect itself.

- The amount of callous growth is regulated by the basipetal (crown-to-base) flow of products synthesized in the crown, especially carbohydrates and growth regulators.

THE PLAN

Taking the time to put plans on paper helps a builder visualize the project

Once a tree has been chosen and has been checked by a professional arborist, it's time to move on to the next steps. The new builder should become familiar with as many types of treehouses as he or she can. There are numerous books, websites, and local treehouses to reference. Talk to a local treehouse builder or architect and ask him or her to assess the treehouse site. Try sketching ideas out on paper and try not to worry about how good the drawing looks. This is a time for imagining things, for taking the dream and turning it into a reality. A good architect, designer, or builder can take a bunch of scribbles and turn it into something terrific.

Perhaps one of the best examples of treehouse planning

Katie's Sketch

S. Peter Lewis's Treehouse

- A child's vision of a tree-house can be a wonderful place to start. Katie Ellis drew a sketch of what she wanted. From her simple drawing, builder Dan Wright constructed her dream.

- Wright determined that the chosen tree could not support a treehouse. He used posts as a foundation.

- One of the main accesses to the treehouse deck is a looped rope ladder. The other access is an escape hatch under the floor.

- Clear, corrugated polycarbonate panels were used for the roofing material.

- Lewis chose a beautiful white pine for a foundation, developing his own fastening system to minimize harm to the tree.

- Cables were put through a conduit and bent to conform to the tree, 37 feet above the ground.

- A steel collar is connected to the cable system with welded eyebolts and turnbuckles.

- A detailed sketch of the platform design shows the essential components. The hexagon shape provides for maximum floor area without being too complex.

comes from S. Peter Lewis, whose book *Treehouse Chronicles* describes his inspiring efforts to build the treehouse of his dreams. He met with structural engineers and had architectural drawings and visualization sketches done of what his treehouse should ultimately look like. The result was a spectacular structure that took four years to build.

But building a structure so detailed is not for most people. Most of us want to build a treehouse that the family can enjoy but that doesn't cost much to erect. Even simple treehouses still require a plan as detailed as possible. From the initial sketches a builder can then make a list of lumber, fasteners, and tools needed for the job.

If a treehouse vision is too much to handle alone, the average backyard builder might want to hire a professional. Before hiring a contractor, make sure that you are familiar with his or her previous work. Call his or her references, realizing that time spent in organizing will save headaches along the way. Show the contractor your sketches, then sit back and watch the dream take shape.

Sketch Becomes Reality

- A simple design was created along with some unique features that echo the surroundings. Dan Wright sketched the idea out and presented it to the client.

- The structure was built between three branching trees as a playhouse for children.

- Knee bracing and cables support the treehouse, and the branches are designed to interweave with the structure.

- The natural branch railing was harvested from the surrounding woods. Climbing handles were added for safety.

Planning Points

- Treehouses should conform to local planning and building codes. Every community has a different set of codes.

- Prior to building, check the local planning department to determine if any laws exist regarding treehouses.

- To ensure community support, canvas the neighborhood for opinions on your treehouse.

- Adding electricity and running water can signal that the dwelling is meant to be lived in and thus subject to different building codes.

CODES & REGULATIONS

Make sure you know the local building restrictions before starting construction on a treehouse

By their nature, treehouses are free-spirited, nonconformist endeavors. Most people think about building a treehouse in the backyard as a right they have as owner of the property. Unfortunately, this doesn't reflect the reality. In most areas, both written and unwritten codes address the building of a treetop dwelling. To ignore them is not a good idea.

First and foremost, a prospective builder should be concerned about the opinion of his or her neighbors. The location of the treehouse could impact their views, for instance. Out of consideration, a treehouse should be attractive and add something to the landscape. In some cases the treehouse might have a view into a neighbor's home or backyard.

Trees on Preservation Lists

- Violating tree preservation laws is a serious offense.

- In most counties, ordinances specifically protect the trees. Typically, a tree has to be of a certain size in order to be protected.

- Local, state, and federal regulations require communi-

ties to address floodplains, storm waters, wetlands, water quality, endangered species, steep slopes, and even air quality.

- If your tree is on a preservation list, care must be taken to keep the tree safe and to not impede its growth.

Treehouse Height Restrictions

- Whereas county ordinances regarding treehouse height restrictions are relatively rare, community planning and zoning laws are more common.

- Most counties allow property owners to build structures within their own boundary lines.

- A professional arborist can evaluate a tree and suggest a height for the treehouse based on the strength and size of the tree.

- In building a treehouse for a child, placing the structure above 8 to 10 feet is not advisable.

Local building codes should be researched. Height allowances, setback requirements, and boundary lines are all potential stumbling blocks to treehouse construction. Regulations differ from county to county, state to state. Most codes and regulations can be found on the Internet and are downloadable. They cover international building codes, green building codes, and list committees and proposals that are upcoming. These comprehensive codes feature time-tested safety concepts, structural, and the latest industry standards in material design. It covers broad-based principles that make the use of new materials and new building designs possible.

Michael Garnier is one of the world's foremost authorities on building treehouses and creating new and innovative support systems. The owner of Out 'n' About Treesort, he waged an eight-year battle with officials in Josephine County, Oregon, that is a lesson in how serious city and county officials can be about building codes and regulations. In the end Garnier prevailed, but his experience should serve as an example.

Make sure you know the local codes that apply to your area and incorporate them into your plan.

Boundary Line Restrictions

- Prior to building, visit the local city hall for a plot map. This will help establish boundary lines to the property. In rare cases, plot lines may contradict fences and established borders.

- No part of the structure should reach within 10 feet of the property line.

- Branches and limbs outside the property line should be trimmed back but without affecting the health of the tree.

- Try to avoid placing your treehouse where it can be seen by a lot of people.

More Notes on Regulations

- Treehouse codes and regulations can be confusing.

- In many cases a treehouse builder will be given an exemption because the structure is considered a nonlivable structure.

- Don't give up too easily on a treehouse if you get into a dispute with a neighbor or county officials.

- A structural engineer can provide information on potential tree stress.

WORKING THE PLAN
Before building in a tree, plan out the basics of the structure on the ground

After the site has been selected and the tree has been cleared for building, it's time to put the plan into action. But don't climb into the tree too soon. As much work as possible should be done on the ground.

A lumber list should be made and costed out. Go over each part of the plan and decide how much wood will be needed, then add 15 percent to ensure that there's enough lumber on hand. Enlist the help of the lumberyard. Show workers there the plan and have them estimate what's needed. Then arrange for the lumber to be delivered.

With the lumber bought and paid for, draw up a schedule. Make sure the schedule is flexible and sensible. Build the

The Treehouse Schedule

- Most treehouse building peaks with the coming of warmer weather in the spring.

- During the winter months, photograph the branch structure of your tree, remove excess ground vegetation, and prune dead branches.

- As the tree blooms, clear any excess soil from around the tree trunk.

- Set the bolts and beams and build the platform. Test the strength of your floor by placing weight on it for a week or so, making sure it will hold the weight.

The Budget

- A budget can be created from a materials list. Pay attention to items that might cost too much and try to think of alternatives.

- Take the materials and lumber list to several supply houses for price quotes.

- Compromises on quality

can be made in paneling and nonstructural elements, but never compromise on the structural supports.

- Be prepared to spend a little more money than expected. The rule of thumb in building is to add 15 percent to the budget.

treehouse during the best time of year in your part of the world. Avoid excessive heat, snow, rain, or intense cold.

Figure out logistics. A power source should be close enough to the tree to allow the use of electric tools. Plan out how you are going to hoist beams, joists, and lumber into the tree. Designate an easily accessible area to sort the lumber and plan on separating the lumber by type. Talk to building helpers to coordinate schedules. Take control of the job and avoid wasting time.

Be prepared to handle any setbacks or problems, especially weather related. Think about what can be done to keep the job proceeding even if the weather stops the building process. Maybe you want to build some simple furniture or review your plans for possible changes. Most of all, keep thinking ahead.

Planning the Interior

- Most treehouses have a simple interior design, but if you desire to do something special, make sure it's carefully planned out beforehand.

- S. Peter Lewis made his treehouse two stories tall after living with a simpler design for several months.

- Materials were priced out and ordered after the interior was reimagined.

- Using scraps of wood and tree branches, Lewis made a chess set of cut branches, odd branch door handles, and funky branch railings to access the drawbridge.

Good Neighbors and the Law

- All fifty states adopted the International Building Codes in 2006. This law states that any structure less than 199 square feet does not require a permit.

- Most legal height restrictions address structures that are 35 to 38 feet high. Several states have amended that code.

- Be open and honest with your neighbors to make sure they are okay with your plans to build a treehouse.

- Draw up a signed agreement with your neighbors in order to have a written record.

RESPECT THE TREE
The first concern of a conscionable builder is the health of the tree

The tree you build in is your partner in the treehouse-building process. You want to make sure that the tree is healthy and that your actions won't do any harm to the tree. You want to make sure that you're building in the right kind of tree and that the tree is free from disease. You also want to pay attention to any symbiotic plants that have wrapped themselves around the tree and are depleting the tree of the nutrients it

needs. Check the tree trunk at the roots and make sure that the symbiont's roots aren't wrapped around it. This situation could eventually lead to the tree nutrients being diverted, which will weaken the tree.

Study the tree trunk for any blistering or unusual flaking of bark, especially if the wood underneath the bark becomes exposed. Also take notice of any wet or black stained areas.

Allow for Tree Growth in the Platform

- A tree needs space to grow. No part of a treehouse should impede a tree's natural growth pattern.

- Platforms should be built close to the trunk but with space left to accommodate the tree's future growth.

- Trees that poke through the structure walls should also have room for growth. In a battle between a tree's growth and a treehouse's walls, the tree will always win but might suffer along the way.

- Every tree is different, so let the tree be your guide.

Free from Straps and Ropes

- Avoid tying anything around the tree trunk or branches. Ropes can gradually strangle a branch, limiting the nutrient flow.

- Trees can sometimes grow over obstacles, but it is much better to completely avoid the risk.

- Ropes on branches or trunks should be considered for only very lightweight treehouses that will be taken down each year to relieve the pressure on the bark.

- Better alternatives are wide webbing straps or slings that will help to spread the load over a greater area.

This could be a sign that the tree is suffering from some type of disease or infestation. Either way, a professional should be brought in to evaluate and suggest a course of action. Never strip away bark from the tree as a solution to anything; you will only do harm to the tree.

As you plan your support system, take into account the effect it will have on the tree. Figure out how you can spread the load over the branches or the trunk. If they are not strong enough, you may want to use cable support or a post or two. The less invasive the support system is, the better chance your tree has to maintain strength and growth. Using proper fasteners can also help to lessen the invasive effect on the tree and increase the support ability.

Whichever system you decide on, always keep your partner's well-being at the root of your decision-making process.

Allow for Tree Growth in the Roof

- The roof should allow several inches of room between roof and tree.

- A rubber gasket or a piece of tire tubing can be used to weatherproof the structure. Use only galvanized nails to attach.

- Skylight-style curbs can be cut around the roof opening. Use a flashing of sheet plastic and duct tape to gently secure the flashing funnels around the tree.

- The more advanced your treehouse design is, the more significant your roof collar should be.

Take Care with Bolts

- The optimum support system uses as few bolts as possible. It's better to use fewer but stronger fasteners to help the tree compartmentalize the wounds.

- To accommodate sway, flexible joints can hold up the support beams.

- Use large bolts, placed no closer than 1 foot or so apart. This will avoid problems with compartmentalization, a condition that causes weakness to the area between the bolts.

- Fixed bolts are generally used for smaller structures.

BUILDING SUPPLIES & TIMBER

Choosing the right materials is critical to the stability, strength, and longevity of a treehouse

Anyone can run down to the local lumberyard and pick up materials, but that's not the way to get the best price. Dig a little deeper, be innovative, and enlarge the search to two or three supply outlets. Browsing through a local used building materials location or an architectural salvage yard could end up being a real money saver. Items like reclaimed posts or uniquely tooled railings can frequently be found. Windows with workable sashes that capture the look of another period can be acquired as well. Specialty items like wood carvings or warehouse doors may be available if you look hard enough.

Another important consideration is the interior lumber. If the plan doesn't call for enclosed walls, you may want to

Timber

- Lumber from a building supply store is of fixed dimension and will have a predictable strength. Found wood can be weaker and should be closely inspected for hidden defects.

- Support beams should be free of large knots and splits and straight when viewed along the long edge. Have one or two extras on hand.

- Douglas fir from a building supplier is well suited for framing a treehouse.

- Cedar works well for floor material. Use a minimum thickness of 1 inch.

Plywood

- Plywood is very strong. It will resist twisting, making the floor more rigid.

- Plywood does not allow drainage or ventilation. Water needs to be prevented from running onto areas of the floor that are not roofed.

- Plywood is useful to make the treehouse more rigid. It can then be faced with other materials.

- Wall coverings are usually nonstructural, so alternative materials, like woven branches or wood shingles, can be used to add visual interest.

upgrade the lumber choice to something more pleasing to look at, like cedar. If the walls will be enclosed, normal-grade Douglas fir will work just fine. If the floor is going to be finished, a nice hardwood like oak or maple might be preferred over cedar or plywood. Take the time to make the right decision.

Having all the necessary building supplies on hand will keep the job running smoothly. Avoid making frequent trips to the store. Decide beforehand what types of saws, hammers, fasteners, cables, screws, nails, ropes, and other items will be needed. Have a tool belt with a tape measure, flat pencils, and a level and have a couple of different-size ladders to work with. To keep the work moving, err on the side of having too much rather than too little.

It helps to make a punch list that covers the building schedule. Figure out how long each task will take and plug it into a calendar. Note suppliers' phone numbers and addresses; program everything into an electronic device if possible. Keep all the information you might need at your fingertips.

Interior Finish

- The wood used in the interior should match the feel of the treehouse.

- In a child's play fort, simple cedar tables and chairs may be just the thing to encourage children to do their homework. Rounded corners on tables, chairs, and railings are safer for small elbows and knees.

- In a rustic treehouse, handmade log tables, benches, and carved animal figures add a nice touch.

- If the treehouse has an antique theme, salvaged windows and doors can act as accentuating elements.

Roofing Lumber

- The roof material should be sturdy, decorative, and long-lasting.

- A sound roof extends the life of the structural materials. Plywood should be covered with felt paper and then topped with wood shingles or shakes.

- Western red cedar, Alaskan yellow cedar, and eastern white cedar work well for roofs. Manufactured shingles make for a more polished look, whereas wood shakes are thicker and rougher.

- A properly installed roof should last a long time.

SUPPORTS

The support system should be unobtrusive, strong, and designed to fit the tree

How you support your treehouse is extremely important. Traditional structures, of course, typically utilize cement foundations, but this option isn't available to treehouse builders. They have to become much more inventive. And although a common priority is to build a great-looking structure that doesn't get overwhelmed by the support system, the system needs to be able to handle the imposed weight as well as avoid damaging the tree. Involving one tree or several, using posts or cables, all the variations share a common purpose.

Advancements in support design have allowed treetop builders to do incredibly innovative things in trees. Variously themed treehouses—Victorians, rustic cabins, artist's

KNACK TREEHOUSES

Simple Spoke Support

- Spoked beams radiating out from the tree trunk make a treehouse appear as if it's floating in the tree.

- Beams should be cut to fit the platform size. A diagonal or scalloped cut on the end of the beam gives it a finished look.

- The beams attach to the tree with a bolt-and-bracket assembly. The beam end closest to the tree rests against the trunk.

- The beam can be trimmed back after completion so it doesn't touch the trunk.

Suspension

- Cables are generally looped at the ends through eyebolts, with a turnbuckle at one end to adjust the tension.

- The looped ends of the cable are secured with clamps.

- An eyebolt through the beam affixes the end of the cable. In order to line the bolt up with the cable, drill the hole through the beam at an angle.

- The top end of the cable hooks to a lag bolt in the tree with a shackle assembly.

installations—are being built all over the world with the help of uniquely designed artificial limbs and cabling. All indications are that more amazing innovations are still to come.

With each new generation of treehouse builders come new support structure innovations. From the original utilitarian emphasis on strength and durability, the focus has recently shifted to eco-friendly ways of achieving the same ends. A few builders have turned to using systems that don't penetrate the tree at all. They use cables that are slung over forked tree branches. The cables are covered by a conduit that does not rub off the bark. The cables are connected to turnbuckles and eyebolts attached to support beams.

The World Tree House Association conducts tests at its yearly meetings. Very early on, it adopted a somewhat standardized "artificial limb" that consists of an alloy steel lag screw stud with integral shear washer. This device was given the name "Garnier Limb" in honor of modern treehouse pioneer Michael Garnier. This set in motion today's trend of exploring new ways to advance treehouse building.

Support across Trees

- Sliding joints can support a flexible or floating framework. When a trunk moves, the support will slide across the joint.

- The simplest sliding joint is a metal bracket in a J-shape.

- A good flexible joint is a sling made of steel cable, fixed to the support and then to a higher branch.

- Brackets should ideally be attached to the tree with just one bolt. Lag bolts should be at least 8 inches long and ¾ inch in diameter.

Unique Support System

- Three Douglas firs, in coordination with two Garnier Limbs and a "knave bracket," provide a fine support system for this treehouse designed and built by Tree-House Workshop, Inc.

- The Garnier Limbs have an "uplift arrestor" so that the beam can slide back and forth but cannot lift off.

- The knave brace is set in a T-configuration with steel diagonal braces. The platform joists are cut to fit a gentle curve in the platform. The platform is fronted by a fascia board made of cedar, bent around the joist members.

RADIATING SPOKES

This system of support works best with a single trunk or in conjunction with other systems

One of the most elegant blendings of engineering and design, the radiating spoke form of support can be used effectively by itself in a single tree or in concert with knee braces, T-brackets, or posts.

Nonrectangular platforms—shaped like hexagons and octagons, for instance—are particularly suited to a support

system built around radiating spokes. This system spreads the load of the house across its members, making it a very sturdy way to go. Without getting too complex, the spokes work extremely well with these interesting shapes even while maximizing the usable area. The platform members also create an attractive geometric shape that can be displayed

Spoke Support

- Treated 4-by-6-inch beams work well in this system.

- Before setting the beams, a builder should drill holes in the trunk where the bolts will go. The bolt holes should be set at the same height, and a bubble level should be used to guarantee accuracy.

- The bolts attach to a bracket where the beam will sit.

- Hoist the beams into position and fasten them to the bolt-and-bracket assembly.

Spokes and Knee Braces

- Using knee braces is a relatively safe method of building because the work is done close to the ground.

- There are several methods to secure the braces. The simplest is to cut a notch in a matching beam that fits an angle cut into the brace. A lag bolt is used to secure

the joint.

- Two pieces of timber can be through-bolted to each side of the brace.

- A pair of triangular pieces of plywood can be fitted across the brace and the beam.

underneath as another design element. Each point in the shape should have a beam attached to the tree with a bolt-and-bracket system. The beams are then supported by knee braces from underneath or from above with a cable system.

A branching tree like an elm or oak lends itself more readily to bracing, whereas a more vertically oriented tree like a Douglas fir or a pine tree—one wherein the lines don't have to weave in and out of branches—is better for cabling. And although knee bracing works in either kind of tree, it can take away from the effect of floating in the tree.

The terrain beneath the tree is also a consideration. Posts are sometimes needed to help buttress the spoke support system. If the tree is sited on a hillside, a partial spoke system can be used. A combination of spokes and posts can also be used to support a deck while posts and knee braces support the main structure.

The point is to be flexible, utilizing various combinations of platform support to accommodate the final treehouse design.

Spokes and Cables

- Knee braces and cables can help achieve a floating treehouse look.

- The beams are cut to fit and drilled while on the ground. They are then hoisted into position and fastened to the tree.

- The lag bolts anchoring the cable need to be fastened high enough that the cables won't interfere with the structure.

- The long end of the cable is attached to the thimble assembly and to a turn-buckle. Turnbuckles can be used to tighten the cables and ensure levelness.

Spokes and Posts

- If a treehouse cannot be totally supported by spoked beams, or if the tree is on a slope, a system of spokes and posts can provide adequate support.

- The more load the tree can support, the less one needs to worry about carrying capacity of the posts and vice versa.

- Tree size can affect how large or small the spoke system needs to be.

- Posts should be set at least 3 feet deep in concrete.

FLEXIBLE BRACKETS
This system of support allows for tree movement, putting less stress on structure and tree alike

A builder should look first to the tree to dictate what type of support system to use. If the treehouse to be built is more than a basic rectangular platform, the best choice for support is probably a flexible support system.

Flexible supports allow for the tree to move in the wind, lessening the stress on your structure. The wind that a tree catches can swing the whole tree around quite a bit. In some parts of the world, the leaning and bending that a tree is subjected to are quite powerful. Nearer the ground, the trunk acts like a giant lever, magnifying the strength of the wind into an incredibly powerful force that moves only 1 or 2 inches. However, 1 or 2 inches can translate to a force that's large enough to lift one

Two-tree Support

- A "bracket" is meant to house a beam that spans two points. The beam should be long enough to move freely in the bracket without sliding out completely.

- Three of the more popular brackets are J-brackets, box brackets, and knee brace brackets.

- When possible, use only one lag bolt per bracket.

- Bolts that are set too close together can cause compartmentalization, a condition wherein the tree between penetrations dies or rots.

Metal Brackets

- Metal brackets can be fixed or flexible. Fixed brackets fit knee braces to a single tree in a radiating or spoked arrangement. The bracket solves the awkward problem of fixing a beam by its end grain to a flat surface.

- Brackets like these are at least ¼-inch-thick steel with high-quality welds at the joints.

- They are treated to resist corrosion.

- Whenever possible, metal brackets should be used in favor of wood brackets.

ton of weight. A fixed system will be under immense pressure and will easily break. If a treehouse will be subjected to these types of forces, a flexible system is the way to go.

When a support system employs one end of a beam that is fixed while the other end allows for tree movement, there is no buildup of pressure, and the platform will withstand strong movement. During a violent storm or high winds the treehouse itself may get damaged, but that is a design concern specific to the house and not to be confused with tree movement.

When in doubt, ask a professional builder.

J-brackets

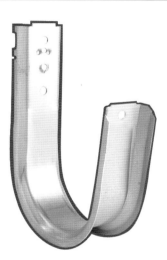

- Brackets in the shape of the letter J allow a beam to be dropped into place after the bracket has been bolted into the tree.

- The open base section of the J-bracket can be made 25 percent wider than the beam to allow movement.

- The typical bracket is made of welded steel with a ¼-inch thickness.

- J-brackets typically need only one bolt. This avoids compartmentalization in the tree.

Box Brackets

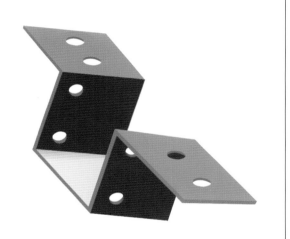

- Box brackets are stronger than J-brackets and are better at keeping the beam from lifting.

- It's easiest to attach the bracket and beam after the bracket has been fitted to the tree.

- With the help of scaffold-ing, it's also possible to slide the bracket onto the beam first and then attach the assembly.

- One version of the box bracket has triangles on 90-degree angles next to the bolt hole. The stronger design prevents the bracket from twisting under a load.

SUSPENSION SYSTEMS

For support that allows for free movement of the tree, it's hard to beat a suspension system

There are few things more beautiful than a treehouse that seems to float effortlessly in its tree, magically defying the laws of gravity.

The first step in achieving that effect is to decide on a cable suspension system. Technically more difficult, it's usually worth the effort, eliminating the need for unsightly knee bracing and posts. The system can be customized to handle the weight and torque of any treehouse structure.

Cable comes in different grades, and each has a rated breaking strength, typically from fifteen hundred to fifteen thousand pounds. Key to any cable system are heavy duty thimbles and tree grips, which are designed for creating

Steel Cables

- Essential elements in a suspension system, cables are available in different tension ratings and sizes.

- A multi-strand steel cable jacketed with plastic fibers reduces friction when you are handling and using the cable.

- Cable should never be wrapped around branches or parts of the trunk, or else the bark will be worn away very quickly.

- Avoid situations where a cable runs diagonally through open spaces. Aside from being dangerous, it will reduce your floor space.

Tree Grips

- Galvanized tree grips, or "dead ends," are used to form a termination on the end of a guy strand.

- Tree-grip dead ends can be used with common-grade cable, reducing the time and cost.

- The five grades of strand are (from weakest to strongest) utilities grade, common grade, Siemens-Martin grade, high-strength grade, and extra-high-strength grade.

- The stronger the strand, the more carbon it contains and the less flexible it will likely be.

terminations or end pieces. The "thimble and tree grip" assembly is collectively referred to as a "dead-end cable." It is hooked with a shackle to a bolt high in the tree. Shackles are rated for tensile strength as well and can have ratings as high as thirty-eight thousand pounds.

The lag bolts, when attached to the eyebolt assembly on the platform beams, should be set high enough to easily clear the structure below. The lag bolts should be set at least 6 inches deep, ensuring that the threads of the bolt are not visible. A turnbuckle assembly attached to the cable system can adjust the tension of the cable once the platform and structure are set. Turnbuckles have safe working load limits as well. The size of the turnbuckle will determine the load and can range up to five thousand pounds. If you have any questions about the combined rating of your system, check with a professional builder or a rigging specialist.

Each bolt, turnbuckle, shackle, thimble, or eyebolt has a stress load rating. The total system is only as strong as the weakest part.

Turnbuckles

- A turnbuckle is a device for adjusting the tension or length of a cable.

- Tension can be adjusted by rotating the loop, causing both eyelets to be screwed in or out simultaneously.

- Turnbuckles have either a "jaw" (pictured above) or an "eye" at each end for connecting to other parts of a tension support system.

- Turnbuckles are available in customized finishes, including brass and bronze, drop forged, and stainless steel.

Shackles

- A shackle is a U-shaped piece of metal secured with a pin or bolt across its opening or a hinged metal loop secured with a quick-release locking pin mechanism.

- Shackles are used as connecting links in suspension systems.

- A "joining shackle" is made in two parts. A fitted stud is kept in place by a steel pin running diagonally through the stud and shackle.

- Before buying a shackle, know the right size, how it's secured, and the rated load limit.

SUPPORT SYSTEM INNOVATIONS

The Garnier Limb allows for a stronger, safer, tree-friendly system of support

In the early 1990s, Michael Garnier hosted the first treehouse association conference. Around the same time, the modern revival in treehouse building began. Garnier, an engineer, and Charlie Greenwood, another icon of the treehouse world, invented the "Garnier Limb," an artificial steel limb that bolts into trees to support anywhere from two thousand to thirty thousand pounds. This innovation made treehouses extremely safe and helped give impetus to the movement.

Garnier Limbs, also known as "GLs," are the best known of all the "attached limb system" designs. Indeed, the term GL has become synonymous with a heavy bolt of any kind that serves to perch a load in a tree. If a treehouse needed

Basic GL

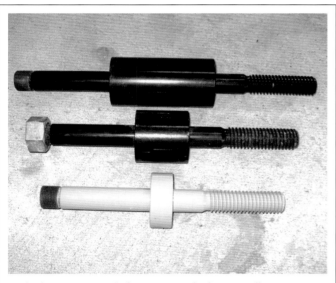

Floating GL

- The basic GL is made from machine-threaded steel round stock with a unique flange or collar.

- A hole is drilled in the tree using a specialized bit that allows the flange to fit flush when fitted.

- The longer collar systems are designed to allow the tree to grow over and around the exposed collar on the outside of the tree.

- The anchor point is capable of withstanding loads from two thousand to thirty thousand pounds.

- A floating Garnier Limb allows the tree to move independently of the treehouse.

- A variation of this system is the Long GL with an "arrestor bracket," allowing the tree to continue to grow and move.

- For heavier loads, the Long GL is usually preferred over the standard GL.

- Holes in the tree are drilled with a special bit. The bit makes a hole and then concentrically inscribes a line in the tree that the GL collar fits into.

another limb the GL would provide it. As a whole, limb system designs have been referred to as "tree anchor bolts" or TABs. But it's the GL that started it all.

From this admirable start, Garnier has continued to experiment. His work has inspired arborists, engineers, and builders to contribute to the improvement of their tree-friendly support systems. Because of their efforts, the evolution of these supports has leaped forward, filling the need to have a safe, reliable device that treats trees well even while withstanding significant shear forces.

A component of larger brackets that accept fitted wooden supports, numerous applications and variations of the basic GL system have been used by custom treehouse builders around the world.

Charlie Greenwood of Treehouse Engineering has developed a high-performance version of the standard GL fastener. Installed in a living oak, it has a load capacity of twelve thousand pounds. This type of fastener is rated at six thousand pounds placed vertically 2 inches out from the collar surface. Many are in service around the world.

T-bracket

- The T-bracket holds a spreader beam, which widens to the width of the bracket at the end.

- The bracket must be balanced vertically and horizontally. The farther the beam projects out, the more length the vertical member of the bracket needs.

- A modified T-bracket using a GL in the center creates a three-point support that can help extend the beam past the tree.

- Each end is supported by a knee brace, which comes back to a GL.

Tree and Fastener Inspection

- Inspecting the connections to your treehouse is essential to maintenance.

- Grab a camera, a pad of paper, and make notes of wear and tear on the treehouse.

- All connections, materials, supports, finishes—every odd detail should be noted.

- If tree connections look strong, and the tree shows no evidence of rot or sap loss, you're in good shape.

ONE OF A KIND
Some treehouses employ a support system designed for the unique needs of tree and structure

For those treehouse builders who want to push the limits of treehouse design, innovations in structural support have given them the ability to construct treehouses that a decade ago wouldn't have been possible. Innovators like Pete Nelson, Jake Jacob, and Michael Garnier are constantly looking for ways to propel treehouse building forward.

In Germany, Andreas Wenning of Baumraum has designed treehouses that combine modern architecture with traditional materials. Everything from fasteners to wood siding has been reconsidered and redesigned. His "winding snake treehouse" wraps around a sequoia like a coiled python. Tom Chudleigh is also a future-minded thinker who created his

Andreas Wenning and Baumraum

- Each Baumraum treehouse project is unique, taking into consideration the environment, the tree, and the clients.

- A range of wood types as well as various options for insulated walls are considered for construction.

- Tree spaces can be outfitted with sitting and sleeping benches, storage spaces, a mini-kitchen, heating, glass windows, lighting, as well as a sound system.

- Every piece is prefabricated in a workshop and then brought to the site.

O2 Sustainable Treehouse

- The geodesic dome is made of T-2 aluminum or steel.

- The dome functions as a skeleton. After a floor and a canopy are added, it's ready for habitation.

- Treehouses are hung via a cable suspension system. The balloonlike basket is accessed through a trap door in the bottom of the house, conveniently docked at floor level.

- Each strut bolts together with ½-inch stainless-steel eyebolts. The triangulated floor structure provides firm support across the entire floor.

spheres to be "wooden cocoons," hanging in their trees with a unique system of cabling and rigging. He's constantly tinkering with his creation to increase its stability and preserve the marvelous finishes applied to the outside of his wooden shells. Builder and designer Roderick Romero has integrated a back-to-nature look with fanciful designs that appear as if they were sculpted from the tree itself. He uses fallen tree branches and limbs and creates "basket railing" designs that look as if the treehouse were sitting in a giant nest. Some of his treehouses have railings that look as if they were swirling around a platform like a wooden tornado.

Revolutionary builder Dustin Feider looks beyond the world of treehouses to the whole concept of how we live. He would like to reconsider how humanity can co-exist with nature. The O2 Treehouse is a combination of formal sculptural sensibilities, functional design, and an environmentalist's passion. His cable suspension system provides a strong, stable, wind-resistant structure. It also ensures that the tree is never harmed or restricted in any way.

Free Spirit Spheres

- Wood spheres are made of two laminations of wood strips over wood frames. The outside is covered with clear fiberglass.

- A range of wood can be used for construction. There are also a number of options for the insulated walls.

- Each wood sphere structural frame is made of four laminations of Sitka spruce and epoxy glue.

- Attachment brackets are fabricated from either steel or aluminum and painted black. Each bracket is drilled, and the screw holes are countersunk.

The Green Treehouse

- This treehouse is constructed out of mostly reclaimed or salvaged wood. The siding also features recycled solar panels as design elements.

- The treehouse is built in a 160-year-old male ficus tree.

- The support system includes six Garnier Limbs with arrestor brackets on the first floor. Four more GLs support the second-story crow's nest.

- The main structure has a seamed steel roof and electrical power generated by a turbine battery.

POST SUPPORTS

Is a treehouse a treehouse when there's no tree to support it?

Although most adults would look at a log fort on stilts as simply, well, a log fort on stilts, for a child, as long as there's a tree poking through the walls, he or she effectively has a treehouse. Recognizing this impulse, Daniels Wood Land creates all sorts of fantastic structures that sit on huge redwood stumps salvaged from northern California's redwood forest. For the lucky owners of these constructions, there's no doubt that they are treehouses.

Two other world-renowned builders, Jake Jacob and Pete Nelson, use posts when they see that it's necessary to augment the treehouse support.

To treehouse resorts around the world, whether they are in Australia or Costa Rica, posts do not negate the fact that their visitors will still be enjoying their stay in a real treehouse.

Green Roof Treehouse

- The trees selected were not strong enough to support the treehouse design, so a post was used to help support the house.

- The platform sits on both a T-brace on a post and a T-brace fastened to a tree with a lag bolt and bracket.

- The wooden top rail is good for structure, and the lower ropes give it a simple and see-through feel.

- A wooden ladder with a hatch provides access.

The Bait Shack Treehouse

- A wildly wacky-looking structure complete with themed accessories and accesses, the Bait Shack has a faux porch with faux door and two lanterns hanging from the porch roof.

- It features a crooked roof with two oversize dormers.

- The design is topped off with a deluxe paint job, weathered windows, and a rust protection package.

- A 3-foot tall platform is supported by a large redwood stump that is hollowed out to provide for a secret stairway.

The Gastineau Treehouse, built by Tree Top Builders, Inc., uses a combination of bracketed posts and beams on lag bolts. Because the treehouse needed to be larger than the tree could support, four posts were buried in cement to support the main structure, while the beams support the deck.

Sometimes the requirements of a job dictate a different method of building a support. The Panther is a one-story treehouse built low to the ground and on three posts and a tree to accommodate the young age of the children.

A treehouse support system should always be dictated by the tree or trees available and the requirements of the project. In some cases, where trees are not strong enough or large enough to support a treehouse, they are incorporated into the design of the treehouse that is supported solely by posts.

The Panther Treehouse

- A combination of posts and tree provides the support. The original treehouse needed repair because it had too many nails and the wrong-size bolts, creating a very unsteady structure.

- New bolts and brackets were attached, and old screws and rails were removed afterward.

- A new shake roof allows the one support tree to poke through.

- A steering wheel and a natural branch rope ladder help create a shiplike feel.

The Gastineau Treehouse

- Posts provide roughly 80 percent of the support for this treehouse.

- The size of the structure would have been a huge burden for the tree and would have required either cutting branches or having lots of wall and roof penetrations.

- Posts support the climbing wall and house, while the tree holds up the wraparound deck.

- A free-form wooden table inside wraps around the tree. The interior has a loft with a 1-foot-high railing and a triangular window opening. The finish is cedar.

TREE STEPS

In addition to thematically suiting the design, a treehouse entrance should be safe and accessible

There are dozens of ways to build steps into a treehouse and just as many types of materials to choose from in building them. The simplest steps are made with an exterior plywood sheathing cut to fit side brackets and then lag bolted to the tree. The step itself fits into a notch created by the brackets and is then bolted, in the middle, to a sturdy exterior post. The steps should be evenly spaced and no more than 12 inches apart, perhaps less if the principal tenant will be a child. The final step should be placed high enough for a child to step easily onto the treehouse deck or into the structure itself.

Plywood steps allow for other variations as well. Some builders, for instance, like ¾-inch plywood or cedar cut into

Triangle Steps

- If building a house with a young child, this is a great way to teach him or her how to construct steps.

- Scraps of ¾-inch exterior plywood can be found at any construction site.

- For flair, the plywood can be painted before the cutting and fastening.

- Measure the height from ground to treehouse and divide that by the distance of separation between the steps. This is the total number of steps to build.

Reclaimed Wood Steps

- A trip to a salvage yard or a reclaimed wood center can result in unique woods that are not normally available and at good prices.

- Redwood 4-by-4 posts are particularly nice to use because you can cut them lengthwise and end up with a nice triangular step.

- Lag screws or bolts are preferable over nails, which are not strong enough.

- For the health of the tree, space the bolts no less than 12 to 18 inches apart.

triangles that are then fastened to brackets bolted in the middle of an exterior post. If you need more riser area, pieces of 2-by-4 can be used to block in between the step and the post. This method is a little more stable and takes less balance to climb, better suiting smaller children.

Doweled Steps

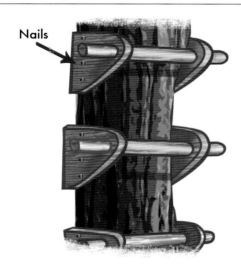

Nails

- Doweled steps require fewer fasteners than other steps.

- Supply store dowels are easy to find, but reclaimed hardwood dowels or even cut bamboo make for a nice touch.

- The diameter of the dowels depends on whom the

steps are being built for, but nothing less than 1½ inches should be used, and for adult climbers the steps should be larger.

- Rounded diagonal side brackets should be constructed out of a wood that weathers well, like redwood or cedar.

Telephone Pole Steps

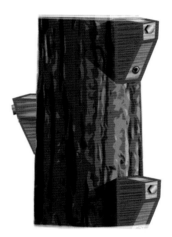

- Staggered telephone pole–style steps fit our natural climbing motion.

- A 2-by-4 is cut diagonally to form a trapezoid shape. The step size should be from 6 to 8 inches. A hole is predrilled into the step, and

a lag screw at least ½ inch long is used to fasten it to the post.

- The larger end of the stud is used as the step.

- A smaller lag screw anchors the step at the bottom.

TREE STAIRS

When an easy climb to the treehouse is important, stairs are the way to go

A staircase is the most efficient and safest way to climb into a treetop dwelling. It can also be used to create a sense of adventure. For a young child, a staircase can symbolize a path to fantasy and freedom. A story can be created just by the way the staircase is utilized. For a twelve-year-old, imagine how much fun a staircase that leads first to a rope bridge

might be. Once the treehouse is reached, another smaller staircase might be built to ascend to a crow's nest. In another creative scenario, a spiral staircase could wrap around the tree and lead to a hatch that opens into the main structure, giving the dweller quick shelter from a worthy foe.

For an adult, a staircase can set a fanciful mood to the

Notched-out Risers

- A treehouse height of more than 6 feet may require connecting platforms, supported by posts. The stringers (stair support railings), made from 2-by-12s, have to be cut accordingly.

- Place the stringers at the appropriate staircase angle and cut them to fit the ground and platform.

- To create the treads, measure from the top to the bottom, evenly spacing your markings.

- Cut a 90-degree notch at each marking, enough to accommodate a 2-by-12 tread.

Gang Plank

- A ¾-inch or 1-inch piece of exterior plywood makes a good gang plank. Cut the board in half and then sand the edges smooth.

- Use 2-by-2s or 2-by-4s as cleats and screw them into the plank. Space at regular intervals.

- For a gang plank longer than 6 feet, use a 2-by-12 board and attach 2-by-2 cleats to it.

- A gang plank can be either removable or fixed to the platform with hinges.

treetop dwelling through the use of salvaged wood treads, boxed posts with finials, and carved railings. Stairs can be functional as well, providing connecting access to multiple treehouse dwellings via walkways and bridges.

A stairway system should be well thought out and built to standard building codes. These codes typically define riser height and tread width, especially if the treehouse is to be used by young children or elderly adults. However stairs are utilized, they set the mood and are the first impression one gets when accessing the structure.

Castaway Stairs

- A split-log circular stair-case is made of logs cut in half. Making one is time consuming and difficult, but the results are quite striking.

- Each stair is cradled by a tree limb with a fork.

- The near end of the limb fastens to the tree with a lag bolt.

- The bottom of the log step rests in a small notch cut into the tree. Galvanized brackets fasten the top of the stair to the tree.

Post Ladder

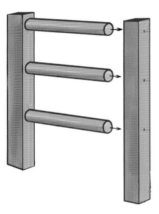

- Use a 4-by-4 post, prefer-ably redwood. Cut the post to the height of the ladder.

- Drill holes of 1½ inches through the post at 12-inch intervals. Cut the dowels to at least 12 inches.

- Fit the dowels in the drilled holes. You may have to sand the dowels to get them to fit well.

- Fasten each dowel with a lag screw in the center of the post. The ladder is portable.

ROPE LADDERS

Rope ladders provide a more adventurous, but potentially more dangerous, way to access a treehouse

Visions of Robin Hood and Tarzan immediately come to mind, swinging into a treetop hideaway and landing safely in the branches of a large tree. For a child or the young at heart, rope climbs increase the sense of playfulness that should ideally be at the heart of every treehouse construction.

There are various ways to make rope ladders, employing all

kinds of knots and lashings, but of common concern to them all is the strength of the rope. Each type of rope has its own ratings system based on the materials used to create it. Furthermore, because the rope ladder will be subjected to the elements, it should be constructed of an extremely durable material. Most natural fibers decay quickly, compromising

Monkey Rope

- Choose the right rope. Strong enough to hold any individual, it shouldn't grate against hands.

- A simple overhand knot can be tied and used for "steps" at 10-inch intervals.

- This style of knot reduces the strength of the overall rope. Make sure to account for knot weaknesses when choosing rope.

- To aid climbing, consider a double knot at the end of the rope or a small attached disc of wood or plastic to stand on.

Loop Rope

- Rope and loops are both three-strand twisted rope. The loops connect by interweaving the ends of the loops with the main rope.

- The loops are connected to opposite sides of the main piece of rope to form steps.

- In most cases a fixed loop knot is used to create the loops. This is the standard tie-in knot for climbers.

- If you are creating your own loop ladder, it should be tested vigorously before use.

safety. There are, however, synthetic materials designed to withstand any type of weather. These can last for years. A rope ladder should also have a smooth surface that won't hurt small hands. You don't necessarily need a soft rope, but it should not have pieces to poke into the skin or cause rope burns.

The looped-rope ladder is perhaps the easiest to use. A treehouse climber steps into a loop of rope knotted at one end and pulls himself or herself up by each successive loop. A tube rope ladder is a more complicated version of this same concept. Perhaps the most difficult rope ladder is the monkey rope ladder wherein the only support for your feet is a large knot. This requires a lot of arm strength and the ability to pull your own weight up. This style of rope ladder usually hangs close to the tree trunk, providing additional foot support as you climb.

No matter the type, rope ladders enhance the feeling of adventure inherent in a treehouse. But remember, always take care to place ropes and ladders in safe spots, not too high off the ground to protect younger people.

Rope-lashing Ladder

- Wooden steps can be lashed together with rope.

- A square lashing is used to bind together two spars or poles at right angles to each other.

- The best rope to use is weather-resistant nylon rope at least ½ inch in diameter. The binding should be inspected from season to season.

- A clove hitch is generally used to start the lashing. The rope is then wrapped around the poles several times and finished with another clove hitch.

Knots to Use

- Figure-8 knots, stopper knots, hitches, and slip knots are all helpful to treehouse builders.

- Knots in conjunction with carabiners and pulleys help move loads.

- Knots and harnesses work as backup safety measures.

- The "monkey's fist" knot adds weight to the end of a rope, good if a builder needs to heave a rope over a branch.

TREE HANDLES

A tree handle in the right place is a welcome sight for any tree climber

Handles are small but essential parts of a treehouse. When you are pulling yourself into the treetop area, they almost always aid in the climb. Handles can be fashioned out of many materials, or they can be as simple as cutting a handhold in the decking.

Handles should be easy for a builder to fasten, made of

strong materials, and complement the design and look of the treehouse. For a Robinson Crusoe–type house, actual tree branches or natural-fiber rope should be considered. For a more modern look, think about sleek handles made of polished wood. A treehouse made from salvaged wood and reclaimed doors and windows calls for salvaged or antique

Simple Wood Handle

- Cedar, redwood, and pine make for nice wooden handles. Sand the handle so the grip is smooth.

- The handle can be fastened to the base with two screws. Make sure the screws are shorter than the handle so they don't poke through.

- The base and handle can be fastened on all four corners with screws.

- Test the strength of the handle once it's installed. Is it strong enough to withstand the stress of constant pulling?

Plastic Premade Handles

- Plastic handles are extremely resistant to torque and are easy to grip.

- Rock-climbing grips can be used as well. They are made with rigid polyurethane, so they stand up well to abuse.

- Kid-friendly rock-climbing grips are round and comfortable with no sharp edges. They are fastened with steel socket-head bolts.

- Plastic handles come in many colorful shades, shapes, and sizes, adding to an upbeat feel.

handles. And of course, a simple tree fort can use a simple wooden handle, a mason's wood float, or a shed handle made of metal. You can purchase playground handles in various colors at any recreation equipment store or online site. You may also want to consider using rock-climbing grips as handles if they fit the style of your treehouse. Whichever handle you choose, make sure it's fastened securely. Long screws or lag screws are always preferred over nails because their grip in the tree is stronger.

Rope handles, threaded through a post or platform and knotted at the back, can be made from ¾-inch nylon, polyester, or natural fiber. Each rope has different qualities that make it desirable, but for strength and flexibility nylon is the best.

The position and number of handles should be well considered. Take into account who will be using them. They are a small but essential part of the overall design. If well placed they can really help make the experience of climbing into a tree safer and more enjoyable.

Natural Branch Handles

- Branches of various shapes and types can be sized to fabricate natural branch handles.

- The handles can be used for doors, windows, and escape hatches, and in cabinetry constructions.

- Stripping off the bark, sanding, and applying a varnish achieve a beautiful finish and protect from insects.

- Any branches you intend to use should be checked for weakness, disease, or infestation. If there are flaws in the branch, throw it away and find another.

Salvaged or Reclaimed Handles

- Salvaged items can bring a sense of style and quality to the construction.

- Hand-forged pull handles come in all sorts of shapes with wax finishes. They can be fastened to the platform, door, or escape hatch.

- Hand-forged iron nails and studs add more style.

- Rather than cutting down trees, using reclaimed wood helps the environment. Reclaimed wood also adds to the narrative attached to the treehouse. Every piece of wood has its own story.

ADVENTUROUS ACCESSES

An inventive access to your treehouse can add a sense of extravagance and excitement

The truly great treehouse builder finds a way to add something new to every aspect of his or her construction. An unusual or particularly apt access point is an element unavailable to most other types of building. It can add ambiance, expand on a theme, and make each trip to the treetop dwelling a new chapter in a child's memory.

Take Cedar Creek Treehouse Observatory, nicknamed the "Stairway to Heaven," for example. It doesn't get more adventurous than a circular stairway 80 feet in the air. This "Stairway to Heaven" rises 8 feet per revolution from the forest floor to the treetop canopy. After climbing the spiral staircase around a huge fir tree, guests can walk across the Rainbow Bridge to

The Cedar Creek Observatory

- The "Stairway to Heaven" shows what can be done when planning and vision meet hard work.

- Each step was knee braced. Vertical poles connect the steps and enclose the climber, creating a safer and more pleasing environment.

- Hoisting the five hundred-pound bridge required a double-pulley rigging.

- Once the bridge was positioned, the treehouse observatory and the 80-foot staircase were connected with cables and a chain link fence.

Steps and Ladders

- The Green treehouse utilizes a unique combination of steps, stairs, ladders, hatches, and reclaimed wood.

- The visitor slides in between the huge branches of a ficus tree to arrive at a small platform surrounded by hardwood ribbing.

- Popping through the salvaged hardwood hatch, a stained glass window casts colored light across the interior.

- A smaller ladder accesses a crow's nest in the branches. A good wind gives visitors a feeling of sailing in the breeze.

the treehouse observatory 43 feet away.

Of course, its not necessary to be that ambitious in building your own access. Roderick Romero designed an access to his Green treehouse using reclaimed redwood posts cut lengthwise into triangular treads. The staircase bisects two huge tree trunks, creating a wraparound walkway that accesses a small platform. From there a small salvaged wood ladder goes up through a hatch to the main deck.

The Tiberi Treehouse is a more typical example of backyard building. A notched riser staircase and a rock-climbing wall access a platform that then connects to the main treehouse via a rope-and-wood bridge. To a young child, this is a fort, a castle, and a getaway all wrapped into one.

Several treehouse builders like Dré Wapenaar, Tom Chudleigh, Lukasz Kos, and Andreas Wenning have made the access to their treehouse designs an adventure in itself. The ladders and steps are a carefully considered design element that serves as an introduction to the treehouse itself, setting the mood and creating a unique welcome to the main structure.

Tiberi Treehouse

- The two platforms are made of solidly supported beams that are in turn bolted, bracketed, and knee braced to the trees. The trees weren't harmed during the construction.

- Rope netting and a wood-planked bridge safely connect the two structures.

- The bridge is fastened to each structure with a system of cables and eyebolts.

- Smoothed, rounded logs and a railing skirt that employed a woven-basket look create a tasteful, Asian flair.

Roderick Romero

- An artist, musician, landscape artist, and treehouse builder, Romero integrates reclaimed and salvaged materials into most of his projects.

- He considers his work to be a kind of treehouse sculpture.

- Romero believes that "nature is the architect."

- Every treehouse builder should share in Romero's determination to allow the tree to dictate what's perched in its branches.

81

UNIQUE ACCESSES

Even a backyard builder can create an access that is entirely new and unexpected

The world of treehouses cries out for builders and designers who push the limits. By its very nature, the act of building in a tree inspires even the most inexperienced builder to dream of new possibilities.

Advances in support systems and methods of building have promoted a treehouse renaissance, allowing designers around the world to push each other to new heights. Some are futuristic (like the Sybarite Design Group treetop modular designs), whereas others are stunningly beautiful (like Lukasz Kos's Tree Lantern architectural masterpiece in Canada). The Canopy Cathedral in Pennsylvania has multiple access points that utilize creative, stunning woodwork, a must-see for all

The Sybarite Treehouse Project

- Captured rainwater, wind baffles to harness energy, and solar cells are all green elements employed to appeal to the eco-minded treehouse enthusiast.

- Tripod-type legs were designed to avoid tree rot and keep the ground surface compacted.

- A glass-enclosed staircase provides a light, welcoming access to the underbelly of the structure.

- The enclosed staircase is temperature controlled to a comfortable level even when snow is on the ground.

The 4Treehouse

- Although very simple, the access takes full advantage of the ambient sights and sounds of the forest.

- A modern-looking ladder uses black dowels as steps, offering varying views of the forest.

- The house is well lit from above and below, allowing safe movement during the night hours. Lights shining through the shuttered walls create a pleasant glow.

- A contemporary wooden ladder leads to a wall ladder that in turn accesses the structure.

ambitious treehouse builders.

S. Peter Lewis's personal passion and vision created a flexible drawbridge to add to his treetop dream. At first glance, it seems to defy the laws of physics and looks nothing like a staircase. In fact, it's a well-disguised engineering marvel.

Roderick Romero regularly uses unique accesses, including such structures as a bridge to a huge branch of a fig tree and salvaged redwood steps that sneak in between two huge stemming branches. In one of his designs, a caged platform acts as entrance to a reclaimed wood step ladder to the treehouse's main platform. You literally feel like you're moving through the tree rather than around it.

Barbara Butler's Coyote Valley treehouse sits high up in the branches of three giant trees. The 24-foot deck wraps around five different tree limbs and is encircled by 60 feet of hand-woven rope net railing. An extraordinary set of double S-curve winder steps circles around two tree trunks toward a large, rustic clubhouse.

These are just a few examples of the incredibly imaginative ways to create an adventurous entrance to a treehouse.

The Canopy Cathedral

- Rusticity and a high-quality finish make the staircase access and railings warm and inviting.

- The rough-hewn railings are lined with finials, pickets, and box posts.

- Ornate railings surround the deck area, providing for tasteful decoration as well as increased safety. A large hemp rope closes off access.

- Inside the cathedral, wide staircases lead up to a second floor and a gorgeous, multi-paned cathedral window consisting of fifty-seven panes of glass.

Treehouse Chronicles

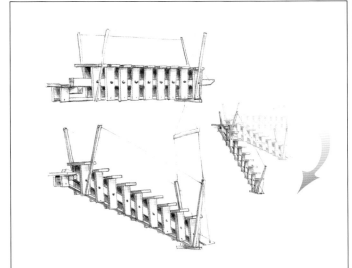

- The builder wanted to make the access memorable and "cool." To that end, he decided to create a collapsing staircase.

- The design centers around a counterweight and swing. Stairs lift up and away from the ground, suspended out of reach.

- When a secret catch gets tripped, treads pivot down to form the stairs.

- A drawbridge swoops down with creaks and groans, adding to the back-to-nature feel of this magnificent personal vision.

DOORS

The door is a visitor's first impression—make it a good one

Every enclosed space needs a door, an entryway that can admit visitors and prevent unwanted intruders from gaining access. Treehouses are no different. How one fills this need is one of the more personal decisions made about a treehouse.

Not unlike the front door to a home, a treehouse door introduces the dwelling to newcomers, telling them a little

bit about both the dwelling and its owner. Whether a door is made from scratch, salvaged from a junkyard, or bought new from a box store, the same basic rules apply to selection and installation. Make sure the door fits its frame snugly. Use strong hinges, and consider using a lock. A few dollars on a good bolt assembly could be the best money spent.

The style of door should fit the overall look of the treehouse.

Ledged-and-braced Door

- A framed, ledged-and-braced door repeats a look seen in old country cottages and barns.

- The door is braced by a diagonal timber fixed with the top of the wood angled toward the top hinge; the diagonal timber gives the door its strength.

- This type of door can be made without the frame but is then simply called a "ledge-and-brace door."

- These doors are usually hung using big T-hinges.

Dutch Door

- The door is divided horizontally; the bottom half can remain shut while the top half swings open.

- The initial purpose was to keep animals out of farmhouses while allowing light and air in.

- A prehung Dutch door has

a unique sealing system that allows it to seal itself as efficiently as any standard door.

- Dutch doors were invented in the Netherlands in the 1600s. They were first used on front doors and then introduced into the kitchen.

As you're building the platform or deck, save the leftover scraps, they might be enough to construct a door. All you need are three 1-by-12s cut to size and a couple of 2-by-4s. Add a handle and perhaps a window, and you're ready to go.

If salvaged lumber, reclaimed windows, and other eco-friendly materials are part of the treehouse, search for a vintage door that will fit the look. Study other treehouses of the same style. Ideas can be picked up just by surfing the Internet. Once a door is chosen, the threshold can be framed to fit. Choose a handle and hinges that complete the look.

In a high-end treehouse, a custom prehung door from a door supply vendor may be the way to go, or perhaps you noticed a terrific door on one of your travels to another country. Choose the door that fits your treehouse and provides the kind of greeting you want to give people when they arrive.

Salvaged Doors

- Salvaged or reclaimed doors rescue the craftsmanship of the past.

- Doors in oak, pine, or walnut are usually available at a salvage yard, and are typically sorted according to tree species.

- Measure the doorway before visiting a salvage yard. Calculate the distance from the inside of one side jamb to the inside of the other and from the threshold to the header.

- After measuring, subtract ¼ inch from each measurement to provide clearance for the door to swing.

Reclaimed/Salvaged Wood

- Hand-hewn timbers from early American forests can be much larger and longer than timbers available today.

- American chestnut, a wood valued for its beautiful finish and resistance to rot, is now available only as a salvaged material.

- Salvage wood can be from 125 to over 250 years old.

- Some artifacts predate the American Revolution.

DIFFERENT DOORS
The perfect treehouse door can both accentuate and expand on a chosen theme

A door is a door, right? True enough, but a creative builder can go the extra mile by turning it into something more. This can be done in a variety of ways, through specialized construction of the door itself, unique stains or paints, or unusual hardware and windows.

A cedar door with a hexagonal window inset changes a simple door into a unique expression of taste. It also lets more light into the dwelling.

Hunting for the right kind of door can be adventurous and fun. There are many salvage or reclaimed wood yards that supply doors from old farms, factories, or homes, often dating back to the 1700s. A salvaged door from a Pennsylvania

Door with Window

- A stylish, economical door can be created by cutting in a porthole.

- Inexpensive porthole windows can be bought at most building supply houses. Use the window itself to trace the window's shape in the door, then cut out a hole with a power saw.

- The window will have a thin collar that overlaps the wood, eliminating the need for sanding the opening.

- Trim for both sides of the window can be cut from 1-by-12 cedar with a jigsaw saw.

Door Hardware

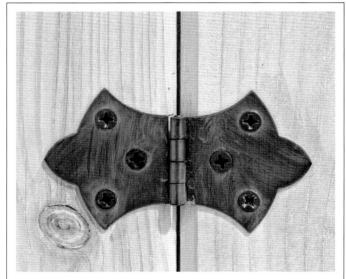

- A door's handle and hinges should match the door's look.

- Standard hinges, strap hinges, spring-loaded, half-mortise, and screen door hinges are all very easy to install.

- For further accessorizing, consider door knockers, bolts, locks, kick plates, and even signs.

- Polished brass, French antique, pewter, and rust are just a few of the many commercially available finishes.

factory with a funky peephole adds both character and history to the treehouse, as does a barn door that once housed animals on a farm in colonial Virginia. Other salvaged windows and trim can be used to outfit the entire dwelling. Match the roofing style to the door, and a treehouse becomes a one-of-a-kind eclectic creation.

Perhaps the look of the treehouse tends toward modern rather than vintage. In that case, consider choosing a floor-to-ceiling, clean-lined door. The handles and any inset windows can be sleek and contemporary with simple, high-end trim. The materials used for the door can also be different, like recycled plastic or aluminum, even solar panels. The doors can operate like hatches, swinging up or sliding to the side.

Or how about a themed entry using a funky, Old World door that leads into a ship captain's quarters? Attach a lantern on the dwelling's front with some rigging here and there, and you are ready to set sail on a new adventure.

Whatever the final choice, a unique door selection can be the first step in creating a truly personal environment.

Tongue-and-groove Door

- An Old World joinery method, tongue-and-groove comes in vertical, angled, and herringbone patterns, as well as variations with fixed louvers to allow for ventilation.

- Most tongue-and-groove doors are milled from kiln-dried lumber.

- Look for pegged, mortise-and-tenon joinery. It will provide a door frame that outperforms a door with dowel-and-screw joints.

- In areas of high humidity, Spanish cedar and Honduran mahogany make wonderful doors, resistant to swelling.

Reclaimed or Salvaged Doors

- A vintage door offers a focal point to any treehouse dwelling.

- Salvaged doors often have extras you don't see anymore in newer doors.

- Beveled glass, ornate trim, and aged wood with superior grain are just a few of the reasons to go with an older door.

- Doors from all over the world are available in salvage.

WINDOWS

A stylish window can still provide adequate light and protection from the elements

So much of the ambiance of a treehouse depends upon adequate windows. It's a beautiful world out there, full of leaves and swaying branches. Nice windows can help bring that world inside even while providing ventilation and protection from the wind and rain. A good rule of thumb when installing windows? The more, the better.

Windows are quite easy to install. Try to do most of the work on the ground, fitting the windows into a suitable frame and installing them in walls that will ultimately be difficult to reach from the outside, discouraging break-ins. Typical window glass can be used, but if the treehouse is prone to twisting, it can shatter. Safety glass (as used in car windshields) is

Simple Shutter Window

- These easy-to-construct shutters can be made out of exterior grade, 1-by-8 tongue-and-groove boards.

- They protect the window glass from the elements, including high winds and flying debris.

- It's important to locate the proper hinges. They may not be available in all areas and have to be ordered from shutter manufacturers.

- Shutter hinges are available in a wide range of styles. Installation will depend on the type of hinge and window design.

Tilt-in Window

- An attractive and functional addition to any project, tilt-in windows provide a breeze without allowing flying debris indoors.

- They can be simply built out of cedar with Plexiglas or Lexan windows and a catch at the top of the window frame.

- Prehung windows offer many built-in options, including grids, simulated divided lights, beveled, etched, or leaded glass, and gothic corners.

- The framing comes in a variety of different wood and metal designs, all with built-in insulation.

better. A material called Lexan can also be used. Hundreds of times stronger than glass, it provides better insulation and is less expensive. There is also the cheaper alternative, Plexiglas, which is not as strong as Lexan and tends to yellow and crack in the sunlight after awhile. Be careful when you use salvaged glass windows, especially if young children are using the treehouse. Because the glass is breakable, place windows high enough so they are out of reach.

If security is a concern, you should know that both Lexan and Plexiglas can be "punched" or shattered with rocks or hammers. However, once you've securely framed them, they will likely withstand most day-to-day perils.

Leaving the windows without coverings or shutters is not a good idea. Weather conditions can warp and destroy the wood around a window, allowing critters of all types to come in and make themselves at home.

After researching and consulting a builder, choose the type of window that will keep the treehouse safe from the elements and unwanted intruders as well as give the maximum exposure to the beauties of nature.

Salvaged

- Preowned windows can be an affordable way to improve the quality of a treehouse.

- Because salvaged windows were made to suit a previous installation, a builder needs to have flexibility in regard to the window's final dimensions.

- Wood can be susceptible to water damage and warping.

- Avoid windows that need a significant amount of paint removal or recaulking. In double-paned windows, avoid windows that show signs of moisture between the panes. Fogging is an indication of a blown seal.

Skylights

- Skylights are especially suited to treehouses, allowing visual access to the branches close overhead.

- A simple skylight can be made from clear, corrugated polycarbonate. It's impact-resistant, virtually unbreakable, and allows up to 90 percent light transmission. Lightweight and easy to work with, it installs using ordinary tools.

- Polycarbonate is weather- and UV-resistant while also providing maximum impact resistance. It's non-corrosive and has a good fire rating.

MORE WINDOWS
Windows add style and charm even while keeping the bugs and critters out

As a treehouse takes on a style of its own, the right set of windows is essential to emphasize any statement a builder wants to make. Without too much expense, a treetop dwelling can be turned into a flying pirate ship with portholes or a storybook gingerbread house with custom-made, prehung, cottage-style windows.

Regardless of the theme, windows are essential to the look and feel of a treetop dwelling. Aside from being decorative, they need to be functional and safe to use, especially if the windows have been salvaged. If the windows are older and preused, most of the time it's advisable to replace the older glass with Lexan or Plexiglas.

Porthole Window

Prehung Window

- Prehung portholes are a must-have for those who love the sea or are building a treehouse with a nautical theme.

- Coming in various finishes (both metal and wood), they are usually flush mounted. Most have a single hinge, two dogs (wing nuts), and

- a protective rubber seal around the glass.

- Portholes also come in fixed, center-tilt, or bottom-pivot styles.

- Make sure that the window has been properly sealed with a bead of caulk behind the nailing flange or fin.

- Once an opening has been prepared, installing a pre-hung window is relatively easy.

- A prehung window has a sash, a frame, a sill, hardware, and most of the trim.

- Prepare the opening by applying sealant around the

- perimeter of the window. Center the window in the opening and partially drive a nail through one of the top corners. Check to make sure the window is level, then finish the install.

- Nail around the outside trim and thoroughly caulk the joints.

For a practical window that harkens back to the early twentieth century, consider looking at drop windows. With a configuration wherein a top window slides vertically into an opening below the sill, they're stylish, sturdy, and safe.

Or perhaps you want something that has more elegance. Panes made of stained glass can paint uniquely fascinating, colorful patterns on the ceilings and walls. Beveled glass divides sunlight into its full spectrum of colors, creating an ambiance that brightens any treehouse.

Fixed Windows

- Fixed windows are sturdy, safe, and easy to maintain; their only downside is limited ventilation.

- Wood does not conduct cold or allow condensation as much as other materials, but it is subject to shrinkage and swelling.

- Wood will warp and rot over time—especially on the exterior.

- Aluminum windows are more durable than wood and are lighter and easier to handle. They can be insulated with a thermal break of extruded vinyl and sometimes foam.

Window Orientation

- A south-facing window lets in the most light and is desirable in all but the hottest climates.

- A north-facing window provides soft, diffuse light.

- The low angle of the sun in the morning and late afternoon can make heat from east- and west-facing windows too intense.

- Consider the view before deciding the placement and size of your windows.

WINDOWS & DOORS

CUSTOM WINDOWS

Windows of all kinds and sizes can be made of special woods and metals

No matter the final shape of a treehouse, for a little investment in time, money, and imagination a builder can design his or her own windows, specific to a unique vision.

Andreas Wenning of Baumraum makes great use of custom windows, giving his treetop structures a light, airy feeling. His large windows sometimes stretch from floor to ceiling or follow the curve of a wall, roof, or floor. His window frames are made of steel or very high-end, finished wood. They are always totally waterproofed. When you reside in some of these structures, you feel encased in your surroundings even as you gaze through the curved glass to a lush, arboreal horizon.

Custom Wood Windows

- Horizontal gliding windows allow for ventilation without taking up additional space when open.

- A bay window is composed of three or more individual units. The center unit is parallel to the exterior wall with side or flanking units aligned at 30- or 45-degree angles.

- Awning windows are hinged at the top and open out from the bottom.

- Stylish casements provide for structural integrity and ventilation. They are hinged so the sash opens outward in a swinging motion.

Important Window Terminology

- "Aluminum cladding" provides a protective shell on the exterior surfaces of wood windows.

- Cladding offers excellent resistance against scratches, cracking, blistering, and flaking.

- To "anodize" is to apply a protective coating to bare aluminum.

- "Dimensional stability" refers to a material's ability to resist changes in its dimensions due to temperature, moisture, or physical stress variations.

The Canopy Cathedral has a wall of custom diagonal windows fitted together to form a huge windowed wall. A canopy of trees surrounds the structure, hence the name. After entering the treehouse, walking up the main, polished-wood staircase is to be awestruck by the filtered light and the sheer size of this amazing set of windows.

Daniels Wood Land creates custom windows that fit its structural themes, whether pirate sloop, king's castle, or a South seas tiki hut. Knotty logs, redwood and cedar, or hand-carved framing are all possibilities.

For Barbara Butler the windows may have hand carvings in colors reminiscent of the region the treehouse is built in. In the Southwest, doors and shutters have carvings of tropical agave plants, wild roses, and classic white doves. In a redwood forest, custom metal window grates provide additional safety for second-story windows.

Windows and window coverings can go a long way to ensuring that a treehouse becomes your own, personally themed environment.

Paneled Windows

- Sidelights and transoms can increase the sense of elegance or drama in any dwelling.

- A sidelight is a window installed on one or both sides of a door, increasing the light and viewing area.

- A transom is a fixed window set above another window or door, giving a more open feeling to a structure.

- All window elements can be custom ordered to fit your plan. They are relatively easy to install.

More Terminology

- Geometric windows can come in a variety of shapes, including rectangles, triangles, trapezoids, octagons, pentagons, half-rounds, quarter-rounds, sectors, and ellipses.

- Green building is aimed at creating structures that are environmentally friendly. Criteria such as sustainability, energy efficiency, and healthfulness are considered.

- To kiln dry is to season or dry wood by artificial heat, controlled humidity, and air circulation.

- Laminated glass is constructed by placing a plastic interlayer between two panels of glass. It helps protect the glass from impacts and prevents shattering.

CUSTOM DOORS & OPENINGS

Doors of all kinds and sizes can make the entry to your treehouse special

The entrance to a treehouse can be as unique or daring as a builder cares to make it. Some found object treehouses use parts of old planes, boats, RVs, and even ships' galley doors. There are no rules.

As the introduction to the treehouse itself, the door must be inviting and inspiring. There are some treehouses where there isn't a door at all but rather an opening, a passageway framed in such a way as to give you a sense of entering a temple or a meditation sanctuary. Materials like bamboo and branches are used to create a feeling that the natural world has been brought inside, that there isn't a need for a door because the environment doesn't need to be shut out.

Custom-cut Doors

- Custom doors allow the builder the freedom to decide what size, shape, and design the door should be.

- A door with a large window pane needs to have thicker glass or plastic installed, especially if the window is more than 18 inches wide.

- The panes can be supplied with trickle ventilators to provide weather-tight airflow through the top of the window.

- The wood finish should be resistant to water damage, termites, warping, and cracking.

Tempered Glass

- Tempered glass is used in applications in which standard glass could pose a danger.

- Four to five times stronger than untempered glass, it does not break into sharp shards.

- "Safety glass," as it's known, is the preferred material for treehouses.

- Acrylic can be used instead of tempered glass in many applications, but it is not fire-resistant.

And then there are doors that have been found in salvage and inspire the entire house. The wood used and the style and structure seem to grow out of the door's design. The builder becomes the instrument the door uses to create the physical structure. Once the door is set and fastened and the hardware is attached and working, the real fun begins.

Treehouses can take a builder beyond the mundane, can inspire her to be more creative and more industrious than she thought possible. If the challenge is accepted and met, that's when the magic begins.

Lofty Lookout Treehouse

- A treehouse resort room with a number of picture and curved-wall windows can help bring the outdoors inside.

- The windows and door were custom ordered from the builder's plans and then fastened to precut openings.

- The door has a custom-made stained glass window that throws off colored beams of light when the sun hits it.

- A rustic, ten-light door opens to the outside deck and a cedar floor with rounded, pine-pole railing.

Do's and Don't's of Doors

- Don't frame the door opening until you know what size your door will be.

- Keep the door dry until it is correctly installed so that it won't warp.

- The door must be installed level, square, and plumb to operate as it was designed.

- Use a bubble level to make sure the bottom and head jamb are level.

WINDOWS & DOORS

95

WOOD ROOFING

Wood shingles are an attractive and practical way to top off your treehouse

When seen at a distance, a roof can tell visitors a great deal about the dwelling. An appropriate choice of roofing materials can both make a statement and accentuate the thematic elements a builder finds important.

Nothing blends into a forest better than wood roofing. Real cedar shingles and shakes are popular choices for roofs because of their rustic appearance. Shingles, the thinner of the two, have smooth, sawn surfaces, whereas shakes may be either sawn or hand-split for a more rugged look.

Fancy-cut wood shingles can be found in a variety of shapes, including fish-scale, cove, and V-cut patterns. Shingles require open sheathing, meaning a series of 1-by-6-inch

Traditional Wood Roof

- A traditional shake-style roof lends a warm ambiance to a treehouse, regardless of the design style.

- In fire-prone areas, wood shingles and shakes may require pressure treatment with fire-retardant polymer, or local building codes may forbid them entirely.

- Where fungus and mildew might be a problem, wood roofs should either be pre-treated with preservatives or treated with a fungicide after the first year.

- Cedar shakes insulate better than asphalt but are more difficult to apply and are not fire-resistant.

Pitched Roofs

- The term *pitch* refers to the angle or slope of a roofline.

- A low-pitched roofline can sometimes allow debris or snow to collect, putting extra stress on the roof.

- A high-pitched roofline doesn't collect as much debris, but it is harder to

- access when repairs are needed.

- If the dwelling is used as a place to sleep and live, then careful attention needs to be paid to all seams and connections, especially at the roof's ridgeline and joints.

boards spaced apart and nailed to roof framing. The spaces allow air to circulate around the shingles to prevent moisture buildup and rot underneath. Shakes, on the other hand, with their deeply grooved textures allowing for air circulation, may be applied over solid sheathing with interlays of thirty-pound roofing felt.

Wood roofing complements many styles of construction, including bungalow, craftsman, Victorian, and alpine. Cedar shakes in particular are an environmentally friendly option for consumers.

Flat Roofs

- Flat wood roofs can be very modern looking, stylish, and imitative of the broad lines of a natural landscape.

- They tend to collect rain and snow, making them a risky design choice.

- Materials for covering flat roofs have improved con-

siderably over the past two decades. With appropriate installation and maintenance, a good flat roof won't leak.

- A glue-down rubber membrane system under the wood is light, quick to install, and requires no special equipment.

Things to Know about Roofs

- To prevent water from pooling and causing leaks, flat roofs are always built on a slight incline.

- Working on a roof, take every safety precaution possible, including harnesses if necessary.

- Always inform someone that you are up there. Better yet, work with a helper.

- Use ladders that are high enough and strong enough for the job.

TREEHOUSE ROOFS

ALTERNATE ROOFING TYPES

There are many cost-effective and attractive ways to top off your treehouse

You don't have to look far to find good roofing materials. New technology has created a variety of safe, attractive, sturdy, weather-resistant shingles that fit any budget. Whether plastic, fiberglass, clay, or asphalt, most shingles come in a variety of colors and styles. They are all weather-resistant and fireproof. And each time someone chooses an artificial roof over

wood shakes, trees are saved.

Many artificial shake roofs have a textured, natural-looking surface that resembles premium shakes. These "look-alikes" last longer than real shakes and are impervious to rot and infestation.

Artificial slate tiles weigh one-third as much as natural slate

Composite Shingles

- Using composite roof shingles is the latest trend in the world of roofing. They are very durable, inexpensive, and attractive.

- Modern manufacturing techniques have made composite roof shingles look almost exactly like traditional shingles.

- Manufacturers sometimes add a chemical that prevents mildew and algae from growing on the roof.

- As an added advantage over wood, composite shingles are fire-resistant and have a life span of over fifty years.

Plastic Roofing Tiles

- Inexpensive to produce and easy to mold into virtually any form, plastic tiles come in a wide range of design choices to complement your treehouse.

- Hard or soft, both options last for an impressively long time.

- Despite the many benefits of plastic, its inability to be effectively recycled, combined with a high environmental cost, makes it unwise to use.

- Plastic roofing is valued both for its light weight and its outstanding insulating properties.

of comparable thickness. After factoring in the expenditure of transportation resources, the energy costs and carbon emissions are both lower. Artificial slate is also kinder to local ecosystems.

Asphalt shingles are economical and versatile. They're relatively inexpensive, easy to install, and available in a variety of qualities, costs, and styles. There are two types: fiberglass and organic-mat shingles. Both are made with asphalt, but fiberglass shingles use a fiberglass reinforcing mat, whereas the organic kind use a cellulose-fiber mat derived from wood.

Asphalt Roofing Tiles

- Versatile and well priced, asphalt is used in as much as 80 percent of the roofing market.

- Asphalt roofing tiles have a great range of quality and style and are compatible with almost any pitch of roof.

- Of the two types of asphalt shingles, fiberglass is most popular for its light weight, thinness, ease of transportation, and high fire rating.

- For durability and longevity, make sure the shingles meet industry standards, even if it means paying more money.

Roofing Installation

- Before installing the shingles, make sure to account for anything that will protrude through the roof.

- The type of roofing should match the pitch of the roof.

- Load your roofing material as close to the edge of the roof as possible for easy access.

- To prevent possible damage, install the roof without walking on the finished portions.

METAL ROOFING
Metal roofing is lightweight, durable, easy to install, and long-lasting

Advances in metals technology have created every type of roofing tile or shingle imaginable. The colors and the textures found in metal roofing are as varied as those of any other material. Suited to almost any treehouse type, metal withstands the elements for many years and still looks great. Inexpensive metal roofing can also keep down the costs of building or renovating your treehouse. Because it is easy to install, even beginner builders can do the work with very little effort.

The most conspicuous benefit of metal roofing is its durability. It's extremely tough and has a longevity that few other roofing types can match. If falling branches are a concern (as they almost always are), metal roofing provides good

Standing Seamed Metal Roofs

- Metal panels are virtually maintenance free and can be installed over almost any type of existing roof system.

- They come in a wide array of color options and styles to match any treehouse style.

- These roofs are best suited to areas that present harsh weather conditions. Resistant to heat and humidity, they also withstand heavy snow and winds.

- A standing seam roof is constructed of many interlocking panels. A raised, interlocking seam allows runoff without seepage.

Stone-Coated Roofing

- An elegant look and hardy composition satisfy even the most refined of tastes.

- The panels are made from structural-grade steel and are coated with aluminum-zinc alloy to enhance the corrosion resistance. Acrylic coating aids the adhesion to the stone-granule coating.

- An acrylic overglaze provides a tough finish for extra protection.

- Stone-coated roofing is strong enough to withstand the elements—hail, wind, fire, freezing and thawing, and even earthquakes—better than most other materials.

protection against punctures. According to most specs, fifty years of service is possible if the roofing is well maintained. And, of course, a metal roof is completely fire-resistant.

The downside of metal roofing, particularly the cheaper models, is that an improper installation can cause leaks. Care needs to be taken to look for continuity in the line of all seals, using quality sealant to minimize reliance on workmanship. Recognize that the ideal sealant bead is uncommon in sheet metal work. Consider thermal movement, weatherability, and the "rain screen principle." On the other hand, many owners are happy to discover that metal is a great conductor of heat, which means that, in cold weather, the roof will help heat the structure. Metal roofs come in a variety of colors and can be made of copper, aluminum, stainless steel, and even lead. Naturally, the price of materials is dependent on the type of metal used for the roofing. Copper roofs are the most expensive material, but they are very attractive.

Given that expense, durability, looks, and easy installation are always important factors to consider, metal roofing is one of the most popular choices in treehouse construction.

Simulated Shake Roofing

- Aluminum shakes do not rust and actually reduce the sound of rain, making it the top choice in metal roofing.

- The shakes are usually coated with Kynar, a plastic coating with an enhanced energy rating. It comes in a variety of colors.

- The low weight per square foot allows for the installation of metal roofing over multiple layers of shingles.

- Given its resistance to moisture, metal roofing can be installed on roofs that have relatively low pitches.

Pros and Cons

- Metal roofs can last for more than fifty years.

- Metal roofs can withstand wind gusts up to 140 miles per hour.

- Most metals can be recycled.

- A metal roof is expensive, yet it should be viewed as a great investment.

- Dents and scratches due to hail and falling debris are a common occurrence.

RECYCLED ROOFING

It's possible to be stylish with a roof even while paying attention to the environment

Using "green" materials for a treehouse roof is not a fad. It's a way of both making a statement and contributing to the overall health of the environment. Using eco-friendly roofing materials may seem like a small gesture in the context of one tiny treehouse, but if every builder made environmentally friendly choices, the benefits in aggregate would be enormous.

The building industry is taking big steps to help provide builders and designers with more environmentally friendly building options. Hazardous asphalt shingles, for instance, are already a thing of the past. They were a petroleum-derived product that was (and still is) a significant contributor to our landfills. Recycled plastics, fiberglass, and wood are quickly

Eco-shake Roofing

- The eco-shake shingle is designed to resemble and replace wood shake shingles.

- Composed of 100 percent recycled materials, reinforced vinyl, and cellulose fiber, eco-shake shingles are a perfect example of what can happen when new technology meets a concern for the environment.

- Their Class A fire rating and Class 4 impact rating are the highest ratings available.

- Freeze- and thaw-resistant, they are sturdy under even 110-mile-per-hour winds.

Recycling Asphalt Shingles

- Asphalt shingles make up roughly two-thirds of America's residential roofing market.

- An estimated eleven million tons of asphalt shingles are disposed of each year just in the United States.

- They are made of the same four basic materials contained in road construction asphalt.

- Using recycled asphalt shingles in road construction can actually improve pavement performance.

becoming standard materials in roofing.

One of the more exciting developments in green building is the movement to recycle old tires. The tread is cut into little squares and then coated with granular-size sand pebbles. The end product is then stacked like any other tile.

Solar-powered shingles are also readily available. A great way to help generate power in a treetop dwelling, they usually need a bank of batteries installed to store the power they generate.

As the list of innovations grows, every builder needs to incorporate them into his or her constructions. The environment will not be saved by any one large gesture but rather by a number of very small ones.

Recycled Wood Pallets

- Recycling pallets is usually quite easy. When you're done with them, recycling centers will pick them up.

- As long as the pallet is in good shape when it is recycled, it will be used repeatedly, cutting down on the amount of new pallets that need to be made, saving wood and trees.

- If the pallet is not reusable, it is broken down and separated from its metal.

- The metal nails, screws, and brackets are recycled as well.

Roof Coating

- Ask your roofing supplier to identify the correct coating to use for your particular roof. You'll need to know the type of recommended roof and the base material (metal, plastic, timber, or tile).

- Using the wrong coating can lead to many problems, including blistering, weathering, and poor adhesion.

- Various roof coatings are made to service various climates and impact situations. Make sure your choice serves your specific needs.

- An annual check of your roof coating is usually a good idea.

UNIQUE ROOFING

A treehouse roof can be as unique and original as the builder who designs it

The most basic of all structural elements, the roof presents inherent limitations that are nevertheless being turned on their ears by some of today's most talented builders and designers. From the viewpoint of a traditional builder, the possibilities being explored in treehouse roofs are truly startling.

Even when the materials being used are rather conventional,

the ways they are being used are altogether unique. In the case of Tom Chudleigh and his spheres, is there really a roof at all, or is the top simply an extension of the walls? Whether made of fiberglass or laminated wood, the uppermost parts of his spheres receive the same treatment as the walls and floor. Essentially the whole structure is protected and strengthened

Slanted Flat Roofing

- Although the slanted flat roof is a simple design, a builder needs to plan ahead, calculating angles and deciding the most suitable materials to use to best handle debris buildup and water runoff.

- The roof is slightly slanted to provide for drainage. It's

waterproofed underneath the roofing material.

- Flat, non-absorbing roofing materials work best.

- Slick metal roofing material is ideal. Debris tends to slide off rather than accumulate.

Free Spirit Spheres

- The walls, floor, and ceiling are covered by a strong wooden shell with layers of fiberglass reinforcement.

- The nutlike shape attaches to a web of rope, replacing the foundation of a conventional building.

- The sphere withstands

harsh weather and impact conditions as the stress load is evenly distributed.

- The sphere functions as a natural adjunct to its environment. If tree limbs fall through the support web, the remaining strands will continue to provide support.

as if all of it were roof.

Andreas Wenning of Baumraum creates slanted or round roofing to conform to his contemporary themes, but his materials are standard stainless steel, composite shake, or recycled rubber tires.

Treehouse builder Dustin Feider uses a combination of wireframe structural elements and $1/16$-inch recycled polyethylene, stretched as a canopy over his geodesic treehouses.

Recycled Fabric

- Made from hemp canvas, recycled milk carton plastic, and 60 percent post-consumer waste eco-resin, the covering is ecologically ideal.

- Instead of nails, nuts, and bolts, a cable suspension system hangs the treehouse from its tree, providing a strong, stable, wind-resistant structure.

- The interior is kept dry by its overlapping roof tile-style panel arrangement.

- Awning material provides a watertight seal around the entry and exit points of the tree's branches.

Dustin Feider

- Feider shows that an environmentally sound structure can be safe and cost-efficient as well.

- His modular designs fit any tree or trees.

- A variety of building materials can be easily switched out to accommodate style, size, and design preferences.

- Feider says, "The treehouse design . . . allows one to experience nature as the birds do in an upper canopy tree haven."

TREEHOUSE ROOFS

THE FUTURE

A history of innovation and creativity in treehouse construction bodes well for the future

Given the rapid pace of innovation in only the last few years, it's impossible to forecast what tomorrow's builders will create. But a handful of individuals are giving road signs, doing their best to break through barriers.

The Solent Centre for Architecture and Design sponsored a competition in which students produced a treehouse study-center concept. The facility was finished in 2008, providing an incredible resource for young people to see and experience firsthand the issues that will face them in the future.

Just south of Mount Rainier in Washington state, a gazebo-style camp has been developed for physically challenged children. Designed for full wheelchair access, it will enable

Sybarite Treehouse Housing Project

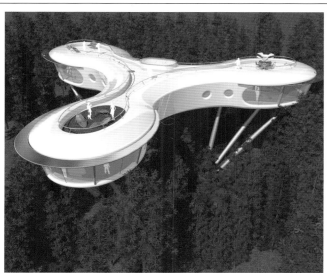

Solar Shingles

- The organic project sculpts architecture into the living environment even while retaining complete functionality.

- The structure provides 200 square meters of rooftop terrace.

- The rooftop design allows rainwater to collect around the perimeter at the roof level. The water is then filtered and stored in a large tank located within the central core of the structure.

- The collected rooftop water can be used for bathing, cleaning, and disposing of waste.

- Solar-powered shingles can blend almost seamlessly with traditional roofing materials, including slate, metal, fiber-cement, and even asphalt.

- Electricity is generated when the sun strikes a semiconductor layer laminated to the shingle's surface.

- The cost of a kilowatt-hour of solar energy is about 25 cents versus 10 cents for a kilowatt-hour of natural gas–generated or coal-generated electricity from the grid.

children to experience the love of the outdoors that their fully enabled friends have.

Innovations in window design have provided builders with new possibilities. UV rays and heat from the sun can be uncomfortable and harmful. Solar control window films reduce heat by rejecting a large percentage of solar energy, infrared rays, and harmful UV rays. Additionally, they can help retain heat during the winter months.

Metal roofing is an exciting option that brings together many end-user benefits. Metal roofing materials are often recycled products that can be recycled again at the end of the usage lifespan. Newer solar technology is now embedded into the roof tile. Design and technology have converged with photovoltaic-coated metal-roofing materials in custom styles and colors.

Camp Primetime

- The gazebo-style platform provides access to the forest for physically challenged children.

- Glulam beams with Kevlar between layers of wood provide stress support adequate to maintain 375 pounds per square foot.

- Because the structure is open to the elements (including snow), the load-bearing capacity is above standard. When in doubt, err on the side of caution.

- Heavy limb support bolts in arrestor brackets were used to fasten the glulam beams.

UK Study Center

- The Solent Centre for Architecture and Design sponsors designs that emphasize environmental and social sustainability.

- The school was established to create teacher-oriented programs.

- The school is devoted to providing opportunities to those who are concerned with teaching the skills and expertise to make a difference.

- The study center's library is available to anyone interested in the study of modern design.

107

THE FORT

To appeal to a child's imagination and sense of fun, nothing beats a treehouse fort

When most people think about treehouses, the image that usually pops up is of a backyard fort for the kids. A treehouse fort is iconic and timeless, and children will always need to defend their refuges from imaginary foes. Above all else, a good fort is a place where kids can be themselves by acting out various roles, be it a pirate, a cowboy, a knight, or a king.

Aside from the parents who build their children treehouse forts, many professional builders specialize in these fanciful hideaways. Barbara Butler believes that all children want to be a part of a great treehouse or tree fort, "to have their own space, high up in a tree, where nooks and crannies are made from tree branches." Children love to play outdoors and climb

Lookout Tower

- The tower of the treehouse fort offers another area of play with easy access from the main treehouse.

- Built around one tree and knee braced from below, the fort has a 360-degree vista unimpeded by supports.

- A zip line runs from the platform, a simple hexagonal structure with a cedar floor, to another tree. A slide is attached to another side.

- A rope-and-wood timber bridge connects the lookout to the main treehouse.

Crow's Nest

- Eight to ten feet above the main structure, a triangular crow's nest sits perched between tree limbs.

- The only access to the crow's nest comes via a nylon, tubular rope climb.

- The crow's nest is set in a level area of branches with

a minimum diameter of 10 inches. The deck is cedar surrounded by cedar railings and pickets.

- The 2–by-10 platform frame is supported by long bolts in brackets.

in trees. What better way to sponsor that sense of exploration than to build an imaginative fort?

Ron Daniels, owner of Daniels Wood Land, creates themed forts and getaways. From crooked bridges to stairways inside a tree stump, it's almost uncanny how he can anticipate what will delight a child. His forts even have playful names like "Monkey Mansion," "Scalliwag Sloop," "Tommy's Turbo," and "The Monstro."

Tree Top Builders, Inc. creates forts with crow's nests, bridges, swings, zip lines, and rope swings. Designed to engage the child's sense of play, these forts have the added benefit of intentionally appealing to adults as well, giving Mom and Dad some fun moments of their own.

Whether you are a child who has put together a platform fort with plywood or a professional builder, the intention is the same: to create a fantasy environment where you can fight dragons, hold your enemies at bay, or make a pirate captain walk the plank. And after the day's imaginative work is done, you can kick back and rest comfortably in your tree-top dwelling.

Fort Fiesta

- By aggressively rejecting the rustic palettes of nature, the playful colors of this fort create an atmosphere of fun and enjoyment.

- An angled catwalk and two straight bridges allow transit from the fort to a platform and then to another part of the fort.

- The colorful rock-climbing walls provide access for the more adventurous child. A scoop slide provides a quick exit.

- The structure is supported by 4-by-4 posts and topped off with a pyramid roof of corrugated tin siding.

Escape Hatch

- A secret access through the structure's floor enhances the sense of adventure essential to a good tree-house fort.

- A rope ladder made of nylon and lumber leads from the ground to the cedar floor hatch 8 feet above.

- The hatch door is hinged so that it swings up and is not visible from the ground below. The ladder can be pulled inside.

- Two-by-four cleats were used to hold the door together.

BRIDGES & WALKWAYS

Few elements enliven a treehouse like an imaginative access stretching between two structures

Bridges and walkways are essential to an enjoyable treehouse experience, allowing the treetop dweller to access difficult places in extravagant, often unexpected ways.

Most solid bridges are usually wooden. They're typically supported by posts and beams. The longer the span, the more support is needed, either via cables hanging from the trees or from larger beams and artificial limbs from underneath.

A rope bridge is like a suspension bridge. The connections at each end of the bridge are extremely important in the support system. A fairly safe version uses two high-strength cables strung at the same height and 2 to 3 feet apart, allowing boards to be set down within a rope netting as a walkway. The

The Fire Treehouse

- The innovative walkway is made of reclaimed timber, while the railings are natural branches with the bark stripped off.

- A swirl of smaller twigs and branches used as horizontal members provides a final, tasteful touch.

- The walkway leads to a salvaged antique wood gate with finials and fleur-de-lis shapes.

- The walkway zigzags through a forested area and is supported by a combination of posts and large eucalyptus trees.

Glenmoore Rope Bridge

- The treehouse deck has a safe and exciting access, and has a zip line escape to another tree.

- The bridge is connected between the structures with two heavy-duty cables attached to eyebolts on each platform.

- The rope railing is a natural fiber covered with nylon netting.

- The 2-by-12 timbers are evenly laid out over 2-by-6 crossbars. The cable threads through two U-bolts fastened to the bottom of each crossbar.

boards are then tied or bolted to the cable to keep them steady and secure. The cable attachments should be connected to a heavy-duty eyebolt attached to the platform or a tree.

There are a few things to remember as you're building your bridge. Be sure to test the walkways and bridges prior to use, making sure they can support the expected foot traffic. Never use a rope bridge in severe weather. Always supervise small children when they use a rope bridge.

Properly built and with appropriate safety precautions, bridges and walkways can be terrific add ons to any treehouse.

Treetop Inn

- A network of rope bridges, wooden walkways, and landings makes climbing to this treehouse a theme park adventure.

- The decks are bolted to both the trees and two 4-by-4 steel columns. The walkways and bridges are supported by the decks and trees.

- A hand-woven rope netting of heavy-duty natural manila rope on each side provides safety and stability.

- The bridge walkways are made out of redwood rounds strung together with heavy-duty cable.

Sphere Bridge Walkway

- A set of stairs wrapping around the tree trunk accesses a landing and a bridge walkway.

- The stairs, bridge, and walkway are all supported by a cable suspension system.

- The stairs fasten to two metal railings winding around the tree to the platform landing. Each stair has an inner and outer bracket used for support.

- The landing is fastened to the sphere with cables and bolts. Wooden treads from the landing to the sphere create a small bridge.

FUN FEATURES

PULLEYS, BEDS, HAMMOCKS
After a treehouse is built, it's time to think about the accessories

The basic shell of the treehouse is finished, but there's still something missing. What can be added to make it an ideal place to play, relax, or work? Each type of treehouse has its own style and needs. It's up to the owner to accessorize according to his or her personal vision.

A child's treehouse is sure to have things in it that an adult would have no interest in and vice versa. A pulley with a bucket

attached, for instance, tends to be one of the most popular additions for kids. It serves as a way to bring food, drinks, and toys up to the treehouse without too much effort.

Beds or sleeping lofts are great additions as well. When the weather is right, and the treehouse is warm enough, a sleepover is about the most fun a child can have without leaving home. Bunk beds and lofts are relatively easy to build and

Pulleys

- A simple pulley can be very useful in hauling building materials to the treehouse.

- A pulley is perhaps one of the easiest accessories to install; a couple of screws will fasten most pulleys to a beam.

- Available at any building supply store, pulleys come in a few sizes. If needed, pick up a plastic bucket as well.

- To hold the bucket, use nylon rope tied to a snap hook. Thread the rope through the pulley and knot the end so it won't pull through.

Hammocks

- A classic choice for durability, comfort, and relaxation, hammocks make a nice addition to any treehouse.

- Rope hammocks can be found almost anywhere. Cotton is best for comfort, but nylon is more durable and will not collect mildew.

- They come in all colors and many designs. If you're planning to leave your hammock outside, nylon is best.

- A soft, quick-drying, water-repellent hammock may be the best choice for children.

don't take up much room. The frame can be made from 2-by-6 lumber attached to 4-by-4 posts with lag screws and a fitted piece of ¾-inch plywood supported by brackets underneath.

Of course, if you're building for adults, you may want to invest a little more and make your loft bed as comfortable as possible. Consider adding a porthole window or run some electricity. Bring up the stereo for those relaxing evenings with your spouse.

A hammock is also a great way to lie around on a sunny day. It is portable and easily installed, and a builder can affix the appropriate bolts at the right distance but then keep the hammock rolled in storage until the right moment presents itself.

Owning a treehouse is a very personal experience, and accessorizing it is a way to bring that personal vision to life.

Bunk Beds

- A treehouse sleepover is even better when bunk beds are involved.

- If space is too limited for built-in beds, fold-up beds can be hung from the wall with a hook and chain.

- A guardrail on the upper bunk may be a good idea

for a restless sleeper. Foam pads help make the night more comfortable.

- The bottom bed can be built on top of storage for pillows, blankets, and spare hammocks.

Sleeping Lofts

- A sleeping loft with a great view can't be beat for a relaxing sense of getting away from it all.

- The interior is furnished with a very spacious, curved sleeping area and bench on both sides of the structure.

- Beneath the bench, drawers made of acrylic glass provide storage.

- The walls are painted soothing white. The interior furniture and floor are made of oak. Reading lights are attached on either side of the loft.

FUN ACCESSORIES

Just a few extras can add immensely to the overall enjoyment of a treehouse

The right choice of accessories can turn a merely great treehouse into a virtual theme park. Rope swings, slides, and zip lines can all create hours of safe fun for a child.

Barbara Butler's colorful treehouses always have themes and appropriate accessories. Many of her more rustic treehouses come with a zip line ride. For a fast, fun (and safe!) trip

from the top of a take-off tower to the ground, nothing beats a zip line. Custom-designed pulley bucket systems can bring up supplies so the clubhouse has all the provisions it needs.

Tree Top Builders, Inc. built a marvelous one-tree treehouse with a rope swing hanging from a limb of the supporting poplar. Adjacent to it is a wooden bench swing for Mom and

Zip Line

- A zip line is an exciting and fast way to move between trees.

- The line should be tethered on both ends with a combination of cables attached to multiple shackles.

- A zip line harness for children or a zip line seat

for adults is a good idea, often along with a cyclone disc seat.

- A zip line is unique in that you must have a trolley-type pulley for it to function correctly. If using cable, the pulley must be designed for cable.

Rope and Bucket

- A simple-yet-useful tool for bringing all sorts of materials to the treehouse in a hurry, a rope-and-bucket system can be installed easily with a small pulley system and a metal or plastic bucket.

- For children, plastic is usually the best bucket choice.

- To support heavier weights, attach a pulley box with a large wheel-and-rope assembly.

- Snap hooks come in various sizes and configurations and are made of brass, steel, and iron.

Dad to watch from as their children swing high in the sky.

Another great accessory but seen less often, fire poles make for delightful quick exits from treetop getaways. When they are set adjacent to a treehouse deck, a fast slide down a slick metal pole makes for a wonderful way to end the day.

A horizontal or tubular climbing net is great exercise and a fun way to move around the treehouse. A horizontal net can stretch to the main deck, while a tubular rope climb can provide access to the ground or a crow's nest. Both types of netting are a cinch to install.

Most accessories are relatively inexpensive and are easy to install. Spend a day with the children, coming up with ideas and adding extras. Before turning the children loose, however, take the time to test everything out, riding and swinging until you're certain of the safety. In the end, accessories can liven up the treehouse experience and provide hours of uninterrupted bliss for adults and children alike.

Rope Swing

- Rope swings can be bought commercially. Made of molded plastic discs 10 to 12 inches in diameter, they come in a variety of colors.

- A ¾-inch-diameter nylon rope is standard. Be sure the supporting limb is sound.

- The length of the rope varies according to need.

- The FH Full Support Swing Seat has been developed for physically challenged children. It has a solid wooden swinging platform and a comfortable central column to cling to.

Fire Pole

- Simple and easy to install, fire poles are available in any length.

- Fire poles normally are constructed of 2½-inch-diameter "cold drawn" brass tubing; the treatment process increases the strength of the brass considerably.

- Poles should be set in at least 36 inches of concrete. Landing mats are optional. A finial brass ball is typically affixed to the top.

- For an inexpensive alternative to brass, consider using a sturdy, 3-inch plastic tube also set in concrete.

MORE FUN ACCESSORIES

There is almost no end to what a creative builder can add to a treehouse

The list of fun accessories for a treehouse can go on and on. The only limit is the builder. And don't forget the kids. When it comes to creativity, nothing beats the imagination of a child.

Rather than just building a simple rope swing, consider a swingset paired with monkey bars, rock climbs, or ladders. Swingsets come in wooden, metal, or plastic and are tested to suit all safety standards. They also have a variety of finishes, from dark wood to power-coated metal.

Slides are another great addition to any treehouse playset or fort. Aside from traditional straight chute slides, there are a number of tube slide types, variously called "wiggle," "tubular," "spiral," and "peek-a-boo." They can easily be integrated into

Swingset

- A swingset attached to the platform is easy to install and inexpensive.

- Two hard plastic brackets are lag screwed to a platform beam for support. A piece of sturdy ½-inch to ⅝-inch rope is then threaded through and tied to each bracket.

- Two holes need to be bored into both ends of the wooden plank seat to fit the rope. The rope should be tied with a bowline knot.

- Set the seat so that feet don't drag on the ground.

Slides

- Slides can be straight or tubular.

- Most children prefer tubular slides. Adults like them as well because they are safer, being fully enclosed. Before ordering, double-check the height of the deck.

- Most tubular slides are made of fade-resistant polyethylene and have weight-capacity ratings. They range in diameter, but 24 inches is the norm for younger children.

- They come in various colors and are easy to assemble per the included installation instructions.

the play area of a treehouse.

Chairs and tables are other near-essential treehouse accessories. Whether made of plywood and timber or of natural branches and cross-sections of trees, they can be freestanding or attached to the structure itself. They can be made out of tree stumps, scrap wood, or even utility spools. A sturdy table, bench, and chair can be used for eating a snack or doing homework.

Birdhouses also make a great addition. The best types are redwood and cedar, which will not deteriorate.

Climbing Nets

- Not only are climbing nets great exercise and fun, but they're also utilitarian.

- A soft nylon or natural-fiber rope netting with eye loops on top can be attached to any play structure.

- A typical climbing net is fabricated from quality ¾-inch, three-strand twisted poly rope using a weave that allows for square mesh openings.

- Most nets are extremely flexible and rugged and have tensile strength ratings, helping you choose the type of net that's right for you.

Simple Table

- An interior table fitting the tree support can be used as a place to eat, do homework, or draw designs for the next treehouse.

- Simple tables can be made from 2-by-4s and ¾-inch plywood.

- Studs should be cross braced or knee braced to the tree itself.

- Create a paper or cardboard template for your table by wrapping it around the tree. Cut the board with a jigsaw and sand the edges. Use nails or screws to assemble.

MORE ABOUT FUN

Treehouses that go the extra mile make for a truly memorable treetop experience

Some builders and designers go all out to make a child's treehouse experience something the child will remember for a lifetime. A simple concept like a rock-climbing wall can transform an average treehouse into something extraordinary. Multiple rock walls only add to the fun and are easy to install and maintain.

For a physically challenging and fun experience, monkey bars come in metal and wood and as either integrated or stand-alone elements. They can be installed vertically, horizontally, straight, or crooked. Because they are easy to put on and easy to take off, there's no excuse for not giving them at least some thought.

Rock-climbing Wall

- Backdrops for a variety of fun and challenging activities, climbing walls are very easy to install.

- For a simple wall, fasten colorful climbing holds onto a piece of plywood. Premolded modular rock walls are also available.

- Traverse walls are more common for younger children.

- Three-dimensional panels offer more climbing options than just a set of basic climbing holds. Bulging shapes and cracks mimic the feel of real rock.

Monkey Bars

- In addition to encouraging imaginative play, monkey bars help promote coordination, balance, and strength.

- Made of durable metal, they are usually 24 inches wide and fastened with nuts and bolts on both ends.

- Metal bars can be straight or curved and are typically powder-coated in a variety of fun colors.

- Various hardwoods offer the firmest, smoothest grip for children's hands. Dowels are usually inserted into 4-by-4 supports.

And who wouldn't want some carved critters to adorn their treetop dwelling? Whether decorated with bears or beavers, carved plants or flowers, a touch of personal art adds decoration and sentimental value. Even the doors and shutters can have carvings.

Stains and paints can liven up a themed treehouse. Stenciled designs or freeform painting can give a treehouse a personal touch that adds to the fun of treetop play. You can create a coat of arms or design your own flag.

········· RED ● LIGHT ·············

When placing recreational equipment in your yard, you should have a fairly large fall zone in all directions. The area around your treehouse should be free of obstacles like fences or bushes or hard surfaces like concrete or asphalt that could lead to worse injuries in case of a fall.

Color Stains and Paints

- Using the correct paints and stains will increase the life of your treehouse as well as accentuate a chosen theme.

- Sample color chips can be very helpful in choosing the stain. Be sure to view the chips outside in the natural sunlight.

- When applying color stains, foam brushes spread the stain evenly and don't leave residue like normal brushes.

- Latex gloves will protect your hands from stain. A full packet of them is typically needed for a job.

Play Area Safety Tips

- Playgrounds should be located away from roads and readily visible from the home.

- Do not use paint containing lead.

- Woods like redwood and cedar are naturally rot-resistant and insect-resistant.

- Wood treated with creosote should not be used in a playground.

- Cover exposed bolts and ends of tubing with caps that cannot be removed without the use of tools.

FUN FEATURES

HAND TOOLS
Having the right set of tools is an essential part of treehouse construction

The plans are drawn, and the site has been chosen. The lumber is delivered, and the tree has been checked by a professional arborist. Before construction begins, however, the prudent treehouse builder needs to go through his or her tools, verifying that everything he or she will need is close at hand and in working order. Lay out the tools you think you'll need on the ground and make a list. If you're missing something, ask a friendly neighbor if you might borrow it for a while. Otherwise go ahead and buy it; you'll probably need it again.

A strap-on tool bag is perhaps the most important piece of equipment a builder can have. It has easy-access pockets

Hammer

- Curved claw hammers are the most familiar type of hammer and what most builders use for driving and pulling nails.

- Roofing ax hammers are useful for rough framing, valued for their cutting and hacking ability.

- Mallet hammers are typically used to form sheet metal and to force tight-fitting metal parts together.

- Sledgehammers, available in a variety of weights, are often used in construction work, useful for driving posts or dislodging trapped objects.

Square and Level

- A bubble level can measure all angles in a 360-degree range. The good ones have impact-resistant vials and durable vial covers.

- A laser level projects a bright, level, and plumb line instantly. They are extremely accurate.

- A square is a multipurpose tool that provides a precisely angled rule. The better ones have a 45-degree miter, a depth gauge, and a level.

- A square typically features easy-to-read length marks—most often at $1/8$, $1/16$, $1/32$, and $1/64$ inch.

and holsters and will hold your most important items, leaving your hands free for climbing and other tasks.

A basic set of hand tools will consist of hammers, nails and screws, a tape measure, a crowbar, a small square, a couple of carpenter's pencils, a hand saw, and a level. Because it's awkward and difficult to fit all of these items in a tool belt at the same time, pack only the tools you need for the job at hand.

The kinds of power tools needed will vary depending on the style of treehouse being built. It's a good idea to use cordless power tools when possible but always with a back-up

battery pack charged and ready at hand. Some power tools, of course, are available only in electric- or gas-powered versions. For most treehouses, a builder will need a circular saw, a jigsaw, disc grinder, drill with various-size bits, chain saw, reciprocating saw, and a table saw.

Lastly, make sure there are plenty of power cords with enough length to reach from the power source to the treehouse platform.

Hand Saw

- The saw's crosscut teeth are typically set in alternating rows to the right and left of center, which helps reduce binding while sawing.

- Most hand saws are rust-resistant or have a Teflon finish, reducing problems with binding and residue buildup.

- Keyhole saws have very thin, pointed blades mounted on a pistol-style grip. They are used for cutting holes and small-radius curves.

- Miter saws are fixed on rollers inside a metal guide, allowing for accurate crosscuts and miter cuts.

Tape Measure

- Hooking to a tool belt, the spring-loaded retractable tape and hooked nose make a good tape measure an essential part of any builder's tool box.

- A plastic-coiled tape measure can take measurements around tree trunks and other difficult shapes.

- Most tape measures can take measurements down to $\frac{1}{16}$ inch.

- A high-tech advance in building, laser measuring tools are fast, accurate, and easy to operate. Just point and shoot.

MORE HAND TOOLS

Knowing precisely which tools will be needed is an essential part of treehouse building

A builder can never have too many tools in his or her arsenal. If a tool is not needed right away, it should be kept handy at the site or in a truck or garage. Appropriate planning will ensure that a needed tool is always only a few feet away.

A good wrench or vise grip, for instance, should never be farther away than the tool belt. They will be used for twisting cable, tightening bolts, and opening hard-to-turn caps on thinners, stains, and solvents. Closed-end or wrenches are essential for tightening bolts of all types. It's a good idea to have a number of them with differently-size heads. Open-end wrenches are valuable as well, particularly adjustable crescent wrenches. For larger bolts, a closed end is preferable.

Vise Grip and Wrenches

- A one-piece wrench with a U-shaped opening, an open-end wrench is often double-ended, with a different-size opening at each end.

- A box-end wrench has an enclosed opening. It will sometimes have an open-end opening on one end.

- Wrenches come in various sizes. In order to tighten GLs or lag bolts, ¾-inch or larger is recommended.

- Pliers that lock into position, vise grips are useful for working in tight spots where a good manual grip is difficult.

Chisels

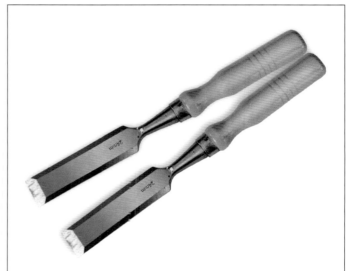

- Used to remove sections of wood while "roughing out" the shape of a pattern or design, chisels are useful in creating a mortise for joining beams.

- A butt chisel has a short blade used for carving and paring.

- A firmer chisel has a longer blade, usually from 3½ inches to 6 inches, and is used mainly for cutting deeply into wood.

- Chisels have wood or plastic handles. The wood handles are available as both tang and socket types.

Chisels are essential as well to help create notches in beams, stair stringers, and door frames. They are small and can be carried easily in a tool belt. The various types of chisels can all be used either with unassisted manual force or in conjunction with a hammer.

Most treehouses will require a variety of ropes and pulleys as well, especially when the project is on multiple levels or relatively high in a tree. Both ropes and pulleys have stress load ratings, which can aid in the buying decision. Ropes and pulleys can be used to hoist a builder into the air with

a harness or to haul tools up onto the platform or to bring some food and drink up to a hungry worker.

In order to smooth wood or size timbers, planes are important tools, too. After planing, a rasp can be used to remove excess wood or to take down sharp edges. The final polish should be done with a file or sandpaper.

Ropes and Pulleys

- A fixed pulley system is a simple way to bring tools and materials to the tree-house platform.

- In coordination with cara-biners, a more robust rope-and-pulley system is used to harness a worker.

- A comfortable harness is

a key component of any rope-and-pulley system. Harnesses typically have a mesh padding for comfort.

- Harnesses often come with gear loops, including a small loop for a chalk bag and another to accom-modate a gear-organizing carabiner.

Planes and Rasps

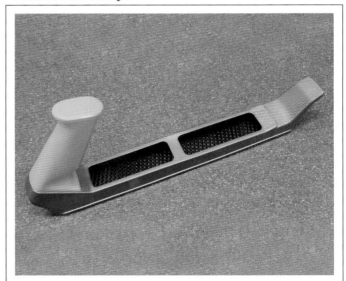

- Used to smooth and shape wood, rasps feature small teeth that cut into a surface.

- Rasps are graded for coarse-ness of cut. The coarsest is called a "bastard cut." A "cabinet rasp" has a very smooth cut and is typically used for finish work.

- Planes are used for trim-ming, beveling, and shaping wood and for smoothing rough spots.

- A block plane is the small-est kind of plane and is used for smoothing the end grain of boards and shaping small pieces of wood.

POWER TOOLS

The efficiency of electric- and gas-powered tools comes with a higher level of risk

The first thing to remember about power tools is that they are always dangerous. Even the most benign-seeming power tools can cause great harm if not operated properly. If there is electricity or gasoline involved, a conscientious builder never forgets that a lapse in attention can cause the loss of a finger or even a life.

That being said, power tools can do jobs that either would be impossible or take a much longer time with hand tools. Most brands of power tools are very reliable and have good warranties.

A jigsaw is almost essential to any treehouse job. There will always be times when you'll need to cut a rough opening in

KNACK TREEHOUSES

Jigsaw

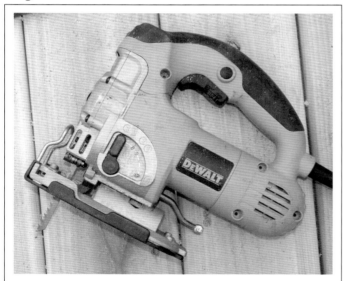

- A versatile and handy tool, a jigsaw performs many of the same functions as band saws and scroll saws.

- Cordless jigsaws are best suited to cutting wood and wood products. Tougher materials require extra power.

- Corded jigsaws provide more power and enable the saw to cut through thick boards and light metal.

- The best jigsaws will offer variable speeds, orbital action, a blower or vacuum, and blade supports.

Circular Saw

- A very powerful and dangerous tool, a circular saw can cut through most any material you'll have on the job site.

- Always wear safety glasses and follow the safety instructions printed in the saw's owner's manual.

- The material to be cut should be supported on a bench or two strong sawhorses, with enough overhang so the cut piece will fall to the ground.

- Never prop up the material to be cut because it could bind the blade and cause a kickback.

panel or plywood, either for a window or a door. A jigsaw can make quick work of the task. It is also good for more delicate cutouts. A small drill hole is all a jigsaw needs to start cutting an intricate shape.

Even more important than a jigsaw, a circular saw is used to cut almost anything—studs to beams, stringers to stair treads. Because it's used so much, a cordless circular saw is a good idea (although there may be a trade-off with torque—cordless power tools are typically less powerful than their counterparts). Just make sure there are spare battery packs to exchange when the power runs out.

Disc grinders are handy when it comes time to cut steel cable or grind excessive material off an object. Always use eye protection when operating a disc grinder. The sparks and flying bits of metal are very dangerous.

And don't forget the drill. A good power drill will be used to drill holes of all sizes and fasten screws, bolts, and brackets. It's not a bad idea to have both corded and uncorded drills on the job site.

Disc Grinder

- Choosing the right grinder is mostly a matter of weighing the disc dimension and size of the motor against the job at hand.

- Valuable especially for installing suspension systems, grinders can cut through all kinds of cables and grind down rough metal ends.

- Grinders should never be used without goggles.

- Newer models have a vibration control system that reduces vibration by 60 percent, making for safer and more precise cuts.

Drill

- In buying a drill, consider how comfortable it is in your hand. Are the forward and reverse toggles and speed switch easy to use?

- There are three types of drills. The T-handle type places the handle near the middle of the drill body. Pistol grips are more traditional, and the right-angle type is designed for use in restricted space.

- Battery-powered drills range from two to twenty-four volts.

- Corded drills are measured in amps. Higher amps mean more power.

MORE POWER TOOLS

Know which power tools you're going to use before you start working

One of the keys to making sure the work on a project progresses smoothly is to have all the tools you'll need near at hand. Nothing is more frustrating than traveling out to a job site only to find that the circular saw is still sitting back in the garage. Make a list of the power tools you'll need and then keep it close at hand, referencing it every morning.

A good reciprocating saw will be used quite often during the building process. Whether trimming platform flooring or making a circular cut around the tree trunk after the floor is laid down, there is no end to the number of potential uses. It will also be used quite often to cut odds and ends off staircases or to widen holes in paneling. It typically doesn't need

Reciprocating Saw

- A very rugged tool, a strong reciprocating saw can tear things down as well as put them together.

- The blade moves back and forth rapidly, sawing from 1 to 1¼ inches per stroke. Such saws do not perform well on thicker lumber.

- Excellent for less exacting work, they can be used either right side up or upside down.

- With appropriate blade changes, a reciprocating saw can cut through metal, tile, or wood.

Power Nailer

- A power nailer enables a builder to finish a job in a fraction of the time that would be required if using hammer and nails.

- A framing nailer is designed for heavy-duty jobs, including framing walls that have 2-by-4 studs.

- The tool uses nails that come in magazine-style packets and in various sizes and lengths.

- An air compressor is necessary to operate the tool, so the site of usage is limited by the length of the compressor hose.

a very wide opening to start cutting.

Power nailers are lifesavers, allowing a builder to assemble framing and platforms rapidly and without tiring the builder. Always take care with a power nailer because it is as dangerous as a loaded gun.

A chain saw is an absolute must on a treehouse job site, especially when pruning branches or vines. But chain saws are the most dangerous tools in a builder's arsenal and should always be treated with the utmost care and respect.

ZOOM

When working in the trees, a conscientious builder will make it a point to tether his or her power tools to ropes and pulleys, keeping them on the ground while he or she works. This will allow the tools to remain close at hand, saving time and energy even while allowing the builder to move around the construction site. Keep the power source on the platform itself.

Chain Saw

- Powerful, popular, and dangerous, chain saws cause more injuries than any other power tool.

- Gloves, earplugs, and safety glasses should be worn at all times. Children and other spectators should be kept at a safe distance.

- Never cut objects over your head. Most injuries are caused by kickback of the blade. To avoid kickback, never cut with the upper part of the blade.

- The chain must be kept sharp to perform well. Sharpening can be done with a round file.

Battery Packs

- Portable battery packs snap into various cordless tools, ranging in voltage from 3.6 to 36 volts.

- Newer battery packs use nickel-metal hydride. The performance is better, and they are easier on the environment.

- Lithium-ion (li-ion) batteries deliver more power and allow for faster recharge times.

- Advances in rechargeable batteries, such as durability and easy, quick-change functions, have made cordless tools more suitable for heavy-duty applications.

SPECIALTY TOOLS
The most unexpected tool might turn out to be what's needed to finish the job

Treehouse building sometimes requires the use of tools that are a little out of the ordinary. While clearing the site of brush, large rocks, concrete, or tangled roots, having the appropriate tool at hand could save hours of sweat and frustration. Walk the site before starting out, noting the conditions. Try to be creative in imagining what type of tool might be needed.

As always, make sure you follow the safety instructions.

An earth auger can be helpful on a site where posts need to be set. It can also be used to dig up roots or ground cover blocking the site. Some augers have springs that absorb ground shock, slowing the impact between the blade and a rock or root and saving wear and tear on the operator.

Earth Auger

- Used for digging holes in hard-packed earth or rugged terrain, it can be operated by a single person.

- The hard carbide tip allows for penetration in even the most stubborn and rocky soils. The tips come in bit sizes of 2 to 12 inches in diameter.

- Power augers run off of small gas engines. They have comfortable handles and are fairly lightweight.

- Antirecoil mechanisms prevent the jolting and bouncing that could kick the auger back toward the operator.

Pick Ax

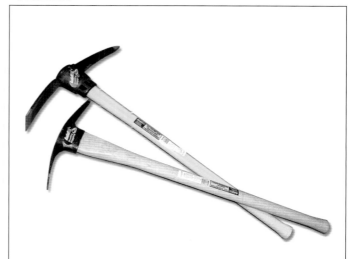

- A hand tool with a hard head attached, a pick ax is excellent for breaking through hardened ground, ice, or loose rocks.

- The chiseled end is particularly well suited for cutting through roots.

- Most pick axes have a 6-inch pick and a hard wooden handle. A longer handle makes digging easier and faster.

- The blade should be kept sharp. Working the blade with a mill file and/or a sharpening stone should be done at regular intervals.

A pick ax is handy to have on the job as well. The pointed end can be used to break up hard surfaces, while roots and rocks can be dug up with less effort than would be possible with a simple spade. Along the same lines, particularly when the ground is soft, a post hole digger is a fast way to sink posts. And for clearing away weeds, shrubbery, or ivy, a simple garden hoe is very effective.

With these tools available on the job site, the work will be a little easier to accomplish.

Post Hole Digger

- A digging tool that weighs about nine pounds, it has two long wooden handles and two blades.

- It's best used by spreading the blades and then dropping it into the dirt, letting the weight of the blades do most of the work to loosen the ground surface.

- If the dirt is hardened, soften it by adding moisture until the tool's blades can cut through.

- It's typically used to dig holes for fences and supports for projects like decks and mailboxes.

Hoe

- Using a simple garden hoe can be a very fast and effective way to move around small amounts of dirt.

- The repetitive chop-and-pull motion can become readily familiar even to children who might want to help out on the job site.

- Great for digging utility ditches and drainage trenches, hoes are also a great way to chop through ice.

- A grape hoe has an 8-inch blade, making it suitable for slicing through even the coarsest weeds.

MORE SPECIALTY TOOLS
Treehouses call for a wider variety of tools than most other building projects

Depending somewhat on the size and ambition of a project, most treehouses call for a surprising array of tools. Given that most power tools can be rented, there really is no excuse for not having, close at hand, the best tools for the job. Once the tools are acquired, the job site should also have plenty of room to set them up. Separate all tools and materials by type so that each has its own space. This makes it easy to know where everything is.

Although sometimes cumbersome to move, a table saw is an invaluable addition to any site. During the setup, remember that a power source needs to be relatively near at hand. Bench-top table saws are lightweight and are designed to

KNACK TREEHOUSES

Table Saw

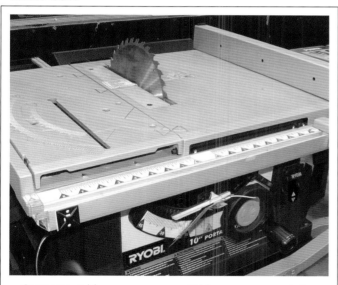

- Contractor table saws are heavier and larger than portable table saws and have an attached stand.

- Table saws are often used to rip long boards or sheets of plywood. The use of an out-feed table makes the work safer and easier.

- Table saws commonly have an adjustable guide called a "rip fence," running from the front of the table to the back, parallel to the blade.

- Never put your fingers in the path of the blade. Always be alert.

Miter Box and Saw

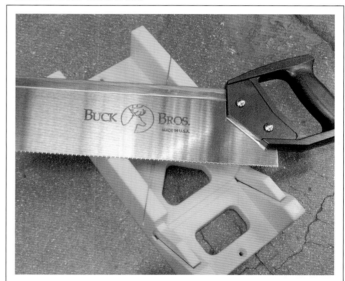

- A simple and easy tool, a miter box allows a saw to make precisely angled cuts in wood.

- Manual miter boxes and saws are typically used for fine cuts in window trim, door trim, and crown molding.

- The most common miter cut is a 45-degree angle, allowing two pieces of wood to join at right angles.

- Power miter saws are useful for projects such as trimming studs to frame a house.

operate while sitting on a table or other support. They can be lifted by one person and carried to the job location. For making doors, windows, or stairs on the site, a table saw can't be beat.

A miter saw is designed to make angled cuts in wood quickly and efficiently. It is a fairly safe tool as well. The saw is short, fine-toothed, and straight and typically has extra support along the top to keep the saw blade from buckling.

A laser level can be especially helpful when lining up decks from tree to tree or when the height of the treehouse needs to be on a certain level relative to another structure. If a parent wants to relax on a porch while keeping an eye on the kids, for instance, the platform of the tree needs to be at least eye level to a sitting adult.

Power sanders are a fast and efficient alternative to hand sanding. Whether finishing floors or smoothing window sills, a power sander will finish the job in a fraction of the time.

Laser Level and Measure

- Construction lasers are rugged, durable, and user friendly. They should never be pointed directly at the eyes.

- Line laser levels are used primarily for single-site interior work, such as for walls or ceilings.

- Some lasers will project different patterns, including crosshairs, single lines, and even combinations of both.

- Laser distance-measuring tools automatically measure distance from point A to point B at the push of a button.

Power Sander

- Orbital sanders polish wood smoothly and quickly, with the added advantage that the random action leaves very few sanding marks on the finish.

- The typical orbital sander uses sanding discs in a 5-inch diameter affixed to a foam-rubber pad.

- Sheet sanders are built to work with partial sheets of standard sandpaper, whereas belt sanders require properly sized sanding belts.

- A good sheet sander will typically cost one-half to one-third of a good random orbital sander.

BOLTS

Bolts are vitally important to keeping your treehouse strong and stable

Essential to almost any kind of construction, bolts are an especially essential element in sound treehouse building. They are used to fasten lumber and trees together, and the kind of bolts required will depend on both the type of tree and the treehouse. As a general rule, of course, the larger the structure, the more bolts will be required. Larger bolts may have to be

specially ordered, something to keep in mind before you start building. Bolts also have stress load ratings, which will impact the size and number of the bolts that are used.

The most basic bolt is a lag bolt. From fastening support cabling high in the treetop to holding up beams underneath the platform, lag bolts serve a variety of functions in

Lag Bolts

- It's important to predrill holes before installing lag bolts. Not doing so could result in splitting the wood. The pilot hole should be approximately three-fourths of the diameter of the lag bolt.

- Lag bolts are primarily made from steel, stainless

steel, silicon bronze, or hot-dipped galvanized metal.

- Stainless steel is produced from alloys. It has a high corrosion resistance.

- The pointed end makes lag bolts look like screws rather than more traditional bolts.

Dead-end Cable and Thimble

- To secure the end of a cable to prevent fraying, the most common method is to turn the end back to form a loop.

- Anytime a sharp bend or loop is formed in a cable, a device called a "thimble" must be used.

- Thimbles guide the cable into a natural curve shape. To secure the end of the cable, wire-rope U-clips are used.

- U-clips are a good way to terminate cables but must be used properly to be effective.

treehouse building. The basic size is 6 to 8 inches, but they can be custom ordered if a larger size is needed.

Bolts often support a "dead-end" cable and thimble assembly above the treehouse. A shackle connects the assembly to the bolt. The dead end can be constructed on the job site using vise grips to wrap the cable around the thimble. A grinder can cut excess cable.

The cable hanging down from the treetop connects to a turnbuckle-and-eyebolt system, which is then fastened to a beam. The turnbuckle is an efficient assembly that can tighten or loosen the cable as needed. As construction progresses, the cable tension should be checked and checked again.

Carriage bolts, with their stylish round heads, are used in woodworking and often as finish bolts in furniture. The collar of the bolt fits into a predrilled hole and twists into the wood as the nut is tightened.

Bolts and brackets are used in conjunction with each other quite often because they make an assembly that is better able to handle heavier loads.

Turnbuckle-and-Eyebolt Assembly

- A metal coupling device used for tightening a rod or wire rope, a turnbuckle helps vary the tension in cabling.

- Turnbuckles are most commonly used in applications that require a great deal of tension. Platform beams that need extra support are a good example of possible applications.

- On a treehouse platform with multiple turnbuckles, they can be used to level the platform as well.

- Turnbuckles have working load limits ranging from 1,200 to 15,200 pounds.

Carriage Bolts

- Used mainly in furniture carpentry, carriage bolts can be used in those treehouses that require an additional, aesthetic touch.

- They have a round head with a square collar and are tightened into place with a nut and wrench.

- They are coarse-threaded and come in diameters from $3/16$ to $3/4$ inch and lengths from $1/2$ to 10 inches.

- They come in galvanized, low carbon, grade 5, and stainles steel and have several finishes to choose from.

SCREWS
For extra strength and reliability, screws are usually preferred over nails

It's hard to overestimate the number of screws that will go into even a moderately sized treehouse. Make sure you stock up on them so you never run out. And as useful and versatile as they are, each type has its own intended role. Before revving up the drill, it's important to know the strengths and weaknesses of each type.

Deck screws are invaluable on the job site. Used in platforms, staircases, and flooring, deck screws come in several colors to match various woods. Most screws will penetrate softwoods, like pine, quite easily, but if drilling into harder woods, like oak, it's a good idea to predrill the hole.

Stainless-steel, square-drive screws with auger points are a

Deck Mate Screws

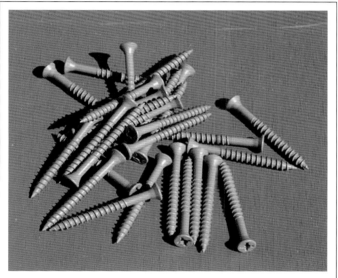

- Anti-Camout ribs (ACRs) match up with a set of ribs on Deck Mate's special driver bits to prevent slipping while driving the screw.

- You can also drive Deck Mates with a standard number two Phillips head.

- The Evercoat coating comes in colors to match your project. It also prevents rust, won't cause stains, and is guaranteed for the life of your project.

- Extra steel under the head means it won't snap off.

Steel Drive and "Star-Drive" Screws

- Steel drive screws can be placed within ⅛ inch of the edge of a board without splitting the wood. They can also penetrate knots without shearing off the screw heads.

- They countersink effortlessly and without predrilling, saving time and effort.

- Most steel drive screws have specially formulated finishes that are rust-resistant and designed for use in treated lumbers.

- The star-drive insert is designed to reduce slippage. It automatically countersinks.

good option to use with pressure-treated wood or premium materials like redwood or western red cedar. They are self-drilling and are great for making railings and simple furniture.

Heavy-duty "star-drive" construction screws are zinc-coated or high-quality, heat-treated, hardened steel. One significant advantage of the star-drive screws is they almost never slip, and it's not necessary to drill pilot holes.

Self-drilling screws, also called "TEK screws," are similar to sheet metal screws but with a "drill bit–style" point that can drill its own pilot hole. They are designed specifically for fastening plywood and other wood products to steel or aluminum. Some TEK screws are coated with a ceramic surface that protects them against corrosion.

Lag screws are very useful in penetrating deep into the wood. They are longer than other screws, with sizes up to 18 inches. Designed for securely fastening heavy timbers to one another, they are also great for fastening wood to masonry or concrete.

Remember that the project will dictate what types of screws to have on hand.

Self-drilling TEK Screws

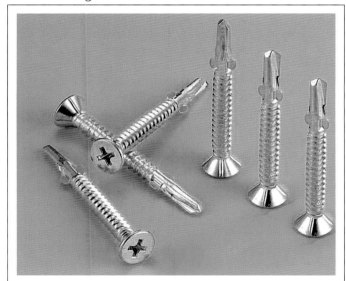

- A screw that drills its own hole can produce a complete fastening system in a single operation.

- Self-drilling screws reduce labor costs and reduce or eliminate the need for drill bits and taps.

- Reamer wings drill through the wood and automatically snap off when they encounter steel or aluminum.

- The "shank slot" holds steel shavings from the screw's drill action and prevents them from interfering with the screw threads as they tap into steel.

Lag Screws

- Generally much larger than traditional screws, lag screws can be found in lengths up to 18 inches (with diameters from ¼ inch to ½ inch).

- They are designed for fastening posts and beams to one another or for fasten-ing wood to masonry or concrete.

- The thickness and length of a lag screw or bolt are the most important elements to consider when buying.

- They generally have a hex-agonal drive head.

NAILS

The most basic fastening device is also one of the most important

Nails are the most common and practical fastener to have on a job site. They are inexpensive and effective and can be used on most parts of a job. Before construction starts, make sure the types of nail that will be needed are accounted for. (Be aware, however, that nails have a tendency to work themselves loose, particularly when used in those parts of the treehouse that will be subjected to swaying motions from the wind.)

The most common kind of nail is called a "wire nail." Wire nails are available in bright or galvanized finishes. In the United States, nails are measured by the "penny," denoted by the symbol "d." Most nails are sold by weight, usually in one-pound boxes. Some supply stores offer them in bulk. Most contractors purchase bulk nails in cardboard cartons holding fifty pounds.

Common Foundation Nails

- Bright nails have no finish. They can cause rust streaks if they are used in siding or decking.

- Hot-dipped nails are galvanized by dipping them in molten zinc. Electro-galvanized nails are plated with zinc and are not as corrosion-resistant.

- Most nails have smooth shanks. Ring-shank nails are used with softwoods, whereas spiral-shank nails are used with hardwoods.

- Most nails have a diamond point. Some have needle points, and a few have a chisel, or duckbill, point.

Outdoor Decking Nails

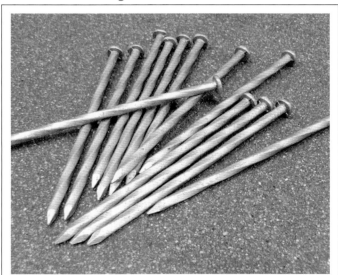

- Hot-dipped galvanized, aluminum, and stainless-steel nails are used to nail cedar and redwood decking.

- Stainless steel is the best choice, but hot-dipped galvanized is more widely used and economical.

- Use 3-inch (10d) nails to fas-ten decking with a nominal thickness of 2 inches. Use 8d nails on decking with a nominal thickness of 1¼ inches. This will allow for nail penetration of approximately 1½ inches.

- To prevent wood from splitting, use thin-shanked nails with blunt points.

Common, stainless-steel foundation or decking nails will not discolor or rust and will last as long as the lumber does. Stainless-steel nails used in fastening cedar or redwood decks have slender shanks and can be nailed at the ends of a board without splitting it. Annular ring threads hold deck boards securely to joists and effectively prevent nail head popping and the resultant obstructions on a deck surface.

For cedar siding or fencing, you might also consider a stainless-steel, threaded, annular ring nail. The ring barbs make this nail the ultimate in pullout protection.

For affixing a treehouse roof, there are various options to consider. The type of nail to use largely depends on the type of roof. Stainless-steel and cooper roofing nails are the most common. They are ring-shanked, providing superior holding power in wood and plywood.

Whatever your need might be, there is a nail to fit it. Do some research and make sure you're outfitted with the correct types.

Stainless-steel Fencing Nails

- Nails exposed to weather will always be vulnerable to corrosion.

- Galvanizing slows the corrosion process by protecting steel nails with a coating of zinc. Hot-dipped is more resistant, whereas electro-coated nails are cheaper.

- For fencing projects, use 1¾-inch cedar fence nails. They have annular rings to prevent them from working loose.

- The nail heads match the texture of the wood and can be driven flush without splitting the surrounding material.

Roofing Nails

- The type of nail and how it is installed can impact its resistance to uplift forces during a windstorm.

- A large variety of nails is used for roofing projects. They all have large heads and ringed shanks.

- Roofing nails are usually treated to prevent rusting. They may also have metal, lead, or plastic washers.

- For Ondura corrugated roofing, use a shingle nail in the valleys. Use only genuine 3-inch Ondura nails to drive through the corrugation crowns.

BRACES & BRACKETS

When other fasteners will not do the job, braces and brackets will usually suffice

For the average treehouse builder bracket-and-brace assemblies may be unfamiliar territory. But there will be a number of occasions during construction when they'll be called for. In choosing an assembly, consider where they will be used and how much stress load they will have to accommodate. This is where a concise plan will help out. Formulate a strategy beforehand, sketching it out on paper.

Metal angle brackets are commonly used in applications involving wood-to-wood reinforcement. The shape is useful for reinforcing beam-to-beam, beam-to-post, beam-to-wall, and post-to-wall connections. They come in various metals and finishes, including galvanized.

Metal Angle Brackets

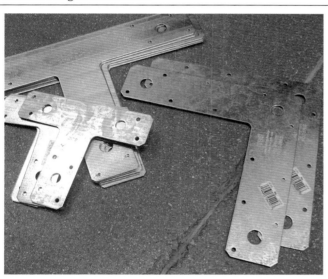

- The versatile L-bracket is useful in numerous connecting, hanging, and retaining applications.

- Used for hanging shelves and mounting electrical components, it can also serve as a construction bracket or as a way to bracket stairs.

- Reinforcing angle brackets reinforce intersecting wooden members.

- T-strap or L-strap brackets can serve as fence brackets, shelf brackets, or deck brackets.

Deck Brackets

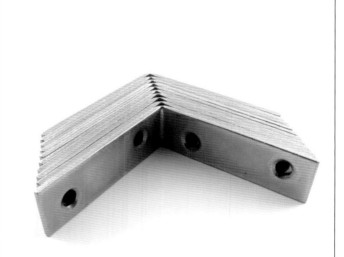

- Available in different shapes, sizes, and finishes, deck brackets are designed specifically for fastening deck materials.

- A wood connector bracket can be made of corrosion-resistant stainless steel, making it perfect for outdoor use.

- The angle brackets are easily mounted with precut factory holes provided for the connection points.

- All-purpose U-brackets are useful in fencing, shelving, and decking. They are easily mounted using either nails or screws.

Deck brackets should be used only in the construction of a deck, whether it be a freestanding deck or one attached to a building. A significant concern in attaching a deck to a building is the risk that moisture may accumulate at the point of attachment fostering rot.

Joist and beam hangers are available in many sizes and styles. It's important to use the right style with the correct number of nail fasteners. All sizes of beams (including huge glulam beams) can be hung with them. A beam hanger has a larger opening than a joist hanger.

Beam Connectors and Hangers

- Hangers came in various sizes and configurations to fit both "2-by" joists or 4-by-4 beams.

- Joist hangers are generally not used on a treehouse platform because they are not configured to withstand the tree movement.

- Larger beam supports are necessary in conjunction with arrestor brackets to support movement when glulam beams spanning a significant distance will be used.

- Joists that are double, triple, and quadruple "2-by" sized can be ordered.

············· YELLOW ● LIGHT ·············

Always be mindful, when attaching a deck to a building, that water might accumulate at the point of attachment. If your treehouse is going to be lived in or used as a resort bed and breakfast, then this is a primary concern. For a typical children's treehouse, it's less of a concern. Nevertheless, deck attachments should be regularly inspected for moisture retention and continued soundness of the wooden materials.

Potential Problems

- The wood that supports your brackets should be clear of knots.

- Use bolts rather than nails when attaching a bracket to a tree.

- Don't bolt a beam between two trees. The tree sway will eventually snap it.

- If the wood is salvaged, make sure it is free from rot and is strong enough to do the job.

- Always consult a professional if there are questions.

ADHESIVES & GLUES

Bonding agents help guarantee that construction fittings are strong and waterproof

Sealants and adhesives are inexpensive, easy to apply, and don't take up a lot of storage space. They are a very important part of your tool kit for building a treehouse. It's important that a builder knows exactly how each brand and type will perform, how to apply it, and what safety precautions need to be taken.

Liquid nails help make a strong connection stronger. By spreading some strategically around a connection, the bond will be much stronger, even if a fastener is being used. Various types are made to be used with wood, ceramic, fiberglass, and drywall.

Wood glues are meant to specifically bond wood together. Most have superior holding strength and are designed to be

Liquid Nails

- The product is recommended for bonding common building materials like concrete and lumber to paneling, drywall, plywood, glass, and plaster.

- It has a strong, instant grab, not much odor, and a durable bond. It can be cleaned up with water.

- Most adhesives conform to GEI standards. GEI is an independent, nonprofit that certifies that products meet certain standards of indoor air quality.

- In some cases, liquid nails can minimize the need for mechanical fasteners.

Wood Glue

- Most wood glues combine strength, sandability, and ease of use with the durability and water resistance of polyurethane.

- Newer glues have a superior strength, are waterproof, and can sit open in the can for roughly ten minutes.

- The best glues resist solvents, heat, and mildew and are unaffected by finishes.

- They can be sanded without softening, and if cleanup is started before the glue dries, simple water is enough to get the job done.

long-lasting water-resistant, and nontoxic. Wood glue is handy to use on furniture in conjunction with nails and screws.

A caulking compound can be used to seal air leaks in a variety of places throughout the treehouse. Caulk forms a flexible seal for cracks, gaps, or joints that are less than ¼-inch wide, including around windows and door frames. Caulking is also used to prevent water damage when applied around openings.

Before using any type of sealant, glue, or liquid nails, be aware of the pros and cons of each product. Most are odorous and can cause skin irritation.

Caulking

- Silicone caulking is resistant to both high temperatures and water. Although most are quite strong-smelling when first applied, after they dry the odor dissipates.

- Silicone caulking can't be painted. Some brands now come in white, brown, clear, and a few other basic colors.

- Latex caulking can be painted. It is water-based, meaning drips and smears clean up easily with water.

- Latex caulking has an odor when applied. It might persist for a few days or even a few weeks.

Sealant Warnings

- Sealants can cause illness, skin irritations, and fires. Handle them carefully.

- If sealants are inhaled, get fresh air immediately. Seek medical attention if discomfort continues.

- If sealants are ingested, drink plenty of water. Do not induce vomiting. Get medical attention immediately.

- If contact is made with the eyes, rinse for at least fifteen minutes and get medical attention.

SPECIAL FASTENERS

New and innovative braces and fasteners are being developed all the time

Something about treehouse building lends itself to innovation. In addition to imaginative designs and creative uses of materials, new braces and fasteners are making an appearance as well.

Michael Garnier, famous for his Garnier Limb, is one of the pioneers of the movement to push treehouse building forward. Aside from the limb he has created, he has developed a treehouse institute that teaches others about treehouse building. He also continues to develop better supports, including floating limb applications and sliding brackets.

S. Peter Lewis has done a great deal for the industry, not only by pioneering the use of innovative "shouldering

Garnier Limb

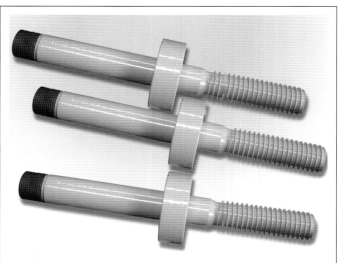

- An invaluable contribution to treehouse design by builder Michael Garnier, the GL is the most commonly known of all the "attached limb systems," or tree bolts.

- It's capable of withstanding significant shear forces, better than any hardware previously used.

- The basic GL is made from machine-threaded, 1¼-inch steel round stock with a unique flanged collar.

- Once installed, the bolt can withstand loads from two thousand to thirty thousand pounds.

Shoulder Bracing

- A collar made from six pieces of angle iron is fastened at the corners with welded eyebolts, forming a hexagon.

- Five cables attached to the eyebolts loop up and over the tree fork. The cables run through PVC pipe to protect the tree.

- From the suspension collar, a hexagon-shaped platform formed by trusses is held tight by an interior and perimeter rim joist.

- The trusses are built of hefty, 5-by-5-inch hemlock from local mills.

bracing" but also by publishing an essential book, *Treehouse Chronicles*. It takes you day by day through his building process, giving the reader true insight about what it takes to conceive and execute a dream treehouse.

Charlie Greenwood, a structural engineer, is another innovator who likes to test his support system ideas on the treehouse in which he lives fulltime. This allows him to have a living laboratory where he can tinker to his heart's content. His latest innovation is the "heavy limb," which can support huge beams and treehouse projects.

Dustin Feider, a young designer and builder, is breaking new ground with cable systems and lightweight treehouse designs using the geodesic dome. His latest endeavor, the "Lotus treehouse," employs a wooden "ship" on a cable line between two platforms.

Whether you are building a simple children's playhouse or an extravagant getaway, it's always a good idea to spend time studying the masters of the trade for inspiration, innovation, and practical, nuts-and-bolts know-how. A few dollars spent on books will save money down the road.

Heavy Limb

- Wood interfaces much like large GLs, heavy limbs (HLs) have threads that are wider and more deeply pitched.

- They are ideal for supporting heavy beams and long knee braces. They spread the weight over a larger surface so that greater loads can be applied with-

out crushing the tree tissue.

- A "limb" can be as long as necessary through the building of extensions.

- Arrestor brackets can be used with HLs, allowing the tree to continue to grow and move.

The Lotus Build

- Primarily a child's play area, the low, semi-enclosed tree platforms utilize a zip line cart.

- Wooden, lotuslike structures were created with a "ship" that could sail back and forth between the hillside and the larger of two structures.

- The original design was too costly and so had to be converted from a design calling for vertical arms made of steel to one that used 2-by-4s.

- The structures were fully built on the ground, taken apart, then rebuilt in the trees.

LUMBER
Each element of a treehouse calls for its own kind of wood

From posts to shingles, from joists to paneling, each aspect of a well-built treehouse is going to need a wood specifically built for the intended use.

Particularly if the wood is going to be exposed to the elements, pressure-treated timbers are the way to go. Resistant to termites as well as rot, most treated woods last for decades and have lifetime guarantees. They can be found in a variety of lumber grades—from knot-free, close-grained woods to grades with more knots, splits, and wane. Pressure treating has little effect on the appearance of wood other than giving it a slight greenish-brown hue.

Joists, the horizontal supporting members that run from beam to beam to support a treehouse platform, are usually 2-by-10s but can run larger or smaller in size depending on

Treated Post Beams

- Before any post is placed in the ground, it should be pressure treated to prevent decay, fungi, and insects.

- The life span of a typical wood post increases up to tenfold when treated properly with a preservative.

- High-quality, properly treated roundwood posts and poles should be clean, free of bark, smooth, and straight.

- Treated wood posts are exceptionally strong, providing a strength-to-weight ratio that is much higher than that of iron or steel.

Lumber Lookout

- Keep an eye on the treehouse lumber for three to six months after the project is complete.

- Weather and tree movement can both damage the wood. As it dries, the lumber will shrink, loosening the joints.

- Lumber does not shrink uniformly across all of its dimensions. The greatest shrinkage will occur across the face of the grain.

- Wood will shrink until it reaches the equilibrium moisture content (EMC). At this point, evaluate structural soundness of roof.

the span they need to support. There are approved formulas for calculating the depth required and reducing the depth as needed.

For the purposes of framing the walls, 2-by-4 studs of Douglas fir are usually a good choice. They provide the rough frame to which interior and exterior wall coverings are attached. They are usually fastened together with nails or screws. They are also used to frame out doors and window openings.

One-by-threes are a good choice for roof lathing. They are laid horizontally across the rafters to provide a structural support for the roofing materials. If the lathing is visible from the inside, the wood can be arranged in a design element appropriate to the structure.

When it comes time to order lumber for the project, add 15 percent to the estimated amount to compensate for unforeseen mishaps and miscalculations. After the lumber is delivered, separate it according to type and intended use. Keep the stacks close to the job site for easy access.

2-by-10 Joists

- Treehouses generally do not have to be built to code, but given their structural importance, setting the floor joists to code is a good idea.

- Building codes detail the maximum distance that floor joists should span. The recommendations are based on the size of the lumber

and the intended spacings.

- Identically sized boards will have a wide range of strength ratings depending on the type and grade of the lumber.

- If squeaking occurs in the floor, the nails may have withdrawn slightly.

2-by-4 Framing Lumber

- If wet wood is used in a project, it will shrink after it's nailed. Green lumber or wet lumber should be stored ahead of time so the wood can dry.

- Common species used in framing are southern pine, spruce pine fir, Douglas fir, and hem-fir.

- Framing wood comes in grades 1 through 2, depending on a board's strength, appearance, and the number of knots.

- When buying framing lumber, reference the information printed on what is called a "grade stamp."

POSTS
To give extra support or to substitute for a tree, nothing beats a post

If a tree cannot support an envisioned structure, or if there is an absence of trees altogether, wood posts make a great substitute. Whether posts are used in conjunction with a cable suspension support, knee braces, or flexible limbs, there are any number of imaginative ways a builder can use his or her foundational posts.

For a rugged product that's resistant to insects and rot, it's hard to beat pressure-treated wooden posts. Their unique ability to fend off decay makes them ideal in any situation where they will be in contact with the ground or moisture. Currently, there are four levels of pressure treatment, regardless of the chemical used as a preservative. These levels are based on the intended use of the product and the measurement in pounds of preservative per cubic foot of wood product.

Pressure-treated Wood

- Over seventy years ago Dr. Karl Wolman invented the process of injecting preservative into wood products.

- Wood is placed into a holding tank, the air is removed, and the tank is filled with preservative placed under high pressure, forcing it deeply into the wood.

- This process makes the wood impervious to insects and fungi, giving it a twenty-year-plus life span.

- Currently there are four levels of pressure treatment, rated for either aboveground use, ground contact, permanent wood foundations, or saltwater.

Redwood

- Redwood has the least volume shrinkage of any commercial, domestic wood.

- Unseasoned wood should air-dry one month before being used in the construction of new structures.

- In places where knots or other flaws aren't a primary

consideration in choosing the wood, "construction heart" and "construction common" are grades frequently chosen.

- Saw-textured redwood holds stains, water repellents, and bleaches up to twice as long as smooth-surfaced wood.

146

Redwood is a great source for posts. It comes in over thirty grades, each with a specific intended use, either seasoned or unseasoned. Heartwood grade, containing small knots and other slight imperfections, can be ordered either surfaced or rough. It can be used in decks, posts, retaining walls, fences, garden structures, stairs, or other outdoor structures, especially on or near soil.

Reddish-brown heartwood from the inner portion of the tree contains elements that render it resistant to decay. The cream-colored sapwood from the outer growth layer of the tree does not possess the heartwood's resistance to decay and insects.

One of the more common preservatives, copper naphthenate, is safe and highly effective against wood-destroying fungi and insects. It also helps prevent mildew, mold, and dry rot. It's used in the pressure treatment of deck posts, railroad crossties, bridge timbers, and many other wood products. It's highly rated by the EPA because it offers minimal hazard to treaters and users alike.

Safety and Pressure-treated Wood

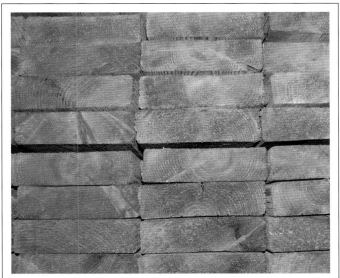

- When working with chemically treated wood, it's a good idea to use a dust mask. The sawdust can be an irritant to the nose, eyes, and skin.

- Retain the sawdust for appropriate disposal. Do most of your cutting over a heavy plastic tarp.

- Under no circumstances should pressure-treated wood be burned. The ash and smoke can contain arsenic.

- Do not use pressure-treated wood for making cutting boards or any other food-preparation surface.

Wood Preservatives

- Wood preservatives are pesticides that protect wood against attack by fungi, bacteria, and insects.

- The active ingredients found in wood preservatives may include creosote, copper, zinc, chromium, arsenic, and other compounds.

- Preservatives are injected into the wood prior to being sold or are applied by the user.

- Posts supporting the treehouse that come in direct contact with the earth should be of naturally durable or preservative-treated wood.

ROOFING

A good roof not only provides shelter but also adds a sense of style

Picking the right roof is like picking the right hairstyle or hat. It's the accessory that ultimately defines the look. Whether you go with a beehive or a bob, baseball cap or top hat, you will inevitably be making some sort of statement. If the opportunity presents itself, why not choose a roof style that stands out and calls attention to itself?

Aside from the design and look, make sure the roof is weather-tight and fastened properly. Each type of material calls for specific fasteners and installation methods. Follow the instructions or get a professional to help out, especially if the treehouse will be used as a living quarters or place to work. The last thing a treehouse resident needs is water dripping onto a computer or a bed.

As treehouses have been redesigned with the environment

Planting Green Roofs

- It's possible to plant a garden that doubles as a roof, providing both shelter and valuable wildlife habitat.

- The climate, the intended use, and final aesthetic appearance should all play a role in the design.

- The Internet has a number

- of helpful resources to help guide green builders, including the World Green Roof Infrastructure Network (WGRIN).

- A green roof must be able to handle a load from fifteen to fifty pounds per square foot, heavier than conventional roof structures.

Armorlite

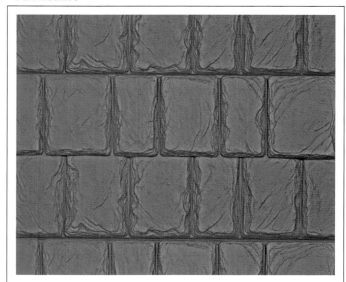

- Light, strong, and environmentally sustainable, Armorlite is made of engineered polymer materials.

- It retains its color and mechanical properties under prolonged exposure to sunlight, moisture, and heat.

- Armorlite roofing is rated at seventy pounds per 100 square feet. The competition averages six hundred pounds per 100 square feet.

- One hundred percent recyclable, Armorlite consumes a minimal amount of energy to ship and manufacture.

in mind, treehouse roofs have been improved as well. Among the many elements that help define a "green" roof (recyclable shingles, for instance), a surprising factor not often considered is the weight of the roof itself. According to Jim Stewart, PhD and environmental scientist, "Lighter weight roofing materials decrease the raw materials used, manufacturing and transportation energy use, workers' and homeowners' safety, landfill use and waste."

Out of this need to create lighter-weight materials comes the innovative roofing material Armorlite. Aside from being very lightweight and durable, it looks good and comes in a number of great color choices.

A roofing product made from 50 percent recycled consumer products, Ondura has a corrugated design that enables it to be both lightweight and strong. It typically can be used over older asphalt shingles without removing them, saving many hours in labor and keeping the shingles out of a landfill.

Whatever materials you decide to use, make them distinctive, durable, and environmentally friendly.

Ondura Roofing

- Ondura doesn't require special skills or tools to install. A hammer, chalk line, saw, and measuring tape are all the typical builder will need.

- The panels are lightweight, weighing only eighteen pounds each, and have no sharp edges.

- The installation manual that comes with a purchase is easy to follow and helps a builder estimate the quantity of materials needed.

- Panels and tiles are made of a tough organic fiber core saturated with asphalt.

Recycled Plastic

- Woodlike products use some recycled plastic from waste bags, milk cartons, jugs, and bottles.

- Resistant to bacteria, insects, moisture, and chemicals, these products can be used as a substitute for wood and metal shingles.

- From shingles to roofing accessories, they can be formed into many shapes and are virtually maintenance- and splinter-free.

- The world's landfills are full of potentially recyclable materials. Building a roof can actually help do the world a favor.

DECKING

The lumber used for the deck should be stylish, safe, and rot-resistant

Because the material that's used in the decking is often used in the interior and other exterior elements, the choice of lumber for decking is one of the most important decisions that a builder can make.

Good, old-fashioned wood is one of the first options. It's easy to install, looks good, and is strong. Unless a preservative is used, however, it grays as it weathers and is susceptible to rot. Treated wood may be the better choice because it has a longer life span.

Redwood and cedar contain natural defenses against rot and insects and last a long time. However, they are soft and easily damaged. The sun will fade their natural color to gray,

Cedar Decking

- Beautifully colored, cedar can last from nine to thirty years.

- Predrilling is not usually required. To prevent splitting, however, predrilling is recommended near the ends of the boards.

- "Architect clear" and

"custom clear" are both optimum grades of cedar. Western red cedar weathers to a deep glow. Others are lighter in color and offer more options for staining.

- Stainless-steel fasteners are advisable with cedar. Other deck fasteners may react to the tannic acid in the wood.

Redwood Decking

- Rugged, knot-textured, garden grades are more economical than architectural grades.

- Heartwood grades such as "construction heart" or "deck heart" are used for structures on or near the ground.

- "Construction common"

and "deck common" grades are used in areas that don't touch the soil.

- Galvanized, stainless-steel, or aluminum hardware is recommended with redwood. A quality water-repellent finish will contain a mildewcide and an ultraviolet inhibitor.

although a regular application of sun-blocking finish will help slow this process. Both of these woods, in a raw state, tend to splinter—a consideration if small hands and feet are going to be playing on them.

Tropical hardwoods are rich in color and extremely attractive, highly durable, and resistant to insects and decay, yet have their drawbacks. They are expensive, heavy, and hard to work with. Predrilling is required due to the hardness of the wood.

The problems that sometimes arise with a deck can often be traced back to the moisture content of the wood at the time it was built or to the moisture it absorbed after installation. One of the few ways to arrest moisture problems is to add a water-repellent finish to the wood or to buy wood that has been treated with water repellent. Still, you cannot control the weather, and too much moisture or lack of moisture can lead to structural problems. The best way to combat this potential problem is to make sure you buy wood that has been properly seasoned.

Tropical Hardwoods

- Many tropical hardwood products (including teak, mahogany, and Brazilian cherry) come from tree farms outside the U.S.

- Many of these trees need at least seventeen years from planting to harvest.

- Ipe (Brazilian hardwood)

is naturally resistant to rot and decay and is eight times harder than California redwood. It has the highest decay-resistance rating.

- Tropical forests, which contain 50 percent of the planet's biodiversity, are threatened by deforestation and illegal logging.

Decking Moisture Problems

- To reduce the risk of deck failings, deck boards at the time of construction should have less than 20 percent moisture content, regardless of the species of wood.

- Grade marks on lumber indicate the maximum moisture content of the wood.

- The moisture content of most treated lumber is high. It will likely still be wet when it arrives at the job site unless it has been kiln-dried after treatment.

- Leave pressure-treated boards out to air-dry. They can potentially shrink unevenly.

SIDING

Protection, appearance, and durability should all be a concern in the walls of a treehouse

To enclose a treehouse, the types of available siding almost defy probability. The final choice a builder makes should depend on the style he or she wants to achieve, the overall design, and, of course, the budget.

The job of siding, like skin, is to protect the interior from the elements and hopefully to do it in style. Whether a builder chooses wood boards, shakes, shingles, steel, aluminum, or vinyl, the siding should last at least as long as the structure itself.

Typically, if it's correctly installed and well maintained, the treehouse's siding will not be a source of problems. It does age, however, and sometimes a loose board might have to

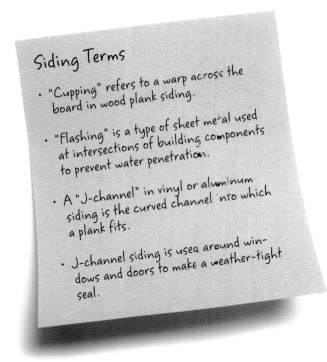

Siding Terms

- "Cupping" refers to a warp across the board in wood plank siding.

- "Flashing" is a type of sheet metal used at intersections of building components to prevent water penetration.

- A "J-channel" in vinyl or aluminum siding is the curved channel into which a plank fits.

- J-channel siding is used around windows and doors to make a weather-tight seal.

Fasten Them Together

- Hot-dipped galvanized, aluminum, and stainless-steel nails are all corrosion-resistant and can be used to nail wood products.

- "Splitless" siding nails have thin shanks and blunt points to reduce splitting. For greater holding power, nails with ring-threaded or spiral-threaded shanks can be used.

- For aluminum siding, use only aluminum nails.

- Use electro- (or hot-dipped) galvanized steel or aluminum roofing nails with vinyl siding.

be fixed or stained. A popped nail or two might need some hammering. When troubleshooting the issues, pay attention to where drainage from rain occurs, looking under the eaves and around doors and windows. The places where siding comes in contact with branches or leaves can also create problems.

Staining is an important element to consider when it comes to siding. Exterior stain is used to preserve the wood as well as to color it to a desired tone. Exterior stains are available in latex- or oil-based formulas. Unlike paint, no primer is needed with stains. However, exterior stains will need to be reapplied more often than paint. The three types of exterior stain—opaque, semitransparent, and transparent—all have their strengths and weaknesses. Before deciding on a stain, test out samples on a stray piece of siding. Let it air-dry and then try to imagine the entire treehouse being this color. Taking a little bit of time to judge the final look may save a lot of time in the end. Nothing is more frustrating than having to go back and restain an entire structure.

Staining the Siding

- When purchasing stain, know your surface measurements and read the label for the manufacturer's recommendations.

- Surface preparation is critical to a successful exterior stain project. Remove dirt by washing with soap and water, then caulk around doors and windows.

- Stain brushes drip less than paint brushes. Use natural bristles for oil and synthetic bristles for latex.

- Apply stain in the direction of the wood grain.

Siding Maintenance

- Aluminum should be monitored for dents.

- Plywood siding expands and contracts at different rates than the framing it's fastened to, causing loose nails, joints, and siding.

- Vinyl is easy to maintain but should be regularly washed to eliminate dirt, stains, mold, or mildew.

- Shakes and shingles will fade over time. Paint or stain helps preserve them.

RAILINGS

Railings can be simple or decorative, but they should always be strong

Railings are like icing on a cake, adding flair to a treehouse. Whether made from simple 2-by-4 lumber or found branches, from elegant Victorian fencing or rustic logs, they'll help set the tone of the treehouse.

When considering an approach to the railing, take into account whom the treehouse will be for. If it's for a child, make sure the railings are safe, sturdy, and spaced such that a child won't be able to fall through. Railings that are naturally branched may look good but may not be safe enough for a young child. When in doubt, think safety first. A treehouse for an adult or a treehouse resort is a different matter. Style can take precedent.

Gates are another aspect of the railing system to consider.

Wood Railings

- Durable and long-lasting, wood railings can stay beautiful for years if cared for properly.

- Straight wood railings are the simplest to make. Curved rails can be innovative and provocative, adding a little extra flair to a treehouse.

- Make sure the rails are fitted tightly and sanded to a smooth touch.

- Railings provide a great opportunity for seasonal decoration. Consider adding flowers twined through posts or beams stretched with ivy.

Natural Branch Railings and Pickets

- The look of any natural branch design is critical to its success. Do some experimenting before committing.

- Choose limbs that are not too wild in shape. They should be large enough to nail to the railing.

- For a tree branch rail, choose a branch at least 2 inches in diameter. Peel off the bark (but leave some pieces) and sand smooth. Apply urethane and install with standard hardware.

- Bamboo makes a great-looking railing system.

Many treehouses don't have gates, but they are actually a great feature. They provide a measure of safety and security, and they can be quite stylish. In fact, a great-looking gate or fence can liven up an otherwise average-looking railing system.

Pickets can also be very important to a treehouse. Whether they're decorative with cutout shapes or salvaged wood with beautifully lathed forms, a builder can have real fun being creative with these elements.

When taken together, the railing, gate, and pickets are as important to the looks of a treehouse as are any other aspect.

MATERIALS

Pickets

- Because pickets are not support members, they can be innovative and vastly different than the railings themselves.

- Dog-ear, flat-top, and gothic picket styles are readily available at most lumber supply houses.

- Salvaged pickets add style to a treehouse. Finials, cross braces, and diagonal trim create a rustic look.

- A wood-and-bamboo fence with 4-by-4 pine posts makes for a classic statement. Thin bamboo pickets can be nailed directly to the framing.

Gates

- An opportunity for personal statements, gates also add another level of security.

- Reclaimed or salvaged gates make terrific additions to any style of treehouse. They add an eclectic feel and charm.

- A simple gate to a child's treehouse can be made with 2-by-4s and cedar planks. A simple wooden handle or the standard metal hardware can be used.

- A wrought-iron gate, whether new or salvaged, makes for a sturdy and safe entryway.

PREP THE SITE

A well-organized site is essential to a productive, trouble-free building experience

After deciding on a treehouse plan and seeing the lumber delivered, it's time to clear the site of all excess shrubbery, boulders, and other obstructions that might block access to the tree. To make the job go faster, at least two people should work on the project.

After clearing the ground around the tree, examine the tree itself and see if any limbs or branches will hinder construction. These will have to be removed. Keep in mind that if the plan calls for the house to be 11 feet off the ground, the roof structure itself will be another 8 or so feet high, and the lag bolts to hang the support cables will be another 8 to 10 feet above the roof. That means the builder will be working at

Clearing Branches

- Make sure all weak or suspect branches, commonly called "widowmakers," are cleared from the tree. Support branches need to be green and strong.

- Look for branches that could be potentially used as handholds or footrests for adventurous climbers. These need to be sound as well.

- Once the dead growth has been cleared, also clear an area to attach long bolts.

- If necessary, clear branches from the ground level up to the roof height to make room for building.

Poison Ivy and Other Hazards

- Always check for poisonous plants and tree damage before starting. If you're unsure whether you have a hazard, ask an arborist to check the tree and surrounding area.

- Remove poison ivy by cutting it first at the root and then pulling off the vines.

- Wear protective clothing.

- Remember that the damaging oil in poison ivy can be present even if the vines look dormant or dead.

- Never burn poison ivy. Inhaling the smoke can cause serious lung problems.

least 24 feet above the ground. In order to safely and effectively work at this height, one needs to hang rope lines over high branches and set up a climbing system with a harness. There should be both a main hookup as well as a secondary, backup safety line. Another pulley assembly with a carabiner should be set up, running from the tree to the ground, so tools can be passed back and forth.

Once the builder is up in the tree, branches can be cut with a hammer ax or a hand saw. Check for any vines that have wrapped around the tree, in particular poison ivy, which has a tendency to strangle tree trunks. Cut the vines from the roots and pull off any part of the plant that stands in the way of building the treehouse. Remember to wear protective gloves, long pants, and a long-sleeved shirt. Do not stand under the tree if someone above is cutting branches or pulling off vines.

Some tree rot is not visible from the outside so a professional inspection and evaluation may be worth the investment.

Excavate the Roots

- Make sure the tops of the tree root are not obstructed by girdling roots and vines.

- Make sure you know your species, specific factors, as root crown cleaning is not a good idea or all trees, such as coastal redwoods.

- Clear any boulders and shrubbery away from the trunk so there is easy access to the tree.

- If roots or vines are wrapped around the tree trunk, clear them away with a pick ax and spade.

Tree Rot

- Prior to building, make sure the tree is sound, top to bottom. Tree rot can cause serious problems.

- Trees should be inspected on a regular basis, especially before and after storms. Larger trees have a greater hazard potential than smaller trees.

- Decay pockets where branches meet the trunk can indicate serious structural problems.

- Inspect the trunk and large branches for cracks. Deep, large cracks indicate structural weakness in the tree and need careful evaluation.

BOLT SUPPORT SYSTEM
A wide range of bolt systems supports various types of treehouses

Setting bolts in the tree is often the first step in the actual construction of the treehouse. For this particular project, the bolts were set 26 feet high in the tree. The builder was harnessed to cables and climbed to a position where the ⁵/₄-inch bolts were to be fastened. Six holes were predrilled, then the bolts were set around the tree. Care was taken to sink all the bolts on the same level around the trunk. (If a builder is off a little in his or

her level, he or she can adjust the cables later.)

On the ground, dead-end cable assemblies were put together using heavy cable wire and thimbles. The wire was wrapped around the thimble (which has a channel to hold the wire) and twisted and braided together using a vise grip. Once the cable was carefully secured, a grinder trimmed off the loose ends.

Top Lag Bolts

- Predrilled bolt holes should be slightly smaller than the bolt itself so it has something to bite into.

- Bolts should be embedded at least 6 inches deep, ensuring that the threads are not visible.

- Bolts are tightened using a large ratchet or pipe wrench. The head of the bolts are hexagonal.

- Be careful to make all holes line up. They should be set far enough apart so as to not over penetrate the tree.

Lag Bolts and Pipe Brackets

- Predrill the lower bolt holes in the same manner as the top bolt holes. Use a bubble level to ensure that they line up.

- Thread the bolt through the bracket before attaching it to the tree.

- Use galvanized or stainless-steel bolts and predrill with a drill bit that's the diameter of the solid core within the threaded area.

- To make it easier to tighten, you can predrill with a wider bit to provide for the unthreaded part of the bolt.

With the six assemblies finished, they were attached to a lag bolt with a steel shackle that hooked around the bolts. Cable pieces were cut to be long enough to connect with the dead-end assemblies and the beams that would support the platform. In this case, 20 feet of cable was sufficient. The six pieces of cable were twisted to the lower end of the dead-end assemblies.

The bolt-and-bracket assembly was then attached to the trunk where the beams were to be set. Six ¾-inch holes were drilled at an identical height. They were all at least 6

inches deep. A bubble level aided in making sure that the bolts were all at the same height. The rubber tubing of the level wrapped around the trunk easily and allowed for a reading. Once all the holes were drilled, the lag bolts were then attached with a ratchet.

Dead-end Cable and Thimble Assembly

- Regardless of whether common-grade or EHS-grade cable is used, it is imperative to install a thimble in the cable loop of the tree-grip dead end.

- Tree grips wrap quickly around the cable, eliminating the time-consuming process of splicing.

- Dead ends are designed to eliminate the labor and hassle of cable splicing.

- The dead end has a "thimble-loop design" created for the arborist industry. It prevents the end thimble from falling out during installation.

Attaching the Assembly to the Top Bolt

- Use galvanized shackles with a sliding pin to connect the tree-grip assembly to the top bolt.

- The assembly should be put together on the ground. The shackle can be tightened by hand and fastened to a carabiner hooking into the thimble.

- The shackle is put on the bolt before it is turned into the tree, so it will never come off the bolt in a wind storm.

- The bottom of the assembly is attached to the hanging cable line that connects to the turnbuckle.

159

SETTING THE BEAMS

Carefully placing and leveling the beams on the support assembly are critical steps

The work of setting a treehouse's beams actually begins on the ground. In this case, treated Douglas fir beams were cut into six 8-foot sections with a circular saw, then the end of each beam was cut on a 15-inch, 20-degree angle, matching the angle of the cable setting. These were now the outside ends. The cable would be angled to clear the roof of the

treehouse on all sides. After the beams were trimmed, ¾-inch holes were drilled 6 inches from the beam's outside end on a 20-degree angle. Eight-inch eyebolts were inserted in each beam and tightened with a nut and washer. The beams were now ready to be attached to the tree.

Setting the beams onto the bolt-and-bracket assembly is

Beams

- Check the 4-by-6 lumber to make sure it's straight and without obvious imperfections. Cut six 8-foot beams.

- Ropes or pulleys can help raise the beams into place.

- Because the lumber will not touch the ground, treated wood is not necessary.

However, it is a good idea to use it or a naturally resistant wood (like redwood or cedar), preventing later damage from insects.

- Rough-hewn lumber can be used for beams when a rustic look is preferred.

Eyebolts Are Set

- Eight-inch galvanized steel eyebolts are preferred. Stainless steel is an alloy of steel with high corrosion resistance. Stainless has become the material of choice for exterior applications.

- Eyebolts should be set and fastened to the beams

while the lumber is still on the ground.

- The eyebolts are set on an angle to match the cable angle hanging from the tree.

- The hole is predrilled to the same size as the bolt to avoid wiggle room.

easier with two people. One person holds the beam steady while the other sets a level. Once a level reading is achieved, the beam can be held while the builder attaches the bracket to the beam using a power drill and lag screws. By the time the sixth bracket and beam assembly are set, a sense of the treehouse will start to take shape.

The next part of the beam-and-cable assembly involved attaching turnbuckles to the eyebolts, then attaching the upside to the cables hanging from the bolts in the tree. With this accomplished, the turnbuckles were then used to adjust the tension and level of each beam. The level of each beam was verified before moving to the next step. Temporary boards spanning the beams underneath held the beams in place so the joists could be attached without nudging the beams out of level.

Eyebolt Information

- Eyebolts are threaded bolts with a loop or "eye" at one end.

- Eyebolts are rated for different types of applications and may pivot or swivel. Load-rated eyebolts are designed for vertical lifting but are not recommended for angular lifting.

- Specifications for eyebolts include maximum load capacity, threaded length, shank length, eye inside diameter, eye section diameter or eye thickness, and total weight.

- "Maximum load capacity" refers to the maximum load that an eyebolt can handle.

Turnbuckles

- The turnbuckle assembly is attached to the eyebolts with a shackle built into the turnbuckle.

- Pliers or a vise grip can be used to tighten the turnbuckle washer.

- The other side of the turnbuckle is attached to the down-end thimble assembly of the cable.

- Selecting turnbuckles requires an analysis of product and performance specifications. Consider diameter, takeup, length, and estimated weight. Use forged-steel or low-carbon steel turnbuckles.

ATTACHING JOISTS

Fastening joists to the beams will stabilize the platform, allowing safe access to the tree

Once a treehouse platform has been stabilized with bracing, joists can be attached to the beams. This is an essential step and needs to be done with care. In this case, outside 2-by-6 joists were cut on a 30-degree angle on both sides to fit in between the span of the beams. The 30 degrees of angle was calculated by dividing the twelve points of attachment into the 360 degrees of the circumference.

The joists were set in place using a rope attachment. Each joist was tied securely and then raised into position. One person can do this job, but two makes it easier and safer.

Having been raised into the tree, each joist was screwed to its beams. After the outside joists were set, the work went

Setting Outside Joists and Temporary Bracing

- Temporary bracings help hold everything in place during construction.

- Using screws in temporary construction allows for easier removal once a job is done.

- Before fastening the joists, cut each end on a 30-degree angle to fit, then preset Deck Mate screws. Use two screws on each end of the joist.

- Set the joist in position and then, using a power drill, sink the screws into the ends of the beams.

Nails versus Screws

- Generally speaking, nails are stronger than screws, but they tend to loosen their grip over time. Wind motion in a tree can hasten a nail's demise.

- Screws resist movement better than nails, but they are also more brittle.

- Screws with cut threads may tend to be more brittle than those with rolled threads.

- If screws are used, their size should at least be equal to (or even greater than) the recommended size of nail.

inward. Three rows of joists were set, each cut at a 30-degree angle. The joists were set with 16 inches between each other. The inner row of joists was set far enough away from the trunk to allow for future tree growth.

With the joists in place, the level of the beams was rechecked, and the turnbuckles were adjusted accordingly. (It's very important to make sure you check the level after each step until the platform is finished.) With the platform secured by the joists, the building progressed to the next step.

ZOOM

The closer you space the joists together, the greater length they can span—up to a point. There are charts that indicate the maximum span you can use based on the type of wood and the spacing you have chosen. Treehouses are not covered by building codes, but it's wise to check with your local building department for specifics about house decking.

Attach the Outside Joist

- Two people can set the outside joist quicker than one. One can hold the board in place while the other fastens it.

- One person on the ground (the "down man") can move a ladder around the structure, while the other person (the "up man") moves across the braced platform.

- Make sure you have a spare battery for the drill. You may want to hang it from a pulley line.

- The person on the ground brings the wood to the platform.

Continue Setting the Joists Inward

- Once the outside joists are set, three rows of joists need to be set inward. This should be done in a circular pattern.

- The up man measures the span that the joist must cover. The down man cuts pieces of joist to size.

- The down man brings the cut pieces to the platform and helps hold them while the up man fastens them.

- This process is repeated for each new row of joists.

SUPPORT CONSTRUCTION

BLOCKING

Appropriately fastened blocking will help stabilize the platform spans and prevent decking problems

With the platform joists in place and the tension in the cables set to level, the last step needed to secure the undercarriage is to set the blocking. The blocking consists of 2-by-6 wood members cut to fit in between the joists. With this particular treehouse it was necessary to block out only two opposing spans, not each span. When setting up blocking row by row,

do not line up the blocking pieces but rather offset them.

Remember to do as much of this work on the ground as possible. Do not cut blocking in the tree or on the unfinished platform. The timber can be cut by a table saw or a hand saw. It's rough framing work so a perfect fit isn't necessary. Calculate how many pieces you'll need and precut them all. You

KNACK TREEHOUSES

Deck Blocking

- To provide extra security for an entry area, add blocking to both the porch side and the opposing side.

- Cut the blocking from the same 2-by-6 lumber used as the joists.

- Blocking creates a rigid rim joist that prevents bounce

and increases the strength of the rail attachment.

- Blocking can be installed throughout the frame to increase the strength of long joist spans, but it isn't always necessary for a structure.

Precut the Blocking to Fit Each Row of Joists

- The up man, or the man in the tree, should make all the necessary measurements. The man on the ground, or the down man, should precut the blocking.

- Blocking pieces are set 16 inches apart.

- The sizes used for joists and for blocking are most often 2-by-6, 2-by-8, 2-by-10, and 2-by-12. These are all the most economical and easiest to find.

- Larger joists allow for greater spans and less blocking area.

164

may want to do more than the number that you need just in case of miscalculation or missteps during the installation.

The blocking is attached using 3-inch screws. Make sure enough screws are packed into your utility belt before climbing the ladder. Make sure the power drill has the proper bit and a fresh battery pack attached. This part of the job will go quickly if two people are doing it, one handing out the blocking, and the other fastening it to the joist.

Remove Temporary Bracing

- Once the blocking is installed, the temporary bracing is removed. Use a power drill to unscrew the fasteners.

- Save the braces after removal because they may be needed for another part of the project.

- Check the level of the completed platform and adjust accordingly.

- Set some weight on the platform to see if it shifts. It might be a good idea to set the platform decking on the joists and wait overnight to see if it changes.

Sistering Joists

- "Sistering" refers to the overlapping of two joists across a beam, creating an extended joist.

- This is necessary only for spans that exceed the length of the longest boards.

- Longer overlaps mean stronger connections. You should overhang at least a couple of feet on each side of the beam.

- Sistering is common when adding to or repairing a deck.

SUPPORT CONSTRUCTION

CLEANUP

It's important to clear the area once the joists and blocking have been attached

After each phase of the building process is complete, it's important to check the various connections, reaffirm the levels, and clean up the mess from construction. When cleaning up, keep a few specific notions in mind.

Pay particular attention to any treated wood scraps. Put them into a separate trash container because they cannot be burned or disposed of with other trash. Most waste material should be delivered to an appropriately permitted landfill. Larger scraps may be used for blocking. Set these pieces aside so that they can be reused. Neatly reorganize the rope-and-pulley systems. These will certainly be used throughout the project. A lot of work will now be done on the platform itself,

Clear the Platform of Ropes and Cords

- Unhook or untie any ropes or cords that are secured to the platform. Set them to the side, away from the action.

- Double-check the ropes to make sure that none has been damaged during use.

- Remove anything from the deck platform that will not be used immediately.

- Double-check the attachment points of the deck platform to remove any protruding screws or gaps in connections.

Clear Ground Area Underneath

- Clear all wood scraps separating those that can be reused.

- Rake the area for smaller debris and dump debris into a trash can. Use gloves to pick up anything smaller and potentially hazardous.

- Clear the area around the tree to at least a 10-foot diameter.

- Make sure that no stray tool parts (like rechargeable batteries or boxes of screws) have fallen into the surrounding shrubbery area.

so the rope lines should not hang lower than the platform height. They shouldn't get tangled with the joists or beams. Only the tool line should be used to access the ground.

Put any tools that are not needed back into their organized area so they can be easily found when needed. Finally, rake the area underneath the tree, disposing of any screws, nails, or chips of wood that could be hazardous. Use a construction magnet to help find nails. It's surprising how easy it is to twist an ankle on a chunk of wood or have a nail pierce the sole of a shoe.

Tools

- When you've finished for the day, put away your tools in a safe place. It's not a bad idea to lock them up. Power tools are expensive and can be a temptation to light-fingered passers-by.

- Most power tools will rust if exposed to moisture.

- Before starting the next day's work, check to make sure that all tools are working properly.

- Take inventory of the tools to make sure that nothing is missing.

Harnesses

- A strong, flexible, and comfortable harness can make building in the treetops easier.

- Make sure both the waist belt and the leg loops match your proportions. A few manufacturers offer adjustable straps or leg loops.

- Most arborist stores and suppliers carry harnesses specifically made for working in trees.

- A tree-specific harness will include extra padding on the leg straps, quick-connect buckles, multiple loops for overhead suspension, and lightweight elements.

SUPPORT CONSTRUCTION

DECKING MATERIALS

The best treehouse decks are usually constructed of sound, weather-resistant lumber

The platform is up, and it's secure. It's time now to begin work on the decking. The first thing to do is sort through the lumber and make sure it's all straight and sound, without too much cupping. If boards are bad, toss them aside. Maybe you can use them in another application, or the lumberyard might accept a return after the job is complete.

During the inspection, look for cracks on the ends and surfaces of boards that might have occurred during drying. These are known as "checks." Checking is caused by shrinkage differences between the surface and the core of the drying lumber. Another potential flaw is "warping," a distortion of the board caused by unequal shrinkage in different directions

Decking Stacking and Drying

- Once the decking materials are delivered to the job site, they need to be properly stacked to avoid warping and twisting.

- Arrange the pieces of lumber side by side, across several 4-by-4 posts. Between each level of wood, use perpendicular spacer strips

of wood to provide for air flow.

- Place weights on top of the stack to keep the top boards from warping.

- To prevent excessive cupping and warping, avoid using deck boards wider than 6 inches.

Cupping and Crowning

- Cupping and crowning can occur in high humidity or after excessive water exposure.

- Cupping is caused by a moisture imbalance through the wood, causing the edges of a board to curl high and its center to drop low.

- The opposite of cupping, crowning is a condition wherein the center of a board is higher than the edges.

- Slight cupping and crowning may occur naturally and should be tolerated. When installing, turn the board over and refasten it.

relative to the wood grain. If a board shrinks unequally in any direction during drying, it will tend to warp. This is especially important in drying oak or other check-prone species. Valuable and check-prone lumber should be sheltered from the elements during air-drying.

When choosing deck materials, be aware that pressure-treated wood is normally recommended for a deck's framing systems. Wood commonly used in different aspects of a deck includes cedar, redwood, and even mahogany. To ensure you have the proper wood type, length, and size for the various components, consult the local building codes.

Once the wood has been sorted through, move it to the ground under the platform's edge. To transport the decking to the platform itself, a person on the ground should walk the decking up a ladder to the platform edge and pass it to the builder on the platform.

For this project, the decking was made of cedar, a great lumber for deck floors and accessories. It naturally resists rotting and is known for its beauty and scent more than its strength.

Wood at the Job Site

- Wood should not be delivered to an excessively wet job site.

- Prior to installation, decking wood should be covered or housed. At least four days should pass before installation begins.

- If boards with too much moisture are installed, the flooring will shrink and show cracks. Nails and screws can potentially work loose during the shrinkage.

- After installation is completed (and if there is time), delay at least a week before sanding and finishing.

Decking Maintenance Tips

- Clean the deck's coated surface with a damp cloth using recommended cleaning products.

- Never use a damp mop to clean a raw wood floor. Water will hasten deterioration in the wood and finish.

- Clean light stains by rubbing with a damp cloth.

- Never let a spill of water dry on the deck.

- Recoat your deck periodically.

SET DECKING IN PLACE

After the decking is on the platform, it needs to be fixed into place

There are various ways to arrange the lumber on a deck. The most basic look, a horizontal pattern, is easy to achieve with a straight, side-by-side placement. To make the deck seem wider, place the boards lengthwise. The most common pattern, a parallel placement, can be spiced up by placing boards with alternating widths side by side.

Starting from the porch area, in front of the treehouse, set the boards side by side with 1/8 inch between them. Flush the outside piece of decking to the outside of the platform joist or leave a 1-inch overhang then fasten that piece to the perpendicular joist underneath it with Deck Mates. Working from the outside in, set a few rows to start the pattern.

With a little more time and precision, a builder can set the decking in a circular pattern. When using materials like

Set a Few Pieces of Decking to Start the Pattern

- Use uncut boards and set them on the deck parallel to each other with ⅛ inch between them. Fasten the first piece down to secure the grouping.

- An overhang of 1 inch will allow water to run off onto the ground instead of soaking the joist.

- Laying a basic decking pattern will proceed much faster than other design patterns. Less lumber and connection hardware are required as well.

- A clean finish is important in a good deck.

Cedar Decking

- Cedar wood is naturally resistant to decay and insect damage.

- Cedar should still be treated if it will be exposed to sunlight or moisture.

- Cedar has less than half the swelling and shrinking ten-

dencies of other domestic softwoods, allowing it to age gracefully through decades of extreme weather.

- Cedar decks have a rich grain, texture, and color that complement any architectural style, from traditional to postmodern.

170

redwood or tropical hardwoods, this makes for a lovely effect.

Deck floor pattern choices are endless. They can add style and can make a deck look larger or smaller or accentuate different areas. Deck floor patterns can be achieved using any decking material. You can stick with a single pattern or combine different patterns for another look. Different deck frames support different patterns, so it is important to choose a pattern design before building. The location of the joists depends on the floor pattern, which will determine all aspects of the framing. Keep in mind that the decking must always be going in the opposite direction of the joists and that each board end must be secured to a joist or double joist. For safety and stability, cut the boards to the appropriate length vis-à-vis the joists. The length of the boards is a crucial consideration. If the boards are too long, they will not be properly supported.

Cedar Wood Grades

- Cedar graded as "architect clear" is the ultimate in durability and appearance and is usually manufactured to individual order.

- "Custom clear" is a cedar with stability, durability, and good looks, usually used in custom residences requiring fine woodwork.

- "Architect knotty" comes with charming rustic characteristics that will not affect its durable performance.

- "Custom knotty" is an economical choice but still sturdy and attractive, providing all the benefits of other grades but without the higher price tag.

Deck Patterns

- A single, diagonal-decking pattern is an easy option, but more joists will be needed.

- A power miter box will assist in cutting the boards at the appropriate angles.

- A double-diagonal decking pattern is a simple design but very attractive.

- A double diagonal needs a double joist in the center of the decking frame.

DECKING AROUND THE TREE
Time invested in appropriately setting the decking will avoid issues down the road

As you set the decking, be aware of potential problems. To prevent splits and chips, nails or screws should not be set too close to the ends of the floor boards. Screws are often the preferred method because they can be more easily removed without causing damage to the wood.

Initially set the decking as close to the tree as possible. You will later come back and cut a circular line 1 to 3 inches from the trunk. You may have to slice off the end of a board on an angle to get it in place, but try to get all the boards close to the tree. You can make all the cuts at the same time, or you can make them as you go, but it's usually easier to cut a neat edge with all the boards in place.

Rough Cutting around the Tree

- Take care to carefully arrange the decking materials around the tree before making the first cut.

- After a line is inscribed around the tree, decking boards can be individually cut and placed.

- As each board is cut, it is fastened to the joists with Deck Mates This work progresses relatively fast, giving a builder a satisfying feeling of accomplishment.

- Nothing beats a good reciprocating saw for making quick cuts around a tree trunk.

Decking around the Tree

- Incorporating trees into the deck is more difficult but provides greater character.

- To maintain a consistent look, design the floor pattern as if the tree were not there. The boards should match up on all sides of the tree.

- Use the tree as a design element by building benches around the opening for the tree.

- Surround the opening of the tree with guardrails. Leaving the space open can create a hazard for anyone who uses the deck, particularly children and pets.

Depending on the tree, a rectangular or square shape can be cut with an even margin. A contoured cut that mirrors the tree's shape can be done as well. In all cases, cut the boards so that they overhang the collar framing around the tree.

If a circle is going to be cut, there are certain methods that will make the job easier. Establish eight equidistant points around the tree trunk. These will act as points on the circumference of the circle. Using a pencil on a string, swing a line from the trunk, connecting your points. You may have to move your position a few times to complete the circle.

As the work progresses, take care not to drop any tools, scrap nails, screws, or other materials that could cause damage to the decking. Remember that you're working in a highly visible area and that it should remain as clean and pristine as possible.

Potential Problems

- Rotten decking usually results from premature failure of water sealant or stain.

- Consistent standing water on the deck can lead to rot and the infestation of carpenter ants and termites.

- If there is deck rot, the decking must be replaced. While replacing the rotted deck pieces, check the deck framing underneath it to make sure it is still structurally sound.

- Fastener penetrations and surface cracks are common paths for water absorption. A protective finish will help.

Composite Decking

- New eco-friendly products give builders more choices at reasonable prices.

- Because of the wood content, natural color shifts do occur in composite products. Twelve to sixteen weeks of exposure to sunlight and rain are typically required for them to achieve a faded color.

- Clips are available for certain deck systems that allow the entire deck surface to be installed without the use of surface fasteners.

- Some offer a wood grain on one side and a smooth, refined look on the other.

TRIMMING THE DECK EDGES

An attractive and thematically suitable trim is usually necessary to make a deck look complete

Now that the deck has been installed, and everything is level and straight, the trimming can be addressed. Grab a circular saw and a reciprocating saw as the main cutting tools and find a framing square (an L-shaped ruler) to mark and cut straight or square lines. As always, a bubble level (or laser level) and a tape measure will also be used. Put a carpenter's

pencil in your shirt pocket and a knife in your pants pocket and get set to work.

The first area to trim will be the decking that butts up against the edge of the platform. A 1/8-inch gap between boards will allow the joist underneath to be seen. Use this as a guide for inscribing a line. Use the reciprocating saw to start the cut,

Using a Circular Saw

- A 6½-inch circular saw is ideal for ripping lumber or cutting it to length, as well as cutting plywood or composite material.

- The base plate can be tilted to make angled cuts. Most saws adjust from 90 degrees to slightly less than

- 45 degrees allowing for beveled ends.

- The blade can be set to the depth required for individual cuts

- Many circular saws are equipped with a ripping fence to guide the blade.

Keeping Square

- To ensure proper angles, framing squares, levels, and gauges are common. Most widely used is a carpentry framing square.

- The typical framing square is a single L-shaped piece of material with markings to indicate incremental lengths.

- Levels can be integrated with framing squares. Framing squares cannot be readily used to plumb studs or lay out rafters for roofing.

- Framing squares are bulky and cannot be carried in an ordinary tool belt.

making room for the circular saw. Be careful that no one is standing below the tree as you cut the trim. Move forward, measuring and cutting as you go, following the form of the deck.

Once this step is complete, the cut around the tree trunk can be done. Use a reciprocating saw, taking time to follow the inscribed line as closely as possible. If part of the wood splinters at the end, don't be concerned. It can be sanded and smoothed later on.

Once the deck is trimmed, a light sanding over the surface will smooth out any roughness. Remember that the bare feet of children might be running across the deck after it's done. You might also want to add a deck finish, providing valuable protection from harsh weather. It's not absolutely necessary, but it is recommended. Also, a wooden skirt below the deck can help hide the platform's undercarriage.

Reciprocating Saw

- Reciprocating saws are available in both corded and battery-powered models.

- Working with a lightweight and easy-to-maneuver cordless reciprocating saw reduces fatigue.

- When it comes to cordless saws, overall power may not be as good as those with cords, but the range of movement is enhanced.

- Having additional battery packs or lithium-ion batteries will let you do plenty of work without worrying about running low on power.

Philippine Mahogany Decking

- Philippine mahogany is a tight-grained hardwood that resists pests and rot.

- Treat it with marine oil, and it looks like teak. It will age to a silvery hue.

- Look for the FSC trademark to ensure that rain forests have not been harvested irresponsibly.

- "Philippine mahogany" is the common name for a group of woods, but they are not a true mahogany, nor are they comparable with mahogany in quality. They are of medium density, with rather favorable properties.

CLEANUP
Make sure the work area is clean and ready for the next step in building

Cleanup. No one likes to do it, but it is a necessary stage if the project is to go smoothly. Cutting and trimming deck materials can be very messy. Throw in staining or clear coating, and there's always going to be some necessary tidying up. Make sure that gloves and protective clothing are worn. A splinter from treated wood or stained wood can cause terrible infections. Start by clearing everything off the deck. Scraps and sawdust can be brushed off and picked up below. If treated wood was used, make sure it goes into a separate pile. Separate usable decking scraps from trash. A plastic trash can will hold a lot of scrap material.

Gather all the tools together and put them back into their

Cleanup Area

- The first thing to do after the day's work is done is to start clearing the deck of all materials.

- Use separate waste containers, one for reusable materials, one for trash, and one for treated wood.

- Use a dust mop to clean the deck. A leaf blower works well to get all the sawdust off the surface, especially if a finish will be applied.

- Heavy-duty trash bags can be used to throw away smaller material and debris.

Power Tool Maintenance

- Properly maintaining power tools is essential to get the most from the products.

- If a tool is faulty, check the power cord and plug. Make sure they are free of cuts or abrasions.

- If the cord is sound, check the switch to see that it is functional and allowing current to flow to the motor.

- Some power tools, including routers, have a pair of brushes that might need to be repaired or replaced as they wear down over time.

place. Locate all batteries and plug them in or store them for another day. Rake the area around the tree, especially if treated wood has been used. An industrial vacuum will help make sure the smaller materials are removed.

The deck can be washed after it has been cleared. There are special cleaners for decking, but warm water and soap will work as well. Make sure to wipe any excess water off the wood. If a finish has been applied, the deck needs cleaning only every one to three years depending upon the frequency of use.

Treated Wood Cleanup

- You cannot handle treated wood the same as other materials. It is very toxic and can cause serious harm.

- Always use gloves and a mask when handling treated wood scraps and sawdust.

- Sawdust and chips can accumulate on clothing. Shirts and pants that have been in contact with treated wood should be washed before being reworn.

- After contact, thoroughly wash your hands and exposed areas with soap and warm water, especially before eating or drinking.

Wood Decking versus Composite

- You cannot refinish a composite deck—you have to simply replace it.

- Fine wood will likely endure for forty years if oiled annually. A wood deck can be refinished every few years to look like new again.

- Composite decking cannot be recycled. After replacing it, it will go into a landfill, where it could remain for hundreds of years.

- Salvaged wood looks brilliant, and it has a certain romance to it that composite decking will never have.

DOUBLE-CHECK EVERYTHING

Even the most experienced builders will occasionally forget some element of their project on the first pass

One of the most important things a treehouse builder can remember is to exercise patience. Rushing a job only creates problems. After each phase of the project, take care to clean up and evaluate the next stage. Troubleshooting should be taken as seriously as the construction itself.

It's not a bad idea to keep a reporter's notebook in your pocket, making a checklist and adding to it as you go. When it comes time to evaluate all the various elements of construction, you may not remember to double-check an element that you remembered earlier in the day.

After part of the project is completed and the area is cleared, check all the fasteners, including eyebolts and turnbuckles.

Check All Fasteners

- At the start of each day, discuss the previous day's work with colleagues, looking for mistakes and flaws.

- Double-check decking fasteners for flaws in the screws or hardware. Correct any mistakes.

- The bolt-and-bracket

assemblies and the eyebolt-and-turnbuckle assemblies should all be checked for unwanted movement.

- Inspect ropes and riggings to make sure they're holding. The next phase of building will involve a lot of platform and tree work.

Deck Prep Before Applying a Finish

- Remove any residue left after washing. You want a truly smooth surface before staining.

- Consider sanding in order to remove splinters. Walking on the deck without shoes should be a pleasure. Sanding will also verify that the heads of nails and

screws aren't protruding.

- The amount of deck sanding to be done will depend on the desired look.

- Power washing the deck safely removes dirt and dust and opens wood pores to allow deep penetration of the deck stain or finish.

Have they withstood the stress of construction? Does the tension need to be adjusted? Look for rough spots in the decking, especially around the trunk. Take time to smooth these spots out with sandpaper. This will have to be done sooner or later, and if done sooner it might save some splinters in your hands. All the deck edges should be checked for splitting or splintering. Underneath the decking, the fasten points need to be checked as well. Have any screws missed their targets? Are any screws coming out of the side of a joist? If any spot needs reinforcement, do it now.

Turnbuckles

- Turnbuckles are used in rigging to join cables to an anchor point.

- They have a screw thread for precise length and tension adjustment. The tension might need to be adjusted more than once as the building progresses.

- Turnbuckles are deep-forged or cast from stainless steel. The continued soundness of a treehouse's turnbuckles is essential to maintaining the integrity of the house.

- They combine very high tensile strengths with ductility and corrosion resistance.

················· YELLOW ● LIGHT ·················

It's best to schedule a treehouse project during the warmer parts of the year. Cold and moisture can play havoc with both builders and materials. In colder parts of the country, avoid snow, heavy rains, and anything that will affect the lumber. Early spring is a good time of the year to start work. Most trees will not have a lot of leaves that get in the way.

Deck Cleaners

- Oxygen bleach cleaners, when mixed with water, create a hydrogen peroxide and soda ash cleaning base, effective in removing mildew stains as well as graying caused by sun exposure.

- They are also effective in cleaning the wood of dirt and deposits. The wood returns to its original color after cleaning.

- Oxalic acid–based cleaners are effective for removing tannin stains in woods such as redwood, cedar, and oak.

- Before cleaning, protect surrounding plants with a plastic drop cloth.

PLATFORM BUILDING

ORGANIZING THE LUMBER

When it comes time to frame the walls, the work should be organized and methodical

After the platform is secure and cleaned, it's time to consider the wall materials. In this case, a stack of framing lumber made from standard-grade Douglas fir had been air-drying for a few days and so was ready to use. The size and amount of the lumber were checked against a materials list, and a portable table saw was set up near the platform.

As with most treehouse construction, the walls would be built on the ground and then brought up to the platform in sections. To make certain that the pieces fit the platform's actual dimensions, the loose lumber was raised to the platform and measured. The base plates, studs, and headers were marked in the positions in which they would be used, and then lowered

Measuring Framing Materials

- Bring the framing materials to the deck and arrange in position. Measure four of the six walls flush to the edge of the platform.

- The front wall is set back to allow for a porch area.

- Measurements are marked on the wood; each board is tagged as to its eventual location.

- The walls are numbered 1 through 6. Walls 5 and 6 are eventually tied together as a front wall with a door dividing them.

Stacking Precut Wood

- After the wood is marked and measured, bring it down to the cutting area, where a table saw should be set up.

- Each stack of wood represents a wall. The stacks should be set well apart from each other.

- Cut the wood from each stack and then restack for easy access during the assembly stage.

- After the wood is cut, the extra pieces should be put into a recycling bin or thrown away.

to the ground. Each wall would be assembled separately.

With the wood on the ground, it was put into separate piles to be easily identified. The boards were cut to size and restacked in an area where the builder would have plenty of room to assemble walls.

The wall members were laid out on the ground. Each piece of wood had specific markings, labeling which wall it belonged to. This would make for an easier assembly.

It takes some patience to organize the wood properly, but it pays off in time savings later on.

Stud-framed Walls

- A wall is a collection of studs, usually 2-by-4s, equally spaced and sandwiched between top and bottom plates.

- The top plate can be either single or double boarded. Double-plating is most common on load-bearing walls.

- A header is a simple beam sized to support the load above the opening it spans.

- When the opening for a window or door is wider than the stud spacing, a header must be inserted to carry the load of the interrupted stud.

Create a Clean Working Area

- A large work area is essential to assembling the walls. All debris should be carried away, and the area raked clean.

- Everything not to be used in the construction can be set to the side.

- Load the nail gun with a new magazine of nails, and roll up all extension cords except for the one powering the nail gun.

- Clear a path from the work area to the platform.

BASE PLATES & FRAMING
A well-conceived base is an essential element for any treehouse

Base plates in treehouses differ quite a bit from those used in normal construction. For one thing, they are not bolted to a slab or substructure as they would be in a house built on the ground. They also don't need to be treated because the wood doesn't touch the ground.

For this project, standard-grade Douglas fir was used for the base plates. Each board was raised into the tree and marked according to eventual placement, then brought back down to the ground for cutting and assembling.

All the marked pieces were cut and placed with the other members of their wall. Each wall would be assembled on the ground, then walked up to the platform. Each marking clearly stated which wall the board belonged to. Even though the plans on paper might show the walls being of equal size, in

Framing a Door

- Cut and insert studs on each side of the door area. They should be the width of the door plus 1 inch.

- Cut 2-by-4s to the height of the door plus 1 inch.

- Headers of 2-by-4s will be nailed together when placed in position.

- Three "crippled studs" should be fitted between the top of the header plate and the ceiling plate.

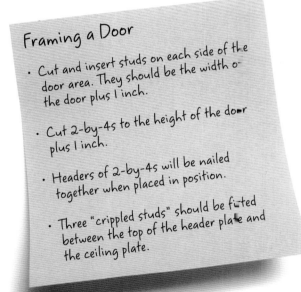

Mark Base Plates on the Deck

- Stud positions were marked on each wall's base plate while it was still in position.

- The positions of the door opening and windows were noted as well.

- Given the hexagonal shape of the platform, 30-degree angles were measured and

marked across each end of the base plates. This would allow them to fit together flush.

- The base plates of the front wall were not angle cut because they did not follow the hexagonal shape.

reality there will be small variations. Once the boards are cut, they will not be interchangeable.

The base plates for each wall were closely inspected. They needed to be straight and knot-free. The wood had been sufficiently dried, so it wouldn't shrink much after it was placed.

A clear path was established from the working area to the platform. A ladder was set up so the builder could take each wall up to the platform after it was assembled.

Cut to Size

- The base plates were all cut to size and appropriately angled. The hexagonal shape of the treehouse made the angle cuts unusually important. A circular saw was used to make the precision cuts.

- The studs, headers, and cripple studs were all cut to their measured sizes.

- After cutting, each wall member was returned to its respective stack.

- The area was cleaned and cleared to make the site ready for the wall assembly.

Framing a Window

- The framing around the rough window opening is meant to support and displace the structural weight above the window.

- In this case, the opening was made slightly larger than the window's actual size. Rough dimensions were provided by the manufacturer.

- The cripple studs that would be placed under the sill and over the header were all cut to size and set aside in an appropriate pile.

- A circular saw was used to cut the window members.

ERECTING THE FIRST WALL

After the lumber has been cut to measure, it's time to assemble the walls

After the boards are cut and organized according to their eventual placement, the next step is to assemble the wall itself. Insofar as this stage allows a builder to see the eventual shape of the treehouse, it can be very fun and satisfying.

In this case, the first wall was laid out on the ground in a shape that mirrored the final form. To accommodate the hexagonal structure, the ends of each base plate were cut on a 30-degree angle. Wall studs on each side were set back a few inches to account for the nontraditional connection. Two studs were nailed together at one end of each wall for extra strength. The builder used a corded nail gun to assemble the walls.

Framing Terms

- A "bottom plate" is the horizontal structural member of a stud-framed wall.

- A bottom plate sets on the subfloor.

- A "cap plate" is the uppermost plate.

- "Cripple studs" are short studs placed between the header and a top plate or between a sill and base plate.

- A nonload-bearing wall supports no load other than its own weight.

Lay Out the First Wall on the Ground

- Before fastening, the wall members were laid out in position to make sure they fit.

- Each board was double-checked to verify that it was straight and free of any knots that could potentially weaken its structural integrity.

- The studs were nailed to the base plate according to the measured marks.

- The top plate was put into position, and the vertical members were lined up with the plate's markings to make sure they matched.

The vertical members of each wall were nailed to the base plates first. Similar to traditional construction, the studs were set 16 inches apart. Once the members were fastened to the base, the top plate was measured again to verify where the studs were going to be placed. A level was used to verify that the studs were straight, and then they were nailed off.

Once the wall was constructed, it was taken by the builder to the platform and hoisted into the tree. With the help of a second builder, the wall was held in its marked position. The base plate was fastened to the decking with star-drive Deck Mate screws. Four to five screws were used to fasten the base plate. The wall was checked to make sure it was straight and level before the other wall structures were fastened to it.

Assembling the walls makes for quick work . . . and it's very satisfying as well.

Finishing the Wall

- After the top plate was positioned according to previous measurements, it was nailed off.

- A bubble level was used to make sure the studs were straight. Before nailing most elements, it's always a good idea to verify the level.

- The completed wall was walked over to the platform and hoisted to the deck. This was done by a single builder.

- The wall was set in position flush to the deck's edge and screwed into both the deck and the floor joist.

Stain and Paint Glossary

- "Color retention" is the ability of paint or stain to resist fading.

- "Cracking" refers to the splitting of a paint or varnish, usually as a result of aging.

- "Elasticity" is the ability of paint or sealant to expand and contract without suffering damage.

- A "knotting compound" is a clear finish or sealant used for sealing knots.

RAISING THE WALLS

With one wall in place, the installation of the remaining elements will progress rapidly

With one wall erected, placing the remaining walls should be a fairly smooth and straightforward process. The only difficulties could potentially come while framing the openings for windows and doors. In this particular instance, the window openings were measured to fit commercially manufactured, prehung windows, so it was a little easier.

Elements of each of the remaining walls were fastened together, and the walls were brought up to the platform. Deck Mate screws were used to fasten the walls together at the top plates. Double-studded ends were connected to those wall ends that had only one stud. There wasn't a need to double-stud each side because the roofing material was

KNACK TREEHOUSES

Repeat Wall Assembly

- The walls were assembled in order, according to their numbers.

- Walls that had window openings were rough framed, per previous markings, to provide space for the windows.

- Walls 5 and 6 were shorter walls. Each had half of a door opening and would be fixed together on the platform with a header.

- Each wall was hoisted to the platform in sequence and fastened to the deck via the base plates.

Framing Connections

- Proper installation of fasteners and connections is crucial to the long-term performance and integrity of the structure.

- Nails, used alone or in combination with metal framing anchors and construction adhesives, are the most common method used to

fasten framing lumber and sheathing panels.

- Nailed joints provide the best performance when the loads are applied at right angles to the nails.

- Nailed joints with the load applied parallel to the nail should be avoided.

going to be very lightweight.

As the walls were set in place, spare decking materials were used for temporary rack bracing. As each wall was rack braced, it was leveled as well in preparation for the installation of the adjacent walls.

The treehouse was now starting to come to life before our eyes, and the excitement that was felt kept us warm despite the freezing weather.

The second top plates were set on top of each wall with a few inches overlapping the adjacent wall structure to give it

a sturdy hold. With the rough framing of the treehouse completed, it was time to clean up and prepare for the next phase of the project.

At every stage of construction, don't be afraid to read the experts for advice. According to Dean Johnson of Hometime, "Prior to starting the layout process, chalk line the locations of the walls and their window/door openings on the deck. These marks will enable you to visualize and check the project's layout before the walls are made. The chalk lines also serve as guidelines when actually raising the walls into place."

Bracing and Leveling the Walls

- As the walls were erected, they were rack braced from the inside with 1-by-6-inch cedar plank ng.

- A level was placed both vertically and horizontally on the frame, making sure everything was straight.

- The walls were checked for

stray nails or screws that had missed their connections and thus were showing on the inside of the framing. Bad connections were removed and replaced.

- Where the base plates met on an angle, an extra screw was used for additional strength.

Attach Top Plates

- A single top plate is allowed under the International Residential Code (IRC), but it is an uncommon construction practice.

- The treehouse had two top plates, one being a cap plate. The door didn't need cripple studs and a header because there wasn't a

door jamb.

- Cap plates were installed with an overlap of a few inches onto the adjacent walls and fastened with screws.

- The walls were leveled and adjusted. The braces were left in place.

SIDING

Explore the various types of available siding before choosing what's right for you

The treehouse siding should be chosen carefully, given that it will be one of the most visible parts of the construction. There are various types of outdoor siding or paneling to choose from, most all of which are sturdy and take color or stain well. Keeping in mind the treehouse theme, decide on a budget and go shopping.

Shiplap siding is a type of drop-lap siding with tight joints similar to tongue-and-groove. It is kiln-dried and can be installed horizontally or vertically. Shiplap is known both for its strength as a supporting member and for its ability to form a relatively tight seal.

Board-and-batten is another simple-yet-effective siding. It's

Shiplap Siding

- A type of siding that works well for buildings that won't receive extensive maintenance, it's also sturdy and can withstand severe climate conditions.

- In post-and-beam construction, rough-sawn shiplap is attached vertically, usually with 6d–8d common nails.

- Milled shiplap siding shows a smooth surface and is more suited to frame construction. It provides a tighter seal and is usually placed horizontally.

- Milled shiplap installs with a minimal amount of effort.

Board-and-batten Siding

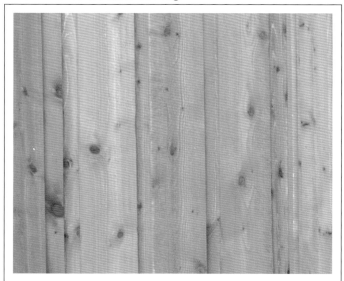

- Typically installed following a vertical pattern, board-and-batten is created by using wide, clear or knotty boards spaced with narrower boards covering the joints.

- Various widths are used to create different looks.

- One-by-three battens and 1-by-10 boards are typical. This can also be reversed, with boards installed over battens to create a deep-channel effect.

- Rough-sawn boards and boards surfaced on one side and two edges are commonly seen.

used either as exterior siding or as interior paneling. It has alternating wide "boards" and narrow wooden strips, called "battens." The boards are usually 1 foot wide. The battens are usually about ½ inch wide. These battens are placed over the seams between the boards.

Good log siding looks identical to real log construction and is much lighter than the real thing. It's easy to assemble and weathers very well.

Attractive and versatile, tongue-and-groove is a popular choice for siding. It can be installed horizontally, vertically, or diagonally. Each method provides for a distinctly different look. Tongue-and-groove siding is available with rough or smooth finishes. Seasoned and unseasoned sidings are also available.

After careful consideration, T1-11 textured plywood paneling was chosen for the project. It was within the budget, would stain well, and was certainly strong enough. The paneling was brought out to the site by the builders, checked thoroughly for defects, and then laid out in a designated "staining area." Ceramic compounds on T1-11 plywood help keep warping to a minimum.

Dura-log Siding

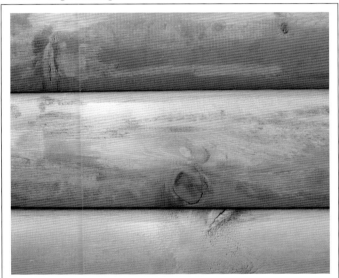

- "Half-log" milled paneling includes a small reveal that creates a dramatic shadow line for a distinctive, real-log look.

- Typically made from pine, half-logs offer the rustic charm of real logs.

- The siding is kiln-dried and attaches to a conventional frame, adding protection from wind and rain without additional caulking or chinking.

- Most siding comes prestained, offering a deeper stain penetration and a more uniform finish than could be done on a job site.

Tongue-and-groove Siding

- Knotty grades are used most often in tongue-and-groove. They are economical and casual looking.

- They also come in clear, smooth grades that have a more formal appearance.

- A random orbital sander will remove the coarse marks left by the rotating cutting knives.

- The edge of the sander also works well for getting into the curved "scalloped" part of the siding.

- Most siding comes in pine, cedar, and redwood.

STAIN & FINISH
Once the basic structure is in place, it's time to add the siding

Each treehouse has its own look and thus requires a slightly different choice in stains or paints. In this case, the builders went with a barn-red stain that fit the rustic surroundings. A few squares of siding were cut and stained to see how they would look. A few different mixtures were applied with a polyester paint roller. While the stain dried, the builders went off to prep other parts of the project.

A few hours later the stain was evaluated, and a mixture was chosen. The next step was to decide how to apply it. A spray-on method didn't achieve a satisfactory look, so a roller was used. The stain was applied at full strength. The result was a very rich color that highlighted the texture of the wood perfectly.

When the panels were dry, the boards were brought up

Stain

- Common plywood and T1-11 siding are much less stable than solid wood siding.

- They are prone to swell, crack, and split due to moisture penetration and temperature change. Special consideration must be given to finishes.

- Application with a brush is preferred, although application by roller or airless spray is also acceptable.

- On common plywood, T1-11 siding, or brushed or abraded plywood, the best finish to use is an all-weather exterior deck or siding stain.

Applying a Finish

- Different shades of stain can be mixed for a unique look. Be sure to mix enough to complete the entire job.

- Of the various methods of application, a roller often provides the most even and smooth finish.

- Lay the boards out in a designated area prior to staining. It will take a few hours for them to dry.

- Make sure you have enough stain for a second coat. This will complete the coverage without any thin spots.

to the platform and set into place. It took two builders to apply them properly. Before nailing it off, some of the siding needed to be cut and fitted over the beams. Given that the back and side walls were flush to the platform's edge, the siding needed to cover the outside joists. As each piece was positioned, the board was marked and cut on the spot with a circular saw; then it was held in place and screwed to the studs with a power drill. Once the panel was fastened, a power nailer finished the job. The nails were placed at regular intervals. With the siding in position the rack bracing

was removed. The siding itself would now hold everything together.

Lastly, holes for windows and the door were cut from the inside with a reciprocating saw. This was done freehanded using the rough framing as a template for the cut.

| *Hoist and Cut to Size* | *Fastening the Paneling* |

- After the panels are dry, bring each up to the deck.

- Raise the siding into position to measure it. Mark any special cuts or notches that will need to be addressed.

- In this case, the siding was cut by a circular saw on the deck, and then fitted to the framed wall.

- The wall was initially fastened to the framing with Deck Mates. If an element needed adjustment, the wall could be unscrewed.

- With the siding in place, verify that it is level and straight, and then nail it off at regular intervals.

- As the walls become stabilized by the siding, the rack bracing can be removed.

- Openings for windows can be cut out of the siding along the lines of the rough openings.

- For this particular project, the opening for the door was cut out on the ground. It had a curved top that needed a precision cut.

ROOFING TYPES

Choose a roofing material that fits the treehouse before building the substructure

As one of the most visible parts of the treehouse, a roof helps define the structure's style. There are many roofing materials to choose from, and they all have different qualities. Style, budget, and durability should all play a role in the decision-making process. A builder should also consider the location of the treehouse. If the house is in an area that gets a lot of rain or snow, the roofing materials should be chosen accordingly. Whichever way you go, remember that the roof is the structure's main protection. Spending a little more on a roof is always a good investment.

Board-and-batten roofing works much the same as its siding counterpart. Easy and affordable, the boards can be

Roof Glossary

- "Blisters" are bubbles that may appear on the surface of asphalt roofing.

- The "butt edge" is the lower edge of shingle tabs.

- In "color-through," color is mixed throughout the roofing material during manufacturing, becoming an integral part of the material.

- A "course" is a row of shingles or roll roofing that runs the length of the roof.

Wood Shingles

- Wood shingles are manufactured from western red cedar, cypress, pine, and redwood trees.

- The industry terms "perfection" and "royal" refer to 18-inch and 24-inch lengths, respectively.

- Asphalt-saturated, nonper-forated, organic felts are common underlayments used in wood shingling.

- The standard for cedar shingles dictates that the shingles be a minimum number one grade. They will be made of 100 percent clear heartwood, with no face defects.

painted or stained and covered with a protective finish to help them withstand the elements.

Wood shingles are highly desirable, although in fire-prone areas they should be pressure-treated with fire retardant. In some places, the building codes may forbid them entirely. In humid climates, where fungus and mildew can be a problem, roofs should be treated with a fungicide. Shingles with pretreated preservatives are also an option.

Tar paper is usually used as a waterproofing layer underneath most shingles. By itself, however, tar paper is not particularly wind- or sun-resistant. It is sold in rolls of various widths, lengths, and thicknesses.

Ondura roofing is a corrugated material that has been impregnated with asphalt. It lasts longer than most other roofing material. It's lightweight and strong, stylish, easily maintained, and easily installed.

For this particular project, the builders chose a brown-colored Ondura corrugation. The color would highlight the barn-red house and the natural trim color.

Tar Paper or Rolled Roofing

- A paper product saturated with tar, simple tar paper is the waterproof material most often used in roof construction. It's very easy to install.

- Tar paper is not sun-resistant, but it works very well underneath most other roofing materials, including asphalt, wood shingles, shakes, and gravel.

- It is often marked with chalk lines at regular intervals to help lay it out straight on roofs.

- It is applied with staples or roofing nails.

Ondura Plastic Roofing

- Ondura can be installed either over purlins (horizontal structural members in a roof) or over a solid decking covered in roofing felt.

- Installation can be dangerous because the sheets are very slick.

- If walking on nailed-down Ondura sheets, step on top of the purlins only, placing your feet across the corrugations. Wear soft-soled shoes.

- Always plan for appropriate ventilation when installing Ondura. Improper or inadequate ventilation will void the warranty.

FRAMING THE RAFTERS

Cut the rafters and check their fittings before bringing them to the platform

With the basic structure of the treehouse built, it's time to cut rafter boards and set them in place. For this particular project, eighteen 2-by-6 Douglas fir boards were used as "hip" and common rafters. They were measured to overhang the frame walls by 6 inches. The ends were cut "dog-eared" style on a 40-degree angle and notched to fit onto the cap plates.

The front rafters were fitted to cover the porch area and fit onto a 2-by-6 beam attached to railing posts in front.

As one builder measured and cut the rafters, another put together a hexagonal collar that would encircle the tree trunk and be used as an attachment point for the tops of the rafters. The collar was made from 2-by-6 wood boards.

Prep Rafters

- Bring the rafter boards to the platform to be measured for length and their angle cuts.

- Once measured, bring them back to the work area so the angle cuts can be made with precision.

- Cut the boards in an assembly-line style. Trim the ends on angles in a half-hexagonal style, or "dog-eared."

- Take the boards back up to the platform to be fastened.

Create the Hexagonal Collar

- In this case the tree diameter was measured with a tape at the rooftop point, 9 feet from the platform.

- For this particular treehouse, six 2-by-6 collar members were cut at 30-degree angles on each end.

- The collar was fastened together around the trunk with a drill and screws.

- With the help of another builder, the collar was rack braced with 2-by-4 boards using Deck Mates. These screws could be easily removed after the collar was fastened to the rafters.

The trunk's diameter was measured, and a few inches were added to the collar in order to give the trunk room to grow. The ends were fastened together with two nails at each connection. Once the collar was assembled, it was set at the high point of the structure on a rack braced with long 2-by-4s. This would hold it in position until it was leveled and the rafters were attached.

The rafters were assembled on the platform. Two builders helped each other fasten them into place. The six hip rafters were connected at each corner first. Two other rafters were

set equidistance between the hip rafters.

The last step prior to attaching the roof was to lay a pair of 2-by-3 nail strips across the rafters, creating a structure to which the roofing could be nailed. This thick lath was used so the nails didn't poke through it. Once these strips were secured, the roofing was ready to be laid into place.

Attaching Rafter Boards

- The next step is to fasten hip rafters first to stabilize the roof structure.

- Any precuts that don't fit can be adjusted on the spot with a circular saw.

- The rest of the common rafters are then nailed off at the attachment points.

Any angle cuts and notches that don't sit well can be adjusted accordingly.

- Once the rafters are attached, the rack bracing can be removed from the collar. Check the rafters and the top plates for sturdiness before continuing.

Attach 2-by-3 Boards across the Rafters

- In this case, 2-by-3 Douglas fir strips were used as purlin attachments.

- The boards are cut to size at the roof line with a circular saw.

- Three horizontal rows of purlin strips are fastened

to the rafters all the way around the roof's diameter.

- Use galvanized steel nails to attach the strips. Because weather is not an issue under a roof, another nail to consider is one with annular ring shanks for superior hold.

ATTACHING THE ROOFING

Few things are as satisfying as finally putting a treehouse under its roof

Regardless of the roofing materials, the basic process of attachment is still the same. In this case, the Ondura roofing sheets were stacked next to the platform, and the path was cleared for the builders to carry each sheet up the ladder to the platform. Two builders would assist each other in the installation. The up man on the roof was harnessed to a rope

rigging for safety. Ondura is slick, and one missed step could easily have sent him flying.

Ondura roofing can be scored with a utility knife and flexed back and forth for a clean edge break. In this case, however, the builders chose to use a circular saw with a carbide-tipped blade. They wore eye protection when cutting.

Bringing the Roofing Material to the Platform

- In this instance, each sheet of Ondura was light enough for one builder to walk it up a ladder to the platform.

- If there isn't enough room on the deck to stack or lay the sheets down, place on the roof one by one.

- Mark the sheets for cutting in position and then take back down to the cutting area.

- For this roof, the process was repeated several times until all the pieces were on the ground and ready to be cut.

Measuring and Cutting

- Draw initial markings and angles on the roofing to show exactly how a cut should be made.

- Cut each piece of roofing with a circular saw, then take back up to the builder on the platform to check the fit.

- If adjustments in the cutting need to be made, the builder can make the cuts on the roof with a circular saw.

- Nail each sheet temporarily to the purlins underneath.

The first sheet of roofing was placed between the hip rafters and nailed down using Ondura nails, which have rubber seals and are colormatched to the panels. The next sheet was placed on the adjacent roof section to the left and lapped over the previous section. The sheet was marked and angle-cut on the spot with the circular saw, and then nailed down. This rough cut would ultimately be covered by a ridge cap. The same procedure was repeated several times until the whole roof area was covered and nailed. This left a few smaller sections that still needed to be fitted with pieces of roofing. These pieces were cut so that a ridge and valley of the new piece fit snuggly into the existing roof's ridge and valley beneath.

Once the roof was complete, all that needed to be done was to attach the ridge caps. The sheets had been set close enough for the caps to cover them nicely. All six rim ridges were fitted with caps, which were then nailed off. The builder hand-tugged the connection points to make sure they were secure.

Nailing the Roof in Place

- After the main sheets are attached, cut smaller pieces of roofing to close any gaps in the roof. They are lapped over the main sheets. Most are marked and cut on the spot.

- After the gaps are covered and temporarily attached, check for alignment.

- Nail the roof using a regular claw hammer. Take care not to drive the nails too deep, which causes spreading.

- In this case, brown Ondura washered nails and shingle nails were used.

Roof Rim

- In setting the hips, the sheets from either side should meet each other with less than 1 inch between them. This is more precise than required.

- In this case, the framing was done in such a way that the upper ends received the nails that would secure the hip cover.

- The hip cover was cut, placed, and nailed with washered nails.

- There are other ways to install Ondura roofing that will produce a tiled effect. For that information refer to the installation guide.

TRIM THE ROOF
After the roof is nailed down, the next step is to start the trimming

Two days into construction, the treehouse was finally looking like a real hideaway in the woods. A dream playhouse for young children was becoming a reality.

As the roof trimming began, anything that was sticking out or not fitting well was adjusted. At the top of the roof, a clean cut around the trunk was made in order to fit a rubber tire gasket. This would serve as a watertight fitting. The roof and surrounding area were cleaned, and all the extra pieces of roofing were thrown away.

The final nailing of the sheets also needed to be done. Shingle nails were driven through the valleys approximately 4½ inches from the top edge of the tile. Care was taken that each nail was driven perpendicularly into roof decking rather than at an angle. The nail heads needed to be in snug

Trim the Overhang

- In this case, after the roof was fastened, it was inspected. The hip cover and the sheets underneath were adjusted to allow for the cables to hang properly.

- A section of sheeting and part of the lower end of the hip cover were cut at all six corners.

- Water seepage was not a concern because the cuts overhung the structure.

- Because the cables had been handled quite a bit during this process, the tension was tested to make sure it was still correct.

Notes on Asphalt Shingles

- For a new roof, felt paper should be laid down underneath the shingles.

- "Drip edges" refer to corrosion-resistant metal strips that protect the exposed ends of the roof deck at the bottom and sides of the roof. They go on the bottom of the roof before the felt paper is applied.

- Install a row of shingles beneath the first regular row of shingles.

- Shingles should not be applied flush. Water has a tendency to pull its way up the shingle.

contact with the tile. Only genuine, 3-inch Ondura washered nails were used. They were driven through the corrugation crowns at the eaves, through the ridge caps at the corrugation crowns and at the lower corners and center of the end laps (protecting against wind lift). The builders were careful not to overdrive the nails so that the roofing wasn't spread out of alignment.

Ondura's corrugated design allowed for ventilated openings at the ridge, rake, and eave.

ZOOM

As siding, Ondura sheets are installed either vertically over framing or horizontally over studs. Short, common, washered nails can be used in the valley. Always use 3-inch nails in side-lap crowns. In both applications, 24 inches is the maximum suggested support spacing. Make sure there is adequate ventilation. The corrugated design ensures that the siding will be lightweight and strong.

Nail Guns

- Nail guns can fire their fasteners into wood and some other materials in a fraction of a second. Although they are extremely useful, they can also be quite dangerous if not used properly.

- Spring-loaded roofing nail guns are the simplest and most affordable nail guns. They use high-tensile springs to fire the nails.

- The most popular type is a pneumatic nail gun.

- A standard air compressor can provide huge amounts of power.

Tips for Wood Shingle Installation

- Lay the material out on the roof and mark it using chalk. Remove it from the rooftop.

- A layer of tarpaper is attached with roofing nails and/or hot tar.

- Install any metal material that will be needed, such as guttering, flashings, and drip edges.

- Attach the outer layer of roofing material per the manufacturer's installation guide.

ATTACHING THE RUBBER GASKET

The roof hole needs to be waterproofed with a rubber fitting around the tree

When a tree penetrates the roof of a treehouse, it's necessary to waterproof the opening. In this instance (as would be the case in most other scenarios as well), the builder chose to waterproof the opening with a rubber fitting made from a simple tire tube. This would make the roof almost airtight and prevent any leakage from rainwater and clutter from falling

debris. Relatively cheap, the tire tube is worth the money many times over. Any leftover rubber tire material was taken to a recycling center.

The circumference of the trunk was measured at the roofline. The builder soon saw that the tire would have to be cut into several pieces in order to make it all the way around. The

Attaching the Rubber Gasket

- In this instance, the tree's diameter was measured by stretching a measuring tape around the trunk.

- A rubber tube was cut into pieces on the ground with a utility knife. Once assembled, the pieces would be long enough to fit the measurements.

- Excess roofing material was trimmed back to provide a clean rim.

- The rubber tubing was fitted into position, and then nailed into the purlins and tree trunk with brown Ondura washered nails. Care was taken not to penetrate the tree too far.

Recycling Rubber Tires

- The amount of wasted rubber produced by the world each year is astonishing. Tires make up a significant portion of this waste.

- Efforts have been made to develop new markets for recycled tires, but vast majorities are still being stockpiled and landfilled.

- A new process, ECOL-Mem, utilizes commercially available porous rubber tubing (PRT) for drip irrigation systems.

- The PRT system helps provide developing countries with safe drinking water, basic sanitation, and solid waste recycling.

builder used a utility knife for the cuts. Each piece was at least 1 foot wide so both the roof and tree were covered properly. To fasten the tubing, Ondura roofing nails were used for both the tree and the roofing connection to the gasket. Nails were hammered in every few inches. The builder used a regular claw hammer instead of a nailer so as not to damage the roof by overdriving or to overpenetrate the tree.

For trees like the one with deeply furrowed bark, the gaps must be sealed with silcone and checked periodically. The shape and orientation of branches encouraged the collection of water toward the center of the tree. Given that this was a playhouse, however, some water seepage was acceptable and it would move down the trunk and out through the 2 inch hole in the floor around the tree. If the tree was meant to be lived in, steps could be taken to make the roof watertight, but it would be costly. The main thing these owners would need to be concerned about was mildew. They would need to keep things as dry as possible and not let water sit.

Caulks and Sealants

- Latex- and oil-based sealants are generally referred to as "caulks." Although they have a relatively poor durability, they are inexpensive and easy to work with.

- Acrylic latex is more durable and elastic and is suitable for both interior and exterior applications.

- Butyl rubber is commonly employed in insulated window assemblies because of its durability.

- Silicone is flexible but not paintable. It is difficult to remove and is unsuitable for porous materials.

Sealant Glossary

- "Abrasion resistance" is the ability of an adhesive to resist mechanical wear.

- An "antiskinning agent" is an additive that retards oxidation.

- An "extender" is an organic material used to improve polymer properties.

- "Mastic" is a highly viscous adhesive with gap-sealing properties.

- "Green time" is the time it takes for adhesive to solidify.

TROUBLESHOOT THE ROOF

With the roofing in place, steps should be taken to verify its soundness

The roofing is set, and it looks fantastic. The debris has been cleaned up, and the day's work is almost done. Before leaving the job site, however, it's important to troubleshoot the work. In this instance, the inspection was done by a single person in harness, tethered to a rigging line. His main purpose was to test the strength of the roof and to spot stray nails or overlaps that were ineffectively installed. The rubber gasket was also looked at again, and a few nails were added at strategic points to achieve a better seal. It was time for a water test.

Before dragging out the hoses, fortuitously rain began to fall. In this case, the roof did its job very well. There wasn't any

Check the Roofing Nails

- After troubleshooting the outside of the roof, look at the inside for stray nails or screws.

- Get on a ladder and check the hip rafters closely to make sure the fit is tight.

- Move the ladder over to the center of the roof and check the rubber gasket fitting for gaps.

- Check all the overlap points carefully and make sure the fits are snug and don't have wiggle room. This could allow leakage.

Roof Maintenance

- Inspecting the roof for signs of damage is something every treehouse owner should do each year.

- Check to see if trees or tree branches are growing too close to the roof.

- Branches that blow in the wind will scratch and gouge the roof. Falling branches from trees can damage or even puncture roofing materials.

- If branches or trees are growing too close to the treehouse, they may have to be trimmed back.

water seepage at all. The owners were cautioned, however, that snowstorms, rain showers, and other severe weather conditions could still result in water seepage. The connections and seals needed to be checked on a regular basis, especially after major storms.

One last thing to consider with roofing is the maintenance. This treehouse has a high-quality roof material that should last the lifetime of the tree, but it would still need to be checked from time to time. The roof of a treehouse is subject to not only nasty weather conditions but also falling tree branches, gathering debris, and curious critters. It doesn't take any time at all to check the roof from season to season, so mark it down as a must-do in the future. Inspect the underside for leaks or water stains and then get out the ladder and inspect the shingles or roofing material itself, looking for loose attachments and punctures.

The treehouse is almost ready to be used, so take a breather and get ready for the next step.

More on Roof Maintenance

- Black streaks on the roof are an indication that there might be a problem with mold, algae, or fungus.

- Fungus flourishes in areas of high humidity and on roofs that receive too much shade.

- A fungus will eat away at the roofing material, eventually causing leaks.

- Trimming nearby trees to reduce shade and to improve air circulation helps with a fungus problem. It's also a good idea to install zinc strips along the ridge of the roof.

Fire Safety

- Never use a wood-burning stove or kerosene heater in a treehouse. Battery-operated or electric heaters are safer. Monitor any heating source closely.

- Cooking equipment should be avoided in a traditional children's treehouse. An outdoor barbecue is a much better idea.

- Matches and cigarette lighters should never be brought into a treehouse.

- Fabric furniture should be avoided. All mattresses and bedding should be portable and, when not in use, kept in dry storage areas.

STAIR SUPPORT
Stair accesses are friendly to children and the aged but rather more complicated to build

Accesses to the treehouse are always important. In this instance, the owners had specific criteria that needed to be met. Access had to be kid-friendly as well as easily navigable by older folks. The owners decided on a staircase rather than a ladder. Because the platform was 11 feet in the air, however, the limited space would more easily accommodate a split

staircase rather than a straight construction. Two flights of stairs would be separated by a small platform. Railings would run the course of the stairs for safety.

The builders decided to place the stair platform about 8 feet from the treehouse deck. Four-by-four, pressure-treated Douglas fir posts would be set in concrete to serve

Digging Post Holes

- In this case, locations for the posts were marked at 4-foot intervals. A handheld clamshell post hole digger was used to dig the holes.

- The tool dug a fairly small hole (the diameter was 4 to 6 inches) to a depth of 3 feet.

- The hole was made slightly broader at the bottom than the top, creating greater stability.

- The dirt that had been dug up was later used to cover the hard concrete.

Set 4-by-4s in the Holes

- A treated post was placed into each of four holes. They were cut longer than necessary so they could be braced.

- The four posts were braced on all sides. Once they were plumb and level, they were ready for the concrete.

- Concrete and aggregate were mixed in a large plastic trash can per instructions on the bag. After a few minutes the mix thickened and was ready to use.

- The concrete was poured into the holes and smoothed with a shovel.

as supports. There would be only a few stairs to the platform, and then the rest would lead to the deck.

To set the posts, the builders dug post holes 3 feet deep and set them 4 to 5 feet apart. While one builder attended to the holes, the other builder mixed cement in a large trash can. Once the holes were ready, the posts were placed, leveled, and braced. A mixture of concrete and aggregate was poured into each post hole. A shovel was used to smooth the area flat around the posts. All that was left to do was wait overnight while the concrete cured.

Concrete Curing

- During curing, crystals grow from a reaction between Portland cement and water—a reaction known as "hydration."

- If there isn't enough water, the crystals can't grow, and the concrete doesn't develop the strength it needs.

- If there is enough water, the crystals grow out like tiny fingers wrapping around the sand and gravel in the mix.

- As fresh concrete cools, the hydration reaction slows down. The temperature of the concrete, not necessarily the temperature of the air, is what's important.

Concrete Terminology

- "Abrams's law" states that concrete strength is inversely related to the ratio of water to cement.

- Low water-to-cement ratios produce greater strengths.

- "Accelerators" are additives used to reduce the setting time of concrete.

- "Hot load" is construction slang used to describe ready-mix concrete that has begun its hydration process while still in the delivery drum of the agitator truck.

ACCESS

205

FRAMING THE PLATFORM
After the concrete has set, it's time to start framing the platform

The next day the builders were ready to begin building the platform landing and staircase. The post bracings were removed, and the four posts were found to stand straight and to be securely fixed into the ground. They were cut to about 43 inches high. The builders wanted six steps from the landing to the ground. Each step had about a 7½-inch rise, so the landing (the sixth step) was about 45 inches high.

The landing would be constructed in the same manner as a deck, although without the support joists underneath (there wouldn't be a load to bear). The rim framing consisted of 2-by-6 Douglas firboards, which were cut and fastened to the posts. Eleven 1¼-inch cedar boards 4 feet long were laid perpendicular to the stairs across the platform and fastened to the frame on both sides. Two Deck Mate screws were used

Stair-building Terms

- "Total run" refers to the horizontal distance covered by the staircase.

- "Total rise" refers to the vertical distance from the surface of the landing to a point level with the surface of the upper floor.

- "Passage width" is the width of the stairway.

- "Run" is the horizontal distance from the leading edge of one tread to the leading edge of the next.

The Landing and Step Count

- In this instance, the full height from ground to platform was 11 feet. At 7½ inches per rise, there were eighteen steps.

- The landing was positioned in lieu of a sixth step.

- The top part of the staircase had thirteen steps cover-

ing an almost 8-foot span, whereas the bottom had five steps covering a little over 3 feet.

- A 2-by-12 beam cut to size was added parallel to the treads under the platform as a fastening for the landing.

to fasten the boards on each end. The result was a very clean-looking, 4-by-5-foot 6-inch platform.

When building a staircase, the "rise per step" for both the top and bottom flights needs to be the same. Local building codes will have the appropriate information. Regardless of code, the stairs will look and feel better if the rise per step, run per step, and all the other dimensions are the same for both flights. The most important thing to remember is that you have to build your platform at the right level in order to have matching upper and lower flights. This number is arrived at by knowing the run and dividing it by the rise per step. Because the upper flight usually has space constraints whereas the lower flight has more latitude in design, the upper flight should be designed first.

Remove the Bracing and Frame the Landing

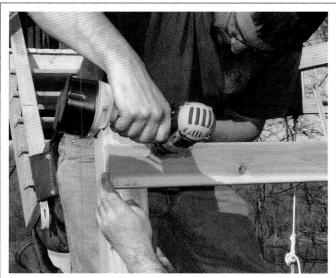

- With the concrete cured, the bracing was removed with a power drill.

- The posts were cut to 42.8 inches, 1 inch shorter than the landing surface to compensate for 1 inch of cedar decking.

- Two-by-six joists were cut to size and fastened to the posts. The boards butted to each other on the ends.

- One-inch cedar decking was laid perpendicular to the orientation of the treads and fastened to the rim joist with Deck Mate screws.

Landing and Stair Codes

- Each area has its own building codes. They usually address decks and stairs and should be followed closely for safety reasons, if not legal ones.

- All decking material should be composed of dimension lumber (with a 2-inch nominal thickness) or span-rated decking in accordance with the American Lumber Standard Committee.

- Any staircase with over three steps requires a railing.

- Stairs must be at least 36 inches across. The stringers should not be spaced farther than 36 inches apart.

STRINGERS

With the platform built, it's time to fasten each of the stringers

Building a staircase can be a very daunting task unless it is planned and executed carefully. A little bit of addition and subtraction will save headaches down the road. Always check with a local building department before designing a stairway and then follow the codes, even if treehouses aren't addressed.

Stringers are an essential part of the staircase. They are the sloped members that support the stairway. Two-by-tens are generally allowed for stairs with four treads or fewer, but for this project, with eighteen treads total, sturdy 2-by-12s were a better choice.

In most cases, you'll need good-quality material with no large knots, either pressure treated or, to resist decay, cut from heart redwood or cedar. If the treads will be ⁵/₄ material, stringers should be placed no more than 24 inches apart.

Prepare the Stringers

- Depending on the width of the staircase, you will need two or three stringers. Most building codes require three stringers for stairways wider than 30 inches.

- The stringers were made as identical as possible. They were stacked together with the cuts aligned.

- Each section was tested for levelness. Small adjustments were made.

- The ends of the stringer boards were cut to rest flush against a skirt board on top and the landing on the bottom.

Alternative Stringer Assembly

- Attach each tread to the unnotched stringers with galvanized, 90-degree angle brackets.

- Fasten each bracket to the underside of the tread, leaving ¼ inch between the end of the tread and the stringer.

- Bevel the top of the tread with a router to assist in water drainage.

- Use brackets to fasten the top edge of the stringer to the deck. Place the brackets on the inside edge of the stringer.

Thirty-six inches apart will suffice for 2-inch-thick lumber. On this project 1-inch cedar treads were used.

To start, the stringers for the top half of the stairs were cut to size (approximately 8 feet). The stringers were then notched for the treads. All the riser measurements were taken using a large L-square. The square was set on the stringer flush against the edge, and the notch was traced along the edge of the square. This process was repeated in a "step-down" fashion from top to bottom until the correct number of notches was laid out. The height of the last riser needed to be less than the others by an amount equal to the thickness of the tread. When the last tread was nailed in place, the step-down to the landing floor would be equal to the others. The first stringer was cut halfway with a circular saw and precisely finished with a hand saw, making sure the cut didn't stray away from the markings.

Back Riser Alternative

- Back risers can create the look and feel of a solid link between one area of the deck and another.

- Stairs with back risers can be susceptible to water damage at the contact point of the tread.

- Cut the riser a bit shorter than normal so it sits about ⅛ inch above the notch in the stringer.

- If using a full-size riser, set the tread so it doesn't fully touch the back of the rise.

Specific Stringer Codes

- If there are no other supports along the stringer's length, stringers should be ½ inch by 2 inches at the minimum. A 1-inch thickness will suffice if supported.

- An effective depth needs to be 3½ inches at the minimum. An effective width is 9¼ inches minimum.

- Stringers must not have direct contact with the ground unless they have been treated with a wood preservative.

- Stringers must be secured at both top and bottom.

209

STRINGERS & TREADS

After the platform is built, it's time to fasten the stringers and treads

With the cuts on the first stringer carefully made, the stringer was set in place to make sure the cuts were correct. It was then used as a template for cuts on the other stringers. After all three stringers were finished, it was now time to fasten them to the platform.

There are a few ways to fasten stringers to the deck. They can be hung to a rim joist with joist hangers, or they can be bolted in place to a joist. The builders of this treehouse preferred mounting the ends of the stringers flush to the deck, then fastening them from behind the rim joist with lag screws.

Once that was done, the other ends of the stringers were temporarily placed on the landing before they were fastened. The lower stringers were measured and cut in the same

Tread Codes

- Although most codes allow for narrower stairs and higher risers, wider treads and lower rises are easier to walk on.

- Treads should be at least 1 inch thick if used with notched stringers. Two inches is optimal.

- Open risers with stringers spaced 30 inches or more apart should be at least 1½ inches thick.

- There should be at least 1 inch of nosing (the overhang of the tread) if the "unit run" (not the actual tread) is less than 10 inches.

Set the Treads in Place

- For the treads, thirty-four ⅝ by 6 decking boards were cut to widths of 30 inches.

- Two boards per step were used, creating a run of approximately 11 inches. This provided more than adequate stepping area as well as a moderate overhang for each tread.

- The treads were fastened to the stringers with two Deck Mate screws on each side of every board.

- The treads were sanded and smoothed to prevent future splitting and splinters.

manner as the top. There would be a total of five steps from the landing to the ground. The stringers were flush-mounted on the ends to a 2-by-12 that was, in turn, fastened to the posts underneath the landing. The sides of the stingers were lag-screwed into the posts as well. The bottoms of the stringers were set on top of three large rocks.

The treads are the horizontal members that you walk on. Typically they are cut from the same material as the upper floor deck or porch. For this treehouse, the cedar that was used for the deck was used for the treads. The wood was measured, marked, cut to size, and then fastened to the stringers. The riser area was left open, a fairly typical decision when dealing with outdoor stairs. The treads are critical to safety. Opt for nonslip stairs if possible.

Check for Splits, Levelness, and Rough Spots

- Troubleshooting the staircase, landing, and the stringer assembly is an essential step before a builder moves on to the railings.

- The levelness and plumbness of each board were checked.

- All the connection points were inspected. If a nail or screw was loose or had missed its connection point, it was refastened.

- The treads were also inspected. If a tread had a significant split, it was replaced. All rough spots were sanded smooth.

Potential Problems

- Wood rot can develop undetected in enclosed, poorly ventilated areas. The subsequent deterioration can lower the load-bearing capacity of the framing.

- Any wood surface with long-term moisture contact may develop fungal growth. The end grain, where cut wood cells are exposed, is the most susceptible.

- The elimination of the moisture source will arrest further growth of the wood rot.

- Uniform building code requires a 6-inch minimum separation between finish grade and wood structures.

RAILING

The railing will stabilize your staircase and give it a professional, finished look

The railing is the final step in putting together a staircase. Not only is it the "icing on the cake," but also it's an integral part of the construction. The railing assembly consists of posts, a cap rail, and vertical balusters or pickets between each post. The most common post materials are 4-by-4s with 2-by-4 handrails. These are what these particular builders chose for their materials, although the balusters would be made of thick bamboo, harvested from the owners' own stand of bamboo plants (which actually needed thinning anyway). Codes regulate the overall height of the railing assembly (usually specifying 30 to 34 inches, although 36 inches is the most common) and may address the maximum width of the

Railing Requirements

- When the railing is 2 to 6 feet from the ground, the minimum height of the railing is usually 36 inches. Over 6 feet, the minimum requirement is usually 42 inches.

- The lower railing can be no more than 4 inches off the deck surface.

- The spread between the balusters cannot be more than 4 inches.

- If utilizing materials like natural branches, it may be harder to follow code. If that's the case, use the code as a simple guideline.

Set Posts on the Platform

- A pair of 4-by-4 deck posts was fastened to the rim joist and deck. They were attached at the top to a header board and screwed into the top railings.

- Three 4-by-4 railing posts were notched and attached to the porch deck area at the rim with two carriage bolts each.

- The tops of the posts were cut into a soft pyramid design.

- Because posts for wooden decks are always susceptible to moisture damage, metal brackets should be considered.

handrails as well. Look up the codes in your area to double-check what may be required. One of the main concerns with the railing on this particular treehouse was that it be made "kidsafe." The coded height worked well in this regard. Once the pickets were spaced close enough together to prevent small bodies from falling through, the owners were content, and building could progress.

To build the railing, 4-by-4 posts were secured with carriage bolts on the deck, the top of the stairs, and the landing. The posts were notched at the bottom so they would fit onto the deck areas and hang over the rim joist at the same time. They were cut long enough to extend 36 inches above the surface of the treads.

The top of the upper rail was about 34 inches above the tread, while the lower rail was about 6 inches above the tread. The railing material was laid out against the posts. Angled cuts were marked for any rails that would be fastened between the posts.

The railings were cut to length and nailed with four 8d galvanized nails.

Railing Assembly

- Wooden railings will deteriorate and weather faster than synthetic products, but they still might be the best option for a budget-minded builder.

- Two-by-four cedar railings were fastened to the posts with Deck Mate screws.

- The posts and railings on the landing were assembled and fastened in the same way as the upper deck.

- Before the balusters were attached, all railings and posts were inspected, verifying that they were tight, plumb, and level.

Alternative Railing Options

- Composite railings are made from a combination of wood and synthetic plastics. They require very little maintenance.

- Aluminum railing is immune to rotting and weathering. Styles range from traditional pickets to modern paneling.

- Inexpensive and low maintenance, wrought-iron railing systems offer a stylish solution, usually protected with a durable finish.

- Vinyl railings are inexpensive and long-lasting. The vinyl is just a skin with metal structural inserts for strength.

EXTRAS

When it comes time to dress up the stair access, gc the extra mile

The staircase is up, the railing is fastened, and so now it's time to attach the balusters and any gates that might be needed. There are a myriad of ways to do this, all of which will add a nice piece of personality to the treehouse. This is where you can have a little fun with the design, adding a little flair to the final product.

One of the more enjoyable ways to outfit a treehouse is to use decorative cargo netting and rope railings. Ropes come in various diameters and colors and can be used for gates as well. While you're at it, you may want to consider using natural branches as balusters. There are as many ways to use the branches as there are branches to use. Straight branches can be used in a traditional way, or wildly shaped branches can be configured in patterns to look like a bird's nest.

Rope and Natural Branch Railings

- Manila ropes, often referred to as "hemp," can be used as railings.

- Braided rope has a number of variations, including solid braid, diamond braid, double braid, or parallel cord.

- Natural branch railings, whether intricate or simple, should be peeled, sanded, and coated with a urethane finish.

- A more freeform way to create branch railings is to build a traditional 2-by-4 structure and attach branches to it.

Post Details and Carvings

- With a little more time invested (and with the right wood), posts and railings can be carved into curves, finials, postcaps, and end-caps. Railings and posts can be carved to thematically match the treehouse.

- Carvings can be insets of suns, trees, landscapes, and coats-of-arms. A Dremel tool can help with the carving.

- Some treehouses have carvings of woodland animals, mythical creatures, even cowboys and Indians. This carving was designed and sculpted by Ron Myhre of TreeHouse Workshop, Inc.

The posts can be carved into various designs and shapes as well. All it takes is a little imagination and some elbow grease. They can be carved like gang plank posts of a pirate ship or porch posts of an old shanty house. The possibilities are endless.

Gates and locks can be just as imaginative. Whether you're installing a piece of salvage or spare parts from an airplane, as long as it's functional, anything goes.

For this treehouse, bamboo was used for the balusters. Cutting was done with a chop saw to prevent splintering. The

bamboo itself was still green when it was installed but would weather to a natural color over time. Each bamboo baluster was predrilled, then fastened to the upper and lower railings using galvanized nails. As a final touch, the upper and lower portions were wrapped with raw twine to enhance the rustic feel.

Gates, Latches, and Ornamental Hardware

- A traditional gate can be built from 2-by-4 Douglas fir and 2-by-5 cedar planks. Whether straight on top or curved, with inexpensive hinges or a traditional latch, it's an easy, inexpensive addition.

- Salvaged gates add a little flair to any treehouse.

- For a more elaborate treehouse, high-end wooden or wrought-iron gates can be installed using decorative hinges, latches, and clavos in a variety of finishes.

- Extras might include ornamental door pulls, door grills, and false-hinge fronts.

Bamboo

- Inexpensive and versatile, bamboo poles are an easy way to rail a treehouse. They come in various diameters and styles.

- Bamboo poles, available as either half-rounds or full-rounds, come in a variety of stained colors.

- If using fresh bamboo, take care to work only with shoots that are of the same circumference.

- Strip the poles of leaves and cut to a size that will fasten flush to the lower and upper railings.

DOORS

The entry to a treehouse provides safety and shelter and makes a style statement as well

There's a real satisfaction to be found in installing a treehouse's door. Whether it's a simple arrangement of 2-by-4s or salvaged teak with hand-tooled hinges, hanging the door means the treehouse is almost finished.

In this instance, the door was made from the material that had been used in most of the treehouse itself: cedar. Three rough-cut boards were enough to build a door that was approximately 31 inches wide, including a ½ inch of space between the boards. The height was 66 inches. The boards were attached to 2-by-4 braces at the top and bottom.

The plan called for the door to have a curved top and a prehung, diagonal window. The builders created an opening for

Assembling the Door

- Three 1-by-10 cedar planks were inspected to make sure they were straight and sound. They were cut to lengths of roughly 66 inches.

- Each board was fastened with Deck Mate screws to Douglas fir braces. One-half inch of space was left between them.

- The screws were set parallel to each other but not in line. This created a better hold.

- The rough spots were sanded to prevent future splintering and splits.

Placing the Window

- A line was drawn around the rim of the octagonal window.

- Following the line, a jigsaw was used to cut an opening between the bracing members.

- The prehung octagonal window was inset into the opening, then fastened with screws through eyelets on the window's flange.

- For the frame, six 1-by-4 pieces of cedar were cut to 30-degree angles, then fitted together using finish nails and wood glue. After sanding, the frame was screwed to the door.

the window by tracing the window shape on the door. The window itself was about 12 inches in diameter. A power jigsaw was used to cut the shape into the door's cedar planks. The window was then fitted to the opening.

Galvanized screws were used to fasten the window's flange to the door. Finally, a 1-by-4 octagonal frame was attached with Deck Mate screws.

The final step was to cut out a half-circle on the top of the door to give the opening a little more flair. A pencil on a string was used to draw the outline, and then a jigsaw cut the shape.

Weather stripping can help prevent the elements, be they rain or cold winds, from entering your treehouse and creating conditions that could ruin your time in the treetops. Although weather stripping is not coded for treehouses, it's always a good idea to follow the codes anyway. You can purchase weather-stripped doors, but it's more economical to do it yourself. All the materials needed are easily available at hardware stores.

A Curved Door

- A half-circle was drawn on the door, running from above the brace on one side to the top of the door to above the brace on the other side.

- The door was carefully cut with a power jigsaw. The edges were sanded smooth.

- The door was brought to the deck to use as a template for the cut in the siding. A pencil was used to draw the line.

- A reciprocating saw was used to cut the rough opening.

Attaching the Door

- Traditional, black-colored door hinges were used to hang the door. It would open from left to right so foot traffic on the deck wouldn't be blocked.

- Two hinges were fastened to the door frame and the door.

- The edges of both the opening and the door were sanded or planed until the fit was right.

- A 1-by-4 exterior door casing was constructed to match the window frame. It was attached to the front paneling.

WINDOWS

The windows of a treehouse open it up to the beauty of its surroundings

All sorts of windows can be used in a treehouse. Whether you are interested in an easy, off-the-shelf insert or something custom-made like the windows created by Andreas Wenning, Roderick Romero, and Ron Daniels, anything goes and usually does. No matter the window type, the installation will involve several key factors, all with one crucial goal: creating a tight, weatherproof seal that keeps moisture away from the wall cavity.

This particular treehouse plan called for six prehung windows. Rough openings had already been made during the framing stage. Each opening was 1 inch wider than the outside measurement of the frame and ½ inch higher. (When

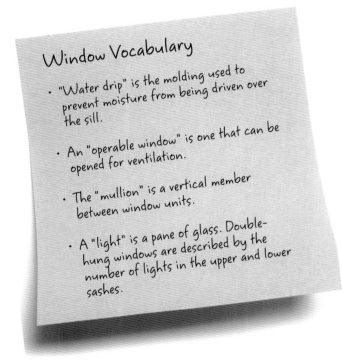

Window Vocabulary

- "Water drip" is the molding used to prevent moisture from being driven over the sill.

- An "operable window" is one that can be opened for ventilation.

- The "mullion" is a vertical member between window units.

- A "light" is a pane of glass. Double-hung windows are described by the number of lights in the upper and lower sashes.

Rough Openings and Window Fastenings

- During construction, six rough-cut openings were made using a reciprocating saw. The stud-framed openings were used as templates.

- The windows were set into place, shimmed, and leveled. Caulking was beaded along the opening for a tight seal, then the windows were screwed into the framework.

- One-by-four casings were cut to fit around each window and fastened with Deck Mates.

- The outside edges of the wood casing were sanded to a rounded finish.

framing rough openings, care should be taken that the sill plate is level and the opening is square, straight, and plumb.) After the paneling had been cut to size with a reciprocating saw, the windows were ready to be set. The flange was placed flush against the outside paneling, and the window was leveled and shimmed. The window was attached with Deck Mate screws at the connection points. A simple, custom-made molding was sanded smooth. It matched the door molding and railings.

Most window manufacturers recognize the importance of proper installation of their products, and so they typically provide a set of detailed installation instructions. Always follow the instructions during an installation.

When a treehouse is in an area that is fairly humid in the summer months, screens are necessary to protect against mosquitoes and other insects. The key to every screen is a strong frame and a good fit. Screens made of fiberglass are long-lasting and weather-resistant. Aluminum mesh is stronger than fiberglass mesh, but it is not as popular due to the fact that it can corrode.

Types of Windows

- Awning windows are designed to provide light and breeze from high on a wall.

- Casement windows open outward to let in light and fresh air. They crank open as opposed to sliding up and down.

- Double-hung windows allow the top to be opened while the bottom remains closed.

- Gliding windows are very easy to open and close. They are perfect for areas such as walkways or when positioned high on walls in living rooms and family rooms.

Types of Window Glass

- Tinted glass absorbs a large fraction of the solar radiation through a window, reducing heat and glare.

- Windows with insulated glazing have two or more panes of glass. These are also called "storm windows."

- A low-emissivity coating controls the heat transfer through a window with insulated glazing. The cost is about 10 to 15 percent more than a regular window, but it will reduce energy loss by as much as 50 percent.

- Reflective coatings reduce solar radiation.

ELECTRICITY

Running power to your treehouse can add to its allure and functionality

Electricity is essential to the modern lifestyle. It's all around us, and yet we don't notice it until it's gone. It powers our world. Why not have it in a treehouse?

Exterior wiring is more challenging than interior wiring. For safety reasons alone, outdoor wiring codes should be followed. Ground fault interrupters (GFIs) are now required in all outdoor areas by the National Electrical Code (NEC). A GFI is an electronic device that supplements conventional circuit breakers or fuses, cutting off power within one-fortieth of a second after disruption.

All light fixtures, outdoor switches, and fittings should be fitted with weatherproof gaskets that inhibit moisture. The

Identify the Power Source

- Most homes have an electrical service panel.

- Power comes into a home from a "service drop," connects to lugs within the service panel, and is then split into separate circuits throughout the house.

- There will usually be enough

power from the main service panel to provide outdoor electricity, but consult an electrician before proceeding. You may need more service or an auxiliary panel.

- Most homeowners should not work on the service panel. A shock from the lugs can be fatal.

Run Lines to the Treehouse

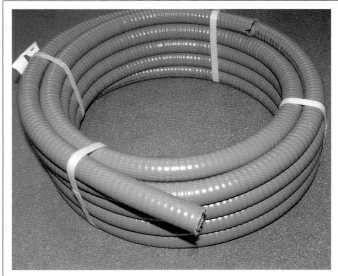

- Outdoor wiring should be installed so that water and other hazards cannot short the lines.

- Contact authorities about building codes in your area. Follow these codes closely.

- Following codes will protect you from possible liability

if any accidents result from the electrical installation.

- Measure the lengths of the conduit and wire that you will need for the project. Running the outside power lines through a conduit is the safest way to protect the wiring. No wires should touch the tree.

switch boxes and the outdoor receptacles should be made from heavy cast metal, and connectors should be fitted with thick gaskets and metal cover plates, making them impervious to moisture.

Three kinds of conduits are made for outdoor use. Rigid aluminum or steel conduits provide good protection to the wires that go through them. Rigid aluminum is easier to work with, but if it is going to be buried in concrete, it must be coated with bituminous paint to prevent corrosion. Rigid plastic conduit, or PVC, comes in two grades, one for aboveground and the other

for below. If PVC is exposed to direct sunlight, it needs two coats of latex paint to prevent deterioration.

Electricity is safe only when you know what you're doing. If precautions are not taken, it can be a killer. Water conducts electricity, so keep wet hands away from electrical equipment and switches. Always firmly grip plugs (not the cord) when unplugging electrical appliances. Yanking the cord can damage the cord, potentially resulting in a shock or fire. Never paint or wallpaper over receptacles or switches. Most work should be done by professional electricians.

Wire the Treehouse

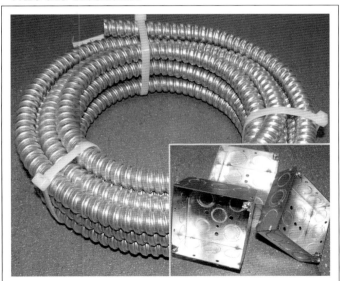

- A conduit containing the wires needs to run up the trunk. Brackets will hold it in place.

- Connect the end point of the conduit to the receptacle. Safely cap or terminate the wires within the receptacle.

- Turn off all the power at the service panel before connecting the outdoor line. Seal the source line and newly installed wiring lines.

- Check each connection. Switch the power back on to the new circuit and test the receptacle at the termination point.

Add Switchplates and Receptacles

- Turn off the power at the main switch.

- Pull the wires from the conduit into the new receptacle box. Push the box into place and screw it to the stud.

- Strip the Romex wiring about 4 inches. Strip the

black and white wires about ½ inch and connect them to the new receptacle. The black wire goes on a gold screw, the white on a silver screw, the ground wire on a green screw.

- Install the receptacle and mount the cover.

221

FURNITURE

With the treehouse complete, it's time to start thinking about appropriate furniture

Whether you're a young child who moves crates onto a platform to make a table or a world-renowned designer of custom furniture, outfitting a treehouse is one of the most enjoyable and creative things you can do. During this stage, consider making furniture from scratch. Inspect the local woods for usable branches or stumps or visit a specialty store. Natural

Tree Furniture is a company based in Kansas and headed by master craftsman Ray Smith. His work epitomizes the ultimate in wood furnishings for casual outdoor living spaces. You bring nature indoors when you purchase one of his pieces.

Over the last few decades, many trees have been cut down to make room for development. Companies like House of

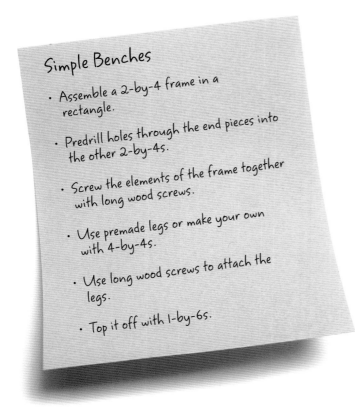

Simple Benches

- Assemble a 2-by-4 frame in a rectangle.

- Predrill holes through the end pieces into the other 2-by-4s.

- Screw the elements of the frame together with long wood screws.

- Use premade legs or make your own with 4-by-4s.

- Use long wood screws to attach the legs.

- Top it off with 1-by-6s.

Tables

- Picnic tables make for easy projects to tackle. Use economical, knotty redwood and build the table top out of 2-by-6 slats.

- Fasten the top to 2-by-4 cleats underneath.

- Cut legs that cross and notch into each other on an

angle via half-lap leg joints. Cut the tops to meet the table top. Machine bolt the table together.

- Tables can also be made from natural sliced tops of huge logs. Add legs or mount on a stump.

Kirk in Virginia are dedicated to saving these logs and putting them to good use. Their planks can be used as tabletops, chairs, and benches. Rustic Furniture in Kansas finds fallen logs and utilizes them to make incredible furniture.

Bunk beds and chairs can be built with common-grade Douglas fir or higher-quality materials. If the treehouse has a rustic look, then salvaged wood may be the way to go. Detailed plans and diagrams can be found on the Internet or in books. And, of course, furniture can be purchased in stores and assembled on site.

There are many ways to make your own furniture and plenty of books and online sites you can access for plans. One company, www.furnitureplans.com, offers a number of projects that anyone can access for very little money. You can also purchase a book by Les Smith and Dan Swesey, *Build Your Own Log Furniture,* which offers many kinds of do-it-yourself projects. All you need is a hammer, saw, and some nails.

Loft

- Make sure there is ample space above the bed. Adults should be able to sit up without bumping their head. Do not make the bed's width less than 3 feet.

- Ensure that the ladder is tightly attached.

- Do not use screws to fix the frame because they might not be able to hold the weight. Bolts will be more suitable.

- Measure the mattress before you fix the box frame. Use the space underneath by constructing a cabinet for storage.

Bunk Beds

- Bunk beds are a terrific addition to a treehouse. You'll need two guardrails, a fire-tested mattress, and a ladder.

- Don't forget the secret nooks and crannies underneath to hold a child's treasures.

- Oak, ash, and cedar are all great woods for bunk beds. They should be sturdy, straight, and give the interior a warm, inviting feel.

- Consider making the bed area a little larger to accommodate a child's growth. The extra space may extend the life of the bed.

LIGHTHEARTED FUN

Above all, treehouses are an opportunity for a builder to enjoy the act of construction

A treehouse is a place to kick back, relax, and enjoy yourself. On a warm summer day, there's nothing better for a child than to play in the treetops. Dad and Mom can kick back in their hammocks and watch the kids have fun.

For this particular treehouse, two swings were added to the construction. One swing had braided nylon rope attached and

knotted to a 2-by-12 rough-cut piece of pine with bark edges. The seat was sanded smooth to protect against splinters. It was fastened to a beam under the platform with a couple of lag bolts and a recycled plastic fastener. The other swing was a small, molded-plastic bucket seat designed for a small child. It had a nylon safety belt and was attached to a beam opposite

Slides

- Slides can create a lot of fun and adventure for a young child. There are plenty of variations to choose from.

- Slides come in simple "rocket" styles, waves, spirals, sidewinders, scoops, and tubes.

- Many are molded from ultraviolet stabilizers and heavy-duty polyethylene.

- Tube slides are generally 24 inches in diameter and come in sections that are easily fitted together. A creative builder can design his or her own wild ride.

Zip Lines

- You can buy zip line kits that have over 100 feet of cable, a steel bar with a handle, carabiners, a cyclone seat, a hardware kit, a velocity trolley, and an instruction booklet.

- Most kits come with a safety backup system.

- A backup system will ensure that, in the event of a trolley failure, the trolley will remain on the line.

- Extras might include bright, flashing LED lights and siren sounds.

the other swing. The owner was there to try out the wooden swing and gave it his stamp of approval on the spot.

A zip line was discussed with the owner, but none was installed at the time. The children for whom the treehouse was built were too young to use it. However, as the children grew older, there was plenty of room for a zip line to run from the platform deck down to a nearby riverbank 100 feet away.

A rope-and-pulley assembly was fastened to one of the hip rafters that overhung the porch. The rope was attached to a small black plastic bucket on the other end.

There was room for other extras, including a rope tube netting, rock-climbing walls, and even a fire pole, but for now the treehouse had everything the owner wanted. It was early spring, and the anticipation of seeing his grandchildren playing in the treehouse in the coming summer caused a huge smile to cross his face.

Cargo Nets

- Flexible yet rugged, heavy-duty cargo climbing nets can be used as either access climbs or play areas.

- They come in various sizes and rope diameters.

- The ropes may be made of polyester, promanila, or polypropylene web net.

- A wide range of colors and styles suits any theme or play area design. There are full lines of UV and chemical-resistant netting and roping solutions. In outdoor or aquatic areas, these will last longer than traditional nets.

Fire Poles

- A standard fire pole can be over 15 feet high, offering a challenging activity for kids and adults.

- A fire pole should be close enough to the platform deck for a young child to access it easily.

- Smaller poles of powder-coated steel are safer and more appropriate for younger children. They can be attached to the platform deck.

- Large brass or stainless-steel poles are available from firehouse supply stores.

ACCESSORIES

There is always another fun and practical item that can be added to a treetop environment

With the building process over, it's time to sit back and enjoy the accomplishment. There are other accessories to think about, but don't rush the process. Let your mind wander. Ideas will come to you.

Perhaps personalizing the treehouse with a family coat-of-arms might be appropriate. Paint it on the front door, have it

imprinted on a custom door mat, or put it on a pennant or a flag and attach it to a wooden pole. Or maybe it would be fun to build a pulley system to bring food and supplies to the deck. How about a pair of hammocks on the underside of the platform, giving Mom and Dad a place to rest while the kids are playing in the treehouse? Mailboxes are a great idea as

Flags and Pennants

- Flags and pennants of all kinds are readily available at flag supply stores or even your local ballpark.

- A treehouse can be dressed up with string pennants, streamers, message flags, code signal flags, and pull-down flags.

- Take the extra step by personalizing a flag with your own design or artwork. Consider creating a lighthearted family coat-of-arms.

- The standard height for a flagpole is 18 feet. Making it shorter or taller can add a little personality.

Pulleys

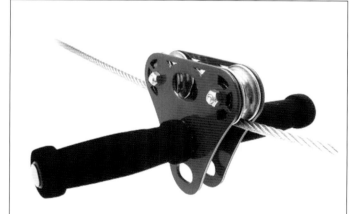

- There are different kinds of pulleys, including the fixed pulley, the movable pulley, the simple pulley, and the compound pulley.

- A pulley can make work seem almost fun for a child. Bringing a large lunch with books and some toys from the ground to a treehouse

- is no problem.

- Pulleys working together can make it easy to lift even very heavy objects.

- A movable pulley moves with the load.

well, giving the kids a place to leave secret notes. If a wooden swing isn't right, then perhaps a tire swing is the way to go.

Zip line perches built on adjacent trees, the perches complete with railings and cantilevered supports, can be a blast. A passageway door leading to an escape-route slide or a ladder table will enhance almost any treehouse. But there's no hurry. Take your time and remember that a little extra effort, done at your leisure, will contribute immeasurably to the overall experience.

Ideally, your treehouse will be just as safe as your family's home. Nevertheless, it's not a bad idea to stow a custom first-aid kit somewhere on the treehouse's premises. Start with a small tool box or tackle box and then buy over-the-counter medicines to address blisters, abrasions, and headaches. Antibiotic ointments, scissors, gauze, Ace bandages, cold packs, heat packs, and hydrogen peroxide are also good ideas.

Hammocks

- A single cotton rope hammock provides support for up to 340 pounds.

- A larger hammock crafted with three-strand, 8-millimeter rope has a weight capacity of 450 pounds.

- Full-cloth, Brazilian hammocks are made of 100 percent cotton. They comfortably wrap the contours of a body, supporting its entire weight.

- Polyester rope hammocks are fade- and mildew-resistant. They can support up to 450 pounds.

Mailboxes

- A mailbox with a name on it will help give kids a sense that the treehouse is their very own.

- The easiest option is to buy a metal or wood mailbox from a supply store and attach it to the treehouse or a staircase post.

- Reclaimed wooden or metal mailboxes can be found and mounted to a post or set in the soil.

- A shadow-box, vertical-mount mailbox uses the latest in high-quality outdoor materials, coupled with contemporary designs.

RESOURCES

Many resources were used in the writing of this book. The Web sites listed here provided a wealth of information that, in turn, can help prospective treehouse builders find the answers to any further questions they might have. Some of the sites contain information about multiple subjects. Browsing through from subject to subject will help enhance your overall understanding of the rich, complicated science that is treehouse construction.

Chapter 1: Treehouse Dreams

Contractors

Andrew Maynard
www.andrewmaynard.com.au

Charlie Greenwood
www.treehouseengineering.com

Romero Studios
www.romerostudios.com

Treehouse Workshop
www.treehouseworkshop.com

Tree Top Builders, Inc.
www.treetopbuilders.net

Green Building

Dustin Feider
www.o2sustainability.com

Free Spirit Spheres
www.freespiritspheres.com

Inhabitat
www.inhabitat.com

Lukasz Kos
www.studiolukaszkos.com

Out 'n' About
www.treehouses.com

Pacific Environments
www.pacificenvironments.co.nz

Inspirations

Daintree Lodge
www.daintree-ecolodge.com.au

Finca Bellavista
www.fincabellavista.net

Longwood Gardens
www.longwoodgardens.org

Matangi Island Resort
www.matangi-island-fiji-resort.com

Solent Centre
www.solentcentre.org.uk

Yellow Treehouse
www.yellowtreehouse.co.nz

Plans and Materials

Treehouse Supplies
www.treehousesupplies.com

Chapter 2: Treehouse Styles

Books

S. Peter Lewis
www.tmcbooks.com

Contractors

John Carberry
www.peacemakertreehouses.com

Skyrooms
www.sky-rooms.co.uk

Ideas

Harry and Joanne Neely
www.harryn.com/treehouse.htm

Play Equipment

Playahead
www.playaheadclimbingframes.co.uk

Chapter 3: Rustic Treehouses

Exotic Ideas

Hana Treehouses
www.maui.net/~hanalani

Malibu Treehouse
www.kirsch-korff.com

Marc's Lodge
www.marcscamp.com

Papua Treehouse Vacation
www.papuatrekking.com

Good Advice

Andreas Wenning
www.baumraum.de

Chapter 4: Tree Selection

Consultants

SavATree

www.savatree.com

Forest Information

Forest and Shade Tree Pathology

www.forestpathology.org

USDA Forest Service

www.na.fs.fed.us

Photos of Pests and Problems

Care of Elm Trees

www.elmcare.com

Forestry Images

www.forestryimages.org

North Dakota State University

www.ndsu.nodak.edu/instruct/stack/TDI

Red Planet

www.cirrusimage.com

Tree Health Problems

Olaf Ribeiro

www.ribeirotreehealth.com

Chapter 5: Planning

Cleaning

Colgate.com

www.colgate.com/app/MurphyOilSoap/US/EN/HomePage.cwsp

Grading of Construction Materials

Sloan's Woodshop

www.sloanswoodshop.com/grading_wood.htm

Legal Information

Building Code References

www.reedconstructiondata.com

Building Codes

www.constructionweblinks.com

International Business Codes

www.iccsafe.org

Materials

About.com

www.woodworking.about.com/od/plywood

Woodmagazine.com
www.woodmagazine.com

Woodsmith
www.woodworkingtips.com

WOODWEB
www.woodweb.com

Tree Evaluation

Elmcare.com
www.elmcare.com

Chapter 6: Platforms & Supports

Construction Materials

Bolts
www.portlandbolt.com

Brackets
www.homedepot.com
www.shortrunpro.com/deck/brackets

Cables
www.cornerhardware.com

Flexible Limbs
www.treehouses.com

Shackles
www.1st-chainsupply.com

Tree Grips
www.treestuff.com

Turnbuckles
www.mutualscrew.com

Chapter 7: Treehouse Access

Green Construction

Building Green
www.buildinggreen.com

Reclaimed Wood
www.heritagebarns.com

Inspiration

Bill Compher
www.cedarcreektreehouse.com

Reclaimed Construction Materials

AltruWood
www.altruwood.com

Duluth Timber
www.duluthtimber.com

Hardwood Flooring and Lumber
www.jgarchitectural.com

Ropes

Fall Protection
www.gemtor.com

Rope Nets and Ladders
www.customcargonets.com

Supplies
www.us-rope-cable.com

Chapter 8: Windows & Doors

Materials

Doors
www.newwoodworker.com
www.sciotosalvage.com
www.todaysgreenconstruction.com
www.vintagelog.com

Dutch Doors
www.dutchdoorstore.com

Ledged-and-Braced Doors
www.jonathanelwellinteriors.co.uk

Portholes
www.nauticaltropical.com
www.seasidetreasures.com

Skylights
www.veluxusa.com

Tempered Glass
www.alumaxbath.com/tech/tgp.htm

Windows
www.simplyshutters.co.uk
www.tilt-inwindows.com

Chapter 9: Treehouse Roofs

Roofing Materials

Asphalt Roofing Tiles
www.gaf.com

Cedar Roofing
www.cedarshakeandshingle.com

Composite Materials
www.omegaroof.com
www.1aboveall.com

Eco Shakes
www.renewwood.com

Metal Roofing
www.metalroofing.com
www.interlockroofing.com

Solar Roofing
www.oksolar.com/roof

Wood Roofing
www.roofingbuilddirect.com

Chapter 10: Fun Features

Inspiration

Barbara Butler, Artist and Builder
www.barbarabutler.com

Toys for Grownups

Hammocks
www.hammocks.com
www.hammock-company.com

Toys for Kids

Cedar Swing Sets and Slides
www.cedarworks.com

Climbing Walls
www.extremeengineering.com/mobile-climbing-walls.aspx
www.rockwerxclimbing.com

Intricate Constructions
www.playnation.com
www.gorillaplaysets.com
www.byoswingset.com
www.swingsetsandmore.com

Swing Sets
www.abcdirectshop.com
www.swingset.com

Zip Lines
www.extextoys.com/funride/html
www.ziplinehomekits.com

Chapter 11: Tools

Helpful Tools

Chain Saws
www.husqvarna.com

Garden Tools
www.spear-and-jackson.com

Heavy Equipment
www.deere.com

Making the Right Tool Decision
www.consumerreports.org

Nail Guns
www.powernail.com

Power Tools
www.lowes.com

www.homedepot.com
www.sears.com
www.craftsman.com
www.makitaoutlet.com
www.skiloutlet.com
www.dewalt.com
www.blackanddecker.com
www.stanleytools.com
www.hitachi-koki.com/powertools
www.cpobostitch.com

Traditional Tools
www.traditionalwoodworker.com
www.cooperhandtools.com

Chapter 12: Hardware

Fasteners

Bolts and Screws
www.instockfasteners.com

www.wholesalebolts.com
www.boltdepot.com

Glues and Adhesives
www.gluefast.com
www.tapplastic.com
www.adhesivewarehouse.com
www.titebond.com

Self-drilling Screws
www.selfdrillers.com

Square Drive Screws
www.McFeelys.com

Stainless Steel Screws
www.stainlessfasteners.com

Chapter 13: Materials

Decking

Bamboo
www.bamboofencer.com
www.calibamboo.com

Green Wood Choices
www.nationalrecycling.com
www.itsrecycled.com
www.plasticlumberyard.com
www.rubbercal.com
www.greenroofs.com
www.ecogeeks.org

Ipe Hardwood
www.ipe-deck.com

Treated Woods
www.pacificwood.com

General Lumber Supplies

Georgia Pacific
www.gp.com

Poles and Timbers
www.americanpoleandtimber.com

Treated Wood
www.osmose.com

Materials Advice

General Advice
www.bobvilla.com

Government Resources
www.epa.gov

Park Service
www.nps.gov/redw

Chapter 14: Support Construction

Consultation and Contractors

Out 'n' About
www.treehouses.com

Plans and Designs
www.thetreehouseguide.com

Playahead
www.playaheadclimbingframes.co.uk

TreeHouse Workshop, Inc.
www.treehouseworkshop.com

Tree Top Builders, Inc.
www.treetopbuilders.net

Environment

Avoiding Threats
www.poison-ivy.org

Good Advice
www.forestry.about.com

Materials and Equipment

Harnesses
www.wesspur.com
www.sitepro1.com
www.sherrilltree.com

Joists
www.awc.org

Tree Evaluation

Inspection Services
www.treeinspection.com

Chapter 15: Platform Building

Cedar Supplies

www.soundcedar.com/lumber/decking
www.wrcla.org

Composite Materials

Fiberon
www.fiberondecking.com

Decking Patterns

Choosing a Pattern
www.renovation-headquarters.com/decking-patterns.htm

EverGrain

www.evergrain.com

Wood Floor Advice

Advice Forum

www.woodfloorsonline.com/techtalk

Disposal

www.1800gotjunk.com

Drying Lumber

http://ohioline.osu.edu/for-fact/0008.html

Eco-friendly Advice

www.buildinggreen.com

Publications

www.deckmagazine.com

Chapter 16: Framing & Walls

Good Advice

Framing Tips

www.homeadditionplus.com/Framing.htm

How-to Articles

www.taunton.com/finehomebuilding/how-to/articles
/anatomy-stud-framed-wall.aspx

Rough Framing

www.hammerzone.com/archives/window/new/ro_framing
.htm

Paints and Stains

Green Supplies

www.ecopainting.com

Overview of Painting Supplies

www.greenlivingideas.com/painting/green-remodeling-with
-eco-friendly-paint

Supplies

www.factorypaint.com/html/paint___stains.html

Panels and Siding

Composite Siding

www.duralog.com

Cost Effective Solutions

www.fauxpanels.com

Rustic Siding

www.lcgsidings.com

Chapter 17: Roofing

Green Materials

Eco-friendly Roofing

www.greenbuilder.com/sourcebook/Roofing.html

Rubber Recycling

www.rubbermulch.com/tire-recycling.asp
www.tireindustry.org/recycling.asp

Good Advice

Roofing Contractors Association

www.nrca.net

Roofing Materials

Caulks and Sealants

www.dap.com

Caulks, Sealants, and Adhesives
www.geocelusa.com

Ondura Roofing
www.ondura.com

Shingles
www.roofing.owenscorning.com/homeowner/shingles

Chapter 18: Access

Online Resources

Carving Templates
www.acetoolonline.com/category-s/4422.htm

Stair Building Guide
www.stairs4u.com

Stair Stringer Design Calculator
www.shalla.net

Supplies

Concrete
www.concretenetwork.com

Construction Chemicals
www.tkproduct.com

Portland Cement Association
www.cement.org

Railings
www.backyardamerica.com

Chapter 19: Additional Options

Good Advice

Accessory Plans for Carpenters
www.woodcraftplans.com

Electrical Checklist
www.pueblo.gsa.gov/cic_text/housing/outdoorcheck
/outdoorcheck.pdf

Tables
www.cakirk.com/TreeSlice.htm

Windows
www.milgard.com/understanding-windows-and-doors
/components/glass

Wiring Tips
www.hometips.com/articles/sunset_books/complete_wiring/
wiresandcables/wiresandcables_028.html

PHOTO CREDITS

Chapter 1

xii (left): Courtesy of TreeHouse Workshop, Inc.
xii (right): Courtesy of Tree Top Builders, Inc.
1 (left): © Freedom Lohr-tokyodv.com
1 (right): Courtesy of TreeHouse Workshop, Inc.
2 (left): Courtesy of T. Chudleigh
2 (right): Courtesy of Lukasz Kos
3 (left): Courtesy of www.O2Treehouse.com
3 (right): Courtesy of Dr. Mitchell Joachim, Terreform ONE
4 (left): Courtesy of Andrew Maynard Architects
4 (right): © dré wapenaar
5 (left): Courtesy of Sybarite
5 (right): Courtesy of Matt Hogan, Finca Bellavista, www.fincabellavista.net
6 (left): Courtesy of Roderick J.W. Romero
6 (right): Courtesy of Lucy Gauntlett, Lucy G Photography
7 (left): Courtesy of Solent Centre for Architecture + Design/Matt Dunkinson
8 (left): Courtesy of Tree Top Builders, Inc.
8 (right): Courtesy of Michael Garnier, www.treehouses.com
9 (left): Courtesy of Longwood Gardens/L. Albee
9 (right): © Gail Johnson | Dreamstime.com
10 (right): Courtesy of Michael Garnier, www.treehouses.com
11 (left): Courtesy of Daintree Eco Lodge & Spa

Chapter 2

12 (left): Courtesy of Tree Top Builders, Inc.
12 (right): Courtesy of Tree Top Builders, Inc.
13 (left): Courtesy of S. Peter Lewis
14 (right): Courtesy of Tree Top Builders, Inc.
15 (left): Courtesy of Longwood Gardens

15 (right): Courtesy of Longwood Gardens
16 (left): Courtesy of Longwood Gardens
16 (right): Courtesy of Harry and Joanne Neely
17 (left): Courtesy of Erica Hogan, Finca Bellavista, www.fincabellavista.net
17 (right): Courtesy of Tree Top Builders, Inc.
18 (left): Courtesy of Tree Top Builders, Inc.
18 (right): Courtesy of Sky-Rooms.co.uk
19 (left): Courtesy of Eric Z. Ayers
20 (left): Courtesy of Megan Ellis
20 (right): Courtesy of Petr Jahoda, www.papuatrekking.com
22 (left): Courtesy of Peacemaker Treehouses
22 (right): Courtesy of Horace L. Burgess
23 (right): Courtesy of Daniels Wood Land, Inc.
23 (left): Courtesy of Daniels Wood Land, Inc.

Chapter 3

24 (left): Courtesy of Anthony Colia
24 (right): Location courtesy of Christena Yeutter.
25 (left): Courtesy of David Greenberg, Treehouses of Hawaii
26 (left): Courtesy of Peter A. Kirsch-Korff
26 (right): Location courtesy of Martin Weissflog.
27 (left): Courtesy of Barbara Butler Artist-Builder Inc.
27 (right): Courtesy of Daniels Wood Land, Inc.
28 (left): Courtesy of Barbara Butler Artist-Builder Inc.
28 (right): Courtesy of Tree Top Builders, Inc.
29 (left): Courtesy of S. Peter Lewis
30 (left): Courtesy of TreeHouse Workshop, Inc.
30 (right): Courtesy of Alsadair Jardine As
31 (left): Courtesy of Tree Top Builders, Inc.
32 (right): Courtesy of Horace L. Burgess

33 (left): Courtesy of Nick McGlynn
34 (right): Courtesy of TreeHouse Workshop, Inc.
35 (left): Courtesy of TreeHouse Workshop, Inc.

Chapter 4

36 (left): © Robert Brown | Dreamstime.com
37 (right): © Joe Gough | Dreamstime.com
38 (left): © Jazzid | Dreamstime.com
39 (left): Courtesy of Porcupine Hollow Farm
39 (right): Courtesy of Porcupine Hollow Farm
42 (right): Courtesy of www.poison-ivy.org
46 (right): Courtesy of Melissa McMasters
47 (left): Courtesy of Iowa State University Plant and Insect Diagnostic Clinic

Chapter 5

48 (left): Courtesy of Katie Ellis
48 (right): Courtesy of S. Peter Lewis
49 (left): Courtesy of Tree Top Builders, Inc.
50 (right): Courtesy of Tree Top Builders, Inc.
51 (left): Courtesy of Tree Top Builders, Inc. and Charles and Lynn Meidt.
53 (left): Courtesy of S. Peter Lewis
57 (right): © Gail Johnson | Dreamstime.com
59 (left): Courtesy of Charley Greenwood
59 (right): Courtesy of TreeHouse Workshop, Inc.

Chapter 6

60 (right): Courtesy of Tree Top Builders, Inc.
61 (right): Location courtesy of Martin Weissflog.
64 (left): © Andrew Kroehn | Shutterstock.com
66 (left): Courtesy of Tree Top Builders, Inc.
67 (left): Courtesy of Tree Top Builders, Inc.
68 (left): Courtesy of Alsadair Jardine As
68 (right): Courtesy of www.O2Treehouse.com
69 (left): Courtesy of T. Chudleigh

PHOTO CREDITS

INDEX

A

access, treehouse, 72–83, 204–15
accessories, 114–17, 226–27
acrylic latex caulking, 201
adhesives and glues, 140–41
Akers, Eric, 19
Alnwick Gardens, 9, 57, 192
aluminum railings, 213
aluminum shakes, 101
angle brackets, 138
arborists, 36, 43, 45, 50
Armorlite, 148, 149
art and study centers, 6–7, 106–7
Artist's Retreat, 31
asphalt shingles, 99, 102, 198
awning windows, 92, 219

B

back risers, 209
Bait Shack Treehouse, 70
bamboo poles, 215
banyan trees, 41
base plates, 182–83
battery packs, 127
Baumraum, 31, 68, 92, 105
beam connectors and hangers, 139
beams, setting, 160–61
beds, 112–13, 223
beech trees, 37
benches, 222
Birdhouse at Longwood Gardens, 15, 21, 40
birdhouses, 117
blocking, 164–65
block planes, 123
board-and-batten roofing, 192–93
board-and-batten siding, 188–89
bolts, 55, 132–33
bolt support system, 158–59
boundary line restrictions, 51
box brackets, 63
box-end wrenches, 122
braces and brackets, 59, 62–63, 138–39

branches, 44, 156–57
branching trees, 40–41
bridges and walkways, 110–11
bubble levels, 120
budget, 52
building supplies, 56–57
bunk beds, 112–13, 223
Burgess, Horace, 22, 32–33
Butler, Barbara, 27, 28–29, 83, 93, 108, 114
butt chisels, 122
butyl rubber, 201

C

cables, 58, 61
cable suspension systems, 64–65
Camp Primetime, 107
Canopy Cathedral at Longwood Gardens, 15, 34, 83–84, 93
Captain Jack's Flying Pirate Ship, 22
cargo nets, 225
carriage bolts, 133
casement windows, 92, 219
castaway stairs, 75
caulking, 141, 201
cedar, 56, 171
Cedar Creek Treehouse Observatory, 80–81, 111
cedar decking, 150–51, 170–71
cedar shingles and shakes, 96
chain saws, 127
chairs, 117
chestnut blight, 46–47
chisels, 122–23
Chudleigh, Tom, 2, 68–69, 104–5
circular saws, 124, 125, 174
cleanup, 166–67, 176–77, 181
climbing nets, 115, 117
closed-end wrenches, 122
codes and regulations, 49, 50–51, 53
composite decking, 173, 177
composite railings, 213
composite shingles, 98

concrete, 21, 205
conifer trees, 36, 42, 43
copper naphthenate, 147
Countryside Education Trust Forest Learning Center, 7
Coyote Valley treehouse, 83
crowning, 168
cupping, 152, 168
curved claw hammers, 120
curved doors, 217

D

Daintree Raintree Resort, 11
Daniels, Ron, 109
Daniels Wood Land, 22–23, 26, 70, 93, 109
dead-end cable and thimble, 132, 133, 159
deciduous trees, 36–37, 43
deck blocking, 164–65
deck brackets, 138–39
deck cleaners, 179
decking, 150–51, 168–69, 170–75, 178
decking nails, 136–37
deck screws, 134
designs, 2–5
disc grinders, 125
door hardware, 86
doors, 84–87, 94–95, 182, 216–17
double-hung windows, 219
Douglas fir, 56
Douglas fir trees, 39
doweled steps, 73
drills, 125
Dura-log siding, 189
Dutch doors, 84
Dutch elm disease, 36, 47

E

earth augers, 128
eco-friendly treehouses, 1
EcoSafe plastic bags, 167

eco-shake roofing, 102
Edwards, Sam, 32, 33
El Castillo Mastate, 5
electricity, 220–21
Ellis Treehouse, 20
elm trees, 36
eucalyptus trees, 38 39
evergreens, 36, 42, 43
eyebolt-and-turnbuckle assembly, 133,
    160–61

F

fasteners, 142–43, 152, 178, 186, 218
Feider, Dustin, 69, 105, 143
fencing nails, 137
fire poles, 115, 225
fire safety, 203
fixed pulley systems, 123
fixed windows, 91
flags and pennants 226
flat roofs, 97
Fort Fiesta, 28, 109
forts, 28–29, 108–9
foundation nails, 136, 137
found object treehouses, 22, 32–33
4Treehouse, 2–3, 82
framing and walls, 45, 180–91,
    194–95, 206–7
Free Spirit Spheres, 2, 68–69, 104–5, 111
fun features, 108–19
furniture, 222–23
future innovations, 106–7

G

gang planks, 74
Garnier, Michael, 8, 9, 11, 51, 66–67, 142
Garnier Limbs, 9, 59, 66–67, 142
Gastineau treehouse, 71
gates, 154–55, 215
Glenmoore treehouse, 14, 110
gliding windows, 219
Global Rescue Station, 4
green roofs, 148, 149
Green treehouse, 69, 80, 81
Greenwood, Charlie, 66, 67, 143

H

hammers, 120
hammocks, 112, 113, 227
Hana treehouse, 25
hand saws, 121
hand tools, 120–23
hangers, 139
hardware, 132–43
hardwoods, 36–37, 43, 151
harnesses, 123, 167
heavy limbs, 143
height restrictions, 50
history of treehouses, 35
hoes, 129

I

ice damming, 99
interior, planning, 53
interior lumber, 56–57
IslandWood, 30

J

Jacob, Jake, 31, 35, 70
J-brackets, 63
jigsaws, 124–25
Joanne and Harry Neely treehouse, 16
joist hangers, 139
joists, 144–45, 162–65

K

keyhole saws, 121
Kitty Kat Treehouse, 27
knee braces, 60
knots, 77

L

lag bolts, 59, 65, 132–33, 158
lag screws, 135
laser levels, 120, 131
latex caulking, 141, 201
L-brackets, 138
ledged-and-braced doors, 84
levels, 120
Lewis, S. Peter, 13, 29, 48–49, 53, 83,
    142–43
liquid nails, 140

Lofty Lookout treehouse, 95
log siding, 189
Longwood Gardens, 9, 34–35
    Birdhouse, 15, 21, 40
    Canopy Cathedral, 15, 34, 83–84, 93
    Lookout Loft, 15, 16
Lookout Loft at Longwood Gardens, 15, 16
looped-rope ladders, 76, 77
lumber, 56–57, 144–45, 150–51, 180–81

M

Madison Square Park, 6, 23, 33
mailboxes, 227
Make-a-Wish treehouse, 30, 31
mallet hammers, 120
maple trees, 40, 41
Marc's Treehouse Lodge, 24–25
Matangi Private Island Resort, 10–11
materials, 144–55
McGlynn, Nick, 32, 33
metal angle brackets, 138
metal brackets, 62
metal roofing, 100–101, 107
Mis Ojos Miran la Catarata, 17
miter boxes, 130
miter saws, 121, 130, 131
monkey bars, 118
monkey rope ladders, 76, 77
Monstro Treehouse, 27
Morocco Treehouse, 6
multiple trees, using, 42–43

N

nail guns, 199
nails, 136–37, 152, 162, 186, 199
natural branch handles, 79
natural branch railings, 154, 214
Nelson, Peter, 6, 31, 35, 70
notched-out risers, 74

O

O2 Treehouse, 3, 68, 69
oak trees, 41
Ondura, 149
Ondura roofing, 193
open-end wrenches, 122

options, 216–27
orbital sanders, 131
Out 'n' About Treesort, 8, 9, 10, 11, 51
Owl's Nest Adirondacks Treehouse, 25

P
Pacific Environment Architects Ltd., 6, 7
paneled windows, 93
paneling, 188–89, 191
Panther Treehouse, 71
Papua Green House, 20
Philippine mahogany decking, 175
physically challenged children, 107, 115
pick axes, 128–29
pickets, 154, 155
pine trees, 38
pipe brackets, 158
pitched roofs, 96
planes, 123
planning, 48–59
plastic bags, 167
plastic premade handles, 78
plastic roofing tiles, 98
platform building, 168–79
platforms and supports, 54, 60–71
play area safety, 117, 119
playhouses, 26–27
plywood, 56
poison ivy, 43, 156
poison oak, 42
poplar trees, 36
porthole windows, 90
post beams, treated, 144
post hole diggers, 129
post holes, 204
post ladders, 75
posts, 20–21, 61, 70–71, 146–47, 214–15
Potomac treehouse, 24
power nailers, 126, 127
power sanders, 131
power tools, 124–27, 176, 181
prehung windows, 90
preservation lists, 50
pressure-treated wood, 144, 146, 147, 177
Pulaskis, 129
pulleys, 112, 123, 226

R
radiating spokes, 60–61
rafters, 194–95
railings, 154–55, 212–13
Ramona Treehouse, 34, 35
rasps, 123
reciprocating saws, 126–27, 175
reclaimed materials. See salvaged/reclaimed
    materials
recycling, 102–3, 105, 149, 200
redwood, 146–47
redwood decking, 150–51
reinforcing angle brackets, 138
resorts, 10–11
rock-climbing grips, 78
rock-climbing walls, 118
Romero, Roderick, 6, 69, 81, 83
roofing, 96–105, 192–203
    allowing tree growth in, 55
    alternate types, 98–99
    attaching, 196–97
    attaching rubber gasket, 200–201
    coatings, 103
    framing rafters, 194–95
    innovations, 106, 107
    installation, 99
    lumber, 57
    maintenance, 202–3
    materials, 148–49
    metal, 100–101, 107
    recycled, 102–3
    terms, 192
    trimming, 198–99
    troubleshooting, 202–3
    types, 192–93
    unique, 104–5
    wood, 96–97
roofing ax hammers, 120
roofing nails, 137, 202
roots, excavating, 157
rope-and-bucket system, 114
rope-and-pulley systems, 123
rope bridges, 110–11
rope handles, 79
rope ladders, 76–77
rope-lashing ladders, 77

rope railings, 214
ropes, 54
rope swings, 115
rubber gaskets, attaching,
    200–201
rustic treehouses, 24–35

S
safety glass, 88–89, 94
salvaged/reclaimed materials
    doors, 85, 87
    handles, 79
    pickets, 155
    windows, 89
    wood, 85
    wood for decking, 177
    wood steps, 72
Samantha's Treehouse School, 7
San Diego treehouse, 1
scavenging found materials, 105
schedule, building, 52–53, 57
screws, 134–35, 162
sealants, 141, 201
self-drilling screws, 135
sequoias, 38–39
shackles, 65
shake roofing, 96, 97
sheet sanders, 131
Sherwood, Samantha, 7
shingles, 96–97
shiplap siding, 188
shoulder bracing, 142
shutter windows, 88
siding, 152–53
silicone caulking, 141, 201
simulated shake roofing, 101
single-trunk treehouses, 12–13
sistering joists, 165
site, prepping, 156–57
skylights, 89
slanted flat roofing, 105
sledgehammers, 120
sleeping lofts, 112–13, 223
slides, 116–17, 224
sliding joints, 59
solar shingles, 103, 106

Solent Centre for Architecture and Design, 106–7
specialty tools, 128–31
specialty treehouses, 30–31
Spheres, 2, 68–69, 104–5, 111
spoke support, simple, 58
spruce trees, 39
squares, 120
staining and painting, 119, 153, 185, 190
stairs, 74–75, 204–5, 206
Stairway to Heaven, 80–81, 111
standing seamed metal roofs, 100
star-drive screws, 134, 135
steel cables, 64
steel drive screws, 134–35
steps, 72–73
stone-coated roofs, 100
storm windows, 219
Storybook treehouse, xii, 59
stringers, 208–11
stud-framed walls, 181
study centers, 6–7, 106–7
styles, 12–23
sudden oak death, 41, 47
support beams, 56, 58
supports
    construction, 156–67
    innovations, 66–67
    planning, 55, 58–59
    styles, 22–23
    unique, 68–69
suspension, 58, 64–65
swingsets, 116
Sybarite Treehouse, 5, 82, 106
sycamore trees, 37

T

tables, 117, 222
table saws, 130–31
tape measures, 121
tar paper, 193
T-brackets, 67
teak, 95
telephone pole steps, 73
tempered glass, 94
Tentvillage, 4, 5

Terreform FabTreehabitat, 3
three-tree treehouses, 16–17
Tiberi Treehouse, 81
tilt-in windows, 88
tires, recycled, 103, 200
tongue-and-groove doors, 87
tongue-and-groove siding, 189
tool bags, 120–21
tools, 120–31, 167
top lag bolts, 158
top plates, 187
treads, 210–11
tree callous, 47
tree grips, 64
tree handles, 78–79
Treehouse Chronicles, 13, 29, 83
Treehouse Chronicles (Lewis), 48–49, 143
treehouse industry, 8–9
Treehouse Institute of Arts and Culture, 8, 9
Treehouses of Hana, 25
TreeHouse Workshop, Inc., xii, 1, 9, 15, 21, 30, 34, 35, 59, 214
tree rot, 157
trees
    cross-section, 44
    diseases, 45–47
    health, 44–45
    injuries, 45
    respecting, 54–55
    selecting, 36–47
    terms, 45
Tree Top Builders, Inc., 71, 109, 114–15
Treetop Inn, 111
triangle steps, 72
tube rope ladders, 77
tubular slides, 116, 224
tulip trees, 40, 41
turnbuckles, 65, 133, 161, 179
two-tree treehouses, 14–15, 62

U

U-brackets, 138
UV finishes, water-based, 177

V

vertical trees, 38–39
vinyl railings, 213
vise grips, 122

W

walls, 184–87
Wapenaar, Dré, 4, 5
weather stripping, 217
Wenning, Andreas, 31, 68, 92, 105
Western Virginia treehouse, 35
window glass types, 219
windows, 86, 88–93, 107, 183, 216, 218–19
wire nails, 136
wood connector brackets, 138
wood glues, 140–41
wood handles, 78
wood pallets, recycled, 103
wood preservatives, 147
wood railings, 154
wood roofing, 96–97
wood shingles, 192, 193, 199
wood windows, custom, 92
World Tree House Association, 59
wrenches, 122
Wright, Dan, 8, 17, 18, 30, 31, 48, 49
wrought-iron railings, 213

Y

Yellow Treehouse Restaurant, 6–7

Z

zip lines, 114, 224